Zhu Xi's Reading of the *Analects*

Zhu Xi's Reading of the *Analects*

Canon, Commentary, and the Classical Tradition

Daniel K. Gardner

Columbia University Press   New York

*Columbia University Press wishes to express its appreciation
for assistance given by the Chiang Ching-kuo Foundation for
International Scholarly Exchange in the preparation of the
translation and in the publication of this book.*

Columbia University Press
Publishers Since 1893
New York   Chichester, West Sussex

Library of Congress Cataloging-in-Publication Data
Gardner, Daniel K., 1950–
    Zhu Xi's Reading of the Analects : canon, commentary, and
the classical tradition / Daniel K. Gardner
        p. cm.
    ISBN 978-0-231-12864-3 (cloth : alk. paper)
    ISBN 978-0-231-12865-0 (paper : alk. paper)
        1. Confucius. Lun yu. 2. Zhu, Xi, 1130–1200. Lun yu ji
    zhu. 3. Neo-Confucianism. I. Title: Canon, commentary,
    and the classical tradition. II. Confucius. Lun yu. English.
    Selections. III. Title.
PL2471.Z7G37 2003
181'.112—dc21   2003040973

⊗

Columbia University Press books are printed
on permanent and durable acid-free paper.
Designed by Chang Jae Lee
Printed in the United States of America

For Jeremy

Contents

Acknowledgments

If Cynthia Brokaw was not interested in hearing me go on endlessly about the grand importance of commentary in the Chinese tradition, or about how the commentarial genre did so much to shape that tradition, she never—or at least rarely—let on. Unfailingly thoughtful, she read countless drafts of the manuscript, prodding me, if not always delicately, to clarify and sharpen arguments. This book owes much to her efforts.

I am grateful to Smith College. More than merely tolerating my scholarly interests in Chinese matters quite far from concerns of the present, Smith has generously encouraged them. A Presidential Fellowship and sabbatical leave gave me the time to complete this book.

Kristina Johnson assisted me in a multitude of tasks, from creating the glossary and bibliography to proofreading the pages. I have relied heavily on her good judgment.

My wife, Claudia, and my son, Jeremy, provided balance throughout the long writing process. In particular, Jeremy, who turns eleven this very day I dedicate this book to him, has been a constant reminder that there are challenges greater—and more rewarding—than writing a book.

My brother, David, died as this book was in its final stages. I hope that Jeremy is endowed with some small portion of his uncle's enormous courage and dignity.

Zhu Xi's Reading of the *Analects*

Introduction

When the Song dynasty (960–1279) was established in the tenth century, the so-called Five Classics—the *Book of Changes*, the *Book of History*, the *Book of Poetry*, the *Book of Rites*, and the *Spring and Autumn Annals*—had long been regarded as the authoritative texts in the Confucian tradition, to be read before all others in the canon. By the end of the dynasty, the Five Classics had been displaced by the Four Books. It was these four texts—the *Greater Learning*, the *Analects*, the *Mencius*, and the *Mean*—that were now to be read first, that were thought to embody the most cherished teachings of the Confucian school.

It was not just that Confucians of the Song had shifted their scholarly attention from one set of canonical texts to another. How they read the canon itself also had changed over the course of the dynasty. An elaborate language of metaphysics had come to be employed in the interpretation of the Confucian texts. Sustained by this new language, traditional Confucian teachings had been given a distinctly different philosophical orientation. Together, the shift away from the once authoritative Five Classics to the Four Books and the reading of the canon in a "new" language mark the Song as a watershed in the history of Confucianism.

Many Song-dynasty scholars were associated with the efforts to refocus canonical attention on the Four Books and to "reread" texts in a contemporary language of metaphysics, but none more closely than Zhu Xi (1130–1200). It was Zhu who was primarily responsible for giving the Four Books precedence over the once authoritative Five Classics. Having studied the *Greater Learning*, the *Analects*, the *Mencius*, and the *Mean* for more than fifty years and having written commentaries on them for more than thirty, in 1190 he published them as a collection entitled the *Sizi*, or *Four Masters*. This was the first time the four texts—which became commonly known in the Yuan period as the *Sishu*, or *Four Books*—circulated together. In writings and in conversation with disciples, Zhu argued that while the Five Classics were still to be read and revered—he himself had written commentaries on four of the five—the Four Books revealed Confucian truths more clearly and effectively and thus should take precedence over all other writings in the canon. In his view, they, not the Five Classics, were the authoritative works in the Confucian tradition.

Zhu Xi devoted much of his life's work to writing commentaries on the Confucian canon, particularly on these Four Books. In writing his commentaries, Zhu drew quite freely on earlier readings, especially those of his predecessors of the Northern Song period (960–1126), a number of whom he took to be his spiritual masters, even though they had lived years earlier and had never personally instructed him. One notable achievement of his commentaries, therefore, is that they bring together the readings of many of the most important thinkers of the Song—such as Cheng Yi (1033–1107), Cheng Hao (1032–1085), Yang Shi (1053–1135), and Xie Liangzuo (1050–1103), to name but a few—many of which are grounded in the language of a new metaphysics. As such, they serve as a sort of synthesis or "summa" of the contemporary, metaphysically informed reading of the canon that had become increasingly prominent in the Song. So influential were the commentaries by Zhu Xi that they quickly became the orthodox reading of the Confucian canon. In fact, as early as 1313, the Four Books, with Zhu's commentary, were officially declared the basis of the civil service examinations, a distinction they claimed until the early decades of the twentieth century.

This book examines Zhu Xi's reading of the *Analects*, one of the Four Books and a text much revered ever since the Han period as the expression of the teachings of Confucius himself. It also looks at how Zhu's reading of this most central of texts helped reshape the Confucian intellectual tradition in the Song, a reshaping that reverberated strongly throughout the next seven centuries in China, as well as in Chosŏn Korea (1392–1910) and Tokugawa Japan (1600–1868), where it likewise was warmly embraced. I focus on Zhu Xi's commentary on the *Analects*, first translating critical passages from the text of the *Analects* with Zhu's commentary and then analyzing Zhu's interpretation in some depth.

My aim is to demonstrate, first, that Zhu Xi was dramatically rethinking the Confucian tradition through his Song reading of the canon and, second, how his reading in particular was different. It therefore is essential that we appreciate how the text of the *Analects* had been read traditionally. To that end, we examine the third-century commentary prepared by He Yan (190–249) and others, which until the Song was regarded as the standard reading of the text. By also translating He Yan's commentary on each passage and comparing it with Zhu Xi's commentary, we can observe the differences in their understandings and begin to analyze the factors that might help explain them.

I have still another purpose. While I am deeply interested in understanding Zhu's reading of the *Analects* and his redefinition of the tradition, no less significant here is my interest in exploring the genre of interlinear commentary and highlighting its importance and usefulness in the study of Chinese intellectual history. As a sort of reflection on the words and ideas of a text, interlinear commentary conveys the commentator's understanding of the meaning of the text while it shapes and conditions future readings and understandings of that text by others, both contemporaries and later generations. How interlinear commentary functions as a genre, how commentators themselves differently understand their responsibilities to the text and to their readers, how different commentaries lend different meanings to a text, how the understanding of a text depends on the particular commentary that accompanies it—these all are concerns motivating this book. In short, one of the book's principal objectives is exploring the role of interlinear commentary in the tradition of Chinese textual exegesis.[1]

Since the Zhou dynasty (ca. 1050–221 B.C.E.), Chinese had been writing—and reading—commentary on the texts especially meaningful to them. By the late Zhou, the *Spring and Autumn Annals*, much revered because of its close association with Confucius, had already attracted a great deal of commentarial attention. The two works, the *Gongyang zhuan* (*Tradition of Gongyang*) and the *Guliang zhuan* (*Tradition of Guliang*), were written as exegeses to it. Similarly, the *Book of Changes* invited commentarial interest very early on. The so-called Ten Wings, which later became an integral part of the *Changes* itself, were written mostly during the Zhou as commentary on the original layers of the text. The *Book of Poetry* and the *Book of History*, too, were subjected to lengthy exegetical treatment in the late Zhou. Much of the *Mencius* and the *Greater Learning*, for instance, is commentary on passages from these two texts.

Later, during the Han period (206 B.C.E.–220 C.E.), a new form of commentary became widely popular: interlinear commentary. Here, the "base" or "target" text is interrupted by the text of the commentary, whose purpose in part is to provide glosses, both phonetic and semantic, for individual characters in the base text and to offer guidance to how the passage is to be read. We have evidence that at this time, all sorts of texts were treated in this way. Interlinear commentaries were written not only on the "Ru," or Confucian, texts, which had become the established curriculum at the Imperial Academy in the early years of the Han, but on a range of other texts as well, such as the *Huainanzi*, the *Chuci* (*Songs of Chu*), the *Laozi*, the *Wuxing* (*Five Virtues*), and the *Taixuan jing* (*Elemental Changes*).[2]

By the close of the Han, few authoritative texts in the Chinese tradition were read without the assistance of an accompanying interlinear commentary. From the second century C.E. through the early years of the twentieth century, the typical reader read the opening passage of the text and then the interlinear commentary on that passage; from interlinear commentary, he would return to the next passage of the text and on again to the interlinear commentary. This process continued passage after passage, from the first lines of text to the very end. Thus the reading of the base text throughout was interrupted—and informed—by the reading of the companion commentary.

When reading interlinear commentary became an established, mainstream practice, so too did writing interlinear commentary quickly become an established, mainstream intellectual activity for literati. From the Han period on, thinkers and philosophers of all kinds devoted considerable effort to preparing interlinear commentary on texts of particular importance and significance for them. In this way, the corpus of Chinese commentary grew to be very full and very rich.

The commentary for those texts regarded as authoritative by the Ru, or Confucian, school is especially rich. Around each of the *jing*, or "classics" in the Confucian canon of authoritative texts, there grew volumes of commentarial writing. Reading the range of commentaries on any one of these texts quickly reveals that there is no one shared "right" reading of the text, that different commentators lend different "reasonable" meanings to words, phrases, lines, paragraphs, and chapters, resulting in fundamentally different readings.

That virtually every passage of the *Analects*, for example, has elicited a wide range of commentarial responses speaks to a critical, if obvious, point, one that deserves to be made explicit at the outset: in addressing a classic, commentators have a range of interpretive options from which they make choices.[3] The choices they make are principally intended to tell us, the readers, something about the classic. But just as significantly, they tell us something about the commentator as well and perhaps even about his contemporary fellowship of readers, insofar as he is a spokesman for them. The choice the commentator makes evolves out of a complex dialectic in which the words of the text, pregnant with possible meanings, interact with the commentator's intellectual concerns and assumptions, which themselves develop out of the contemporary zeitgeist. This interaction between text and commentator results in the particular commentary, which thus may serve as a window on the intellectual disposition of the commentator—as well as that of his age.

Thus I am arguing that while the canon does indeed have an openness and indeterminacy that give rise to a multiplicity of interpretive voices in the form of commentary, these voices are always produced in a historical context. That is, in practice, canonical indeterminacy is limited by historical circumstance. The state of the tradition, the terms of contemporary debate, and the particular sociopolitical realities all come together in the individual commentator to condition (to one degree or another) his interpretive response to a canonical text. For all the variety and interpretive differences it manifests, the commentarial tradition is subject to and reflective of a distinctive historical logic.

Reading the various commentaries on a canonical text allows us not only to observe that the Confucian interpretive community was, in fact, an ever changing one but also to chart in detail how ideas, beliefs, and values important to that community underwent historical change at the hands of different interpreters over the centuries. Thus, as a genre that illuminates the Confucian past and that documents especially well the vibrancy and changing nature of that past, commentary is indispensable to the study of Chinese intellectual history.

This book is in part a study of Zhu Xi's reexamination of one of the most central and influential texts in the Confucian tradition, the *Analects*. In equal part, by focusing on the importance of the commentarial form and the way it functions to shape meaning, it is also a study of genres. The variety of issues I address here, both implicitly and explicitly, include: Why did Zhu Xi choose to write interlinear commentary as a vehicle for expressing his understanding of the *Analects* and of the Confucian tradition? How did Zhu, as a commentator, understand his relationship to the base text, the *Analects*? How did Zhu negotiate between the words of sages past and the beliefs and conventions of contemporary readers? How did Zhu's commentary shape other people's reading and understanding of the text? How was Zhu's commentarial reading of the *Analects* influenced and mediated by the earlier tradition of commentary on the text? In turn, how did his commentary mediate the reading of the text by other commentators over the next seven hundred years?

By translating the two most acclaimed commentaries on the *Analects*, the first by He Yan and his colleagues and the second by Zhu

Xi, and by analyzing Zhu's "reading" of the classic against He's earlier "reading," I hope to illustrate the dynamic and complex relationship between the classical text and the interlinear commentary. It quickly becomes evident that as a vehicle of intellectual expression, interlinear commentary does not simply draw inspiration and meaning from the text but simultaneously gives meaning to it, significantly shaping and reshaping its reading.

Background of He Yan's and Zhu Xi's Commentaries on the *Analects*

That the *Analects* has continually attracted attention over the centuries from a variety of commentators, He Yan and Zhu Xi among them, comes as little surprise to the modern reader, who is well aware of its central importance in the formation of Confucian thought. While a detailed history of the text is beyond the scope of this study, a few brief remarks will provide some background.

Thought in the Han to be notes written down and compiled by the Master's disciples, the *Analects* is widely viewed by contemporary scholarship as a composite work of multiple layers that took shape as a book only in the Han period. During the early years of the Han, at least three different recensions of the *Analects*—the Lu version, the Qi version, and the old text version—circulated. Only in the Later Han were the various versions reconciled, after which the so-called *LuLun* came to be the standard and authoritative edition of the *Analects* text.[4]

Throughout most of the Han period, the *Analects* was not even counted among the canonical texts by the Confucian school. During Emperor Wu's reign, when Confucianism was promoted and the institution of the Erudites of the Five Classics (*wujing boshi*) established, only the *Book of Changes*, the *Book of History*, the *Book of Poetry*, the *Book of Rites*, and the *Spring and Autumn Annals* were regarded as canonical, classified as *jing*.[5] At this time, the *Analects* was considered *zhuan*, or commentary, viewed as Confucius's own oral commentary on the Five Classics, texts of the ancient sages, each of which Confucius was believed to have had a hand in editing, writing, or transmitting.

As a result of the Han's elevation of Confucianism and the increasingly popular appeal of the Sage himself during the dynasty, the *Analects*, the direct words of the Sage—or so it was thought—attracted greater and greater attention. By the Later Han, it had become required reading for all schoolchildren, for anyone aspiring to literacy, and was to be learned and memorized before the Five Classics themselves. Indeed, the heir apparent was typically provided a tutor for the *Analects*. The fact that the *Analects* had achieved canonical status was recognized in the Later Han's expansion of the Five Classics to the Seven Classics, to include the two small texts: the *Analects* and the *Classic of Filial Piety*.[6]

Since the Han period, there have been almost countless commentaries written on this revered text. Without doubt, the two that have had the greatest influence on the Chinese tradition over the centuries are the ones discussed here: the *Lunyu jijie* (*Collected Explanations of the* Analects) (248 C.E.), attributed to He Yan and his colleagues, and the *Lunyu jizhu* (*Collected Commentaries on the* Analects) by Zhu Xi. The *Collected Explanations of the* Analects brings together earlier remarks by Han-dynasty and Wei-dynasty (220–265) commentators—notably Kong Anguo (fl. ca. 120 B.C.E.), Bao Xian (6 B.C.E.–65 C.E.), Ma Rong (79–166), Zheng Xuan (127–200), and a certain Zhou of the Han; and Chen Qun (d. 236), Wang Su (195–256), and Zhousheng Lie (fl. 230) of the Wei—with He's and those of his co-compilers.[7] It is the oldest extant complete commentary on the *Analects* and served as the standard guide to the text for nearly a millennium, from the Wei period through the late Song–early Yuan period. So prominent was it that Huang Kan (488–545) wrote a subcommentary on it in his *Lunyu yishu* (*Subcommentary on the* Analects) (545), as did Xing Bing (932–1010) four centuries later in his imperially sponsored *Lunyu zhushu* (*Commentary and Subcommentary on the* Analects) (999).[8]

Zhu Xi's *Collected Commentaries on the* Analects, like He Yan's *Collected Explanations of the* Analects, brings together with his own observations the remarks of earlier commentators (some thirty or more), especially those by Cheng Yi, Cheng Hao, Xie Liangzuo, Yang Shi, Fan Zuyu (1041–1098), Yin Tun (1071–1142), Hu Yin (1098–1156), and You Zuo (1053–1123), all of the Song. This is the commentary, with its decidedly Song "bias," that in the fourteenth century displaced He's. From then until 1905, Zhu Xi's was the commentary prescribed by the imperial state and read, indeed memorized, by all Chinese aspiring to literacy and official status. In sum, these two works, He Yan's *Collected Explanations of the* Analects and Zhu Xi's *Collected Commentaries on the* Analects, were more widely read than any other commentaries on the *Analects* in the Chinese tradition.

He Yan and the *Analects* in the Third Century

He Yan's commentary on the text of the *Analects* is not the focus of this study but serves as a sort of a foil enabling us to better understand Zhu Xi's commentary. Because he is not particularly well known to Western readers, He deserves an introduction. The more familiar we are with He Yan and his times, the better we can appreciate his commentary; and the better our appreciation of He's commentary is, the sharper the significance of Zhu's reading of the *Analects* will be.

He Yan's precise role in compiling the *Collected Explanations of the* Analects is unclear. We are informed by the preface to the *Collected Explanations* that the work was completed by an editorial board of five—Sun Yong, Zheng Chong, Cao Xi, Xun Yi, and He Yan—but nowhere are the responsibilities and contributions of each recorded. Still, ever since Huang Kan first expressed his scholarly opinion in the *Lunyu yishu*, his influential subcommentary on the *Collected Explanations*, that He Yan had overseen the project, this has been the accepted view of the Chinese tradition.[9] It likewise has been the traditional view since Huang Kan that all remarks in the *Collected Explanations* without specific attribution should be regarded as He Yan's own and not remarks by the other members of the editorial board. Indeed, by the beginning of the Tang period (618–907), it was He's name alone that had come to be associated with the *Collected Explanations*; even those of the other board members had been put aside. The reason for this, in the judgment of the editors of the *Siku quanshu* (*Complete Library of the Four Treasuries*), was that He was the editor in chief, as Huang Kan first argued, the member of the board principally responsible for the project.[10] There is little contemporary evidence to support any of these claims and assumptions. Of He's role in the *Collected Explanations of the* Analects, all we can conclude with any certainty is that he was a co-editor. Beyond this, the opinions of Huang Kan and the later Chinese tradition notwithstanding, we know little. In this book, I refer to the *Collected Explanations of the* Analects as He Yan's commentary, but more for convenience's sake—as a sort of shorthand—than as a nod to tradition.

If He's precise role in the project is uncertain, so too are the reasons for his participation. Nowhere in the contemporary record is the motivation cited for his involvement in the *Analects* commentary. Thus, whether it was an inspired and invested He Yan himself who initiated and designed the project or whether it was a colleague on the editorial board who conceived of it and solicited the assistance of the others, including He Yan, we cannot know. In fact, by concluding with the formulaic "respectfully submitted" (*shang*), the preface even suggests that the members of the editorial board may simply have been commanded to write it, perhaps by those at the Wei court eager to provide the Wei with the appearance of legitimacy.

To understand the commentary, it is not essential that we know why He Yan became involved in it or the nature of his involvement. It is helpful, however, to know something about the intellectual concerns of the day, and since we can be sure that He Yan was closely connected to the text, knowing something of his life is helpful as well. I provide a brief discussion of He Yan here in the hopes of shedding light on He's life in particular and on the intellectual atmosphere of the second and third centuries more generally. For whatever the precise authorship of the *Collected Explanations* is, understanding the contemporary context of intellectual pluralism enables us to appreciate better the concerns it expresses.

The contemporary historical record provides only limited information about He Yan and his life. We learn that his great-grandfather was a butcher and that his grandfather, He Jin, was a general-in-chief under the Han. His mother, née Yin, became a concubine of the great Han general and founder of the Wei dynasty, Cao Cao (155–220), when He was a boy of six or so. As a consequence, He was brought up in the Wei palace, cared for with all the other princes, including the crown prince, Cao Pi (187–226). But because he presumed to wear the dress and ornamentation of a crown prince, Cao Pi resented him and referred to He not by name but by the term "false son." At an unspecified age, He was married to one of the palace princesses, the princess of Jinxiang, who may also have been a half sister.[11]

The various sources describe He Yan at an early age earning a reputation for being especially gifted, "bright and intelligent as a god."[12] But at the same time, he was also thought by others to be effeminate, fond of makeup, egotistical, and dissolute. Here, though, we should keep in mind that the sources, especially the dynastic history written during the Jin period, whose founders were professed enemies of He Yan, may be prejudicial. Indeed, Emperor Ming (r. 227–239) refused to employ He because, in the words of the dynastic history, he, like many in his coterie, was "a floating flower" (*fuhua*), renowned for a life of flamboyance and dissipation.[13] Such an impression of him is reinforced by accounts in the *Shishuo xinyu* (*New Accounts of Tales of the World*) that relate his special fondness for "five-mineral powder," a hallucinatory drug.[14]

He Yan achieved no particular political prominence under the first two emperors of the Wei, Wen and Ming—whether the cause was sibling rivalry, He's reputation for debauchery, or simply an intellectual orientation that these rulers found uncongenial. But with the death of Emperor Ming in 239, He's political fortunes took a turn. A child emperor now came to the throne, and another member of the Cao clan, Cao Shuang, was appointed regent. He thereupon became a member of Cao Shuang's inner circle, one of his clique, and soon found himself appointed president of the Ministry of Personnel (*libu shangshu*), a position that enabled him to bring friends and acquaintances— one of whom was the influential philosopher Wang Bi (226–249)—into important posts. During the Zhengshi reign (240–249), He succeeded in retaining control over most official appointments. Then in 249 the Sima family, which had posed a military threat to the dynasty from almost the beginning, succeeded in a coup d'état and took over the government. Cao Shuang and members of his faction, including He Yan, were executed.[15]

Clearly, the post-Han decades of the Three Kingdoms era (220–280) were precarious times. The strong, centralized government that had characterized the early centuries of the Han had been ended long ago by the internal rebellions and civil wars during the second century. Three ruling houses, all with imperial aspirations, now divided up the empire. In each of the capitals, political intrigue, assassination attempts, and coups d'état were common, according to the dynastic histories. Under such circumstances, attitudes toward political service grew ambivalent. The once dominant Confucian imperative to serve increasingly gave way to fear and resignation, and behavior characterized by some scholars as "nihilistic"[16]—the sort of dissolution and irreverence attributed to He Yan in contemporary accounts—had become commonplace.

This retreat from the political imperative of Confucianism was accompanied by a gradual philosophical retreat from Confucianism itself. As early as the second century, interest in the teachings of Confucianism had begun to wane. No doubt the civil wars raging throughout China and the unabashed corruption of the eunuch-dominated court had dampened the interest of the literati not only in government and politics but also in Confucian ideals themselves, which had failed to maintain the political and social order they had promised.

Paradoxically, the nature of contemporary Confucian learning itself may have also helped diminish interest in Confucianism in the second century. The dynastic history of the Later Han explains that while the detailed chapter-and-verse exegesis (*zhangju*) characteristic of the school had become tremendously popular in the second century, especially at the Imperial Academy, it had also become increasingly long-winded and arid and was now robbing the school of much of its intellectual vitality, prompting students to turn to other, more frivolous pursuits.[17]

There is little doubt, too, that with the collapse of the Han, beginning in the late second century, whatever constraints the imperially sanctioned Confucian orthodoxy once might have imposed on the intelligentsia loosened enormously. Men were now freer than ever to find inspiration in a variety of modes of thought, the result being that their commitment to Confucian teachings declined.

In short, by the later years of the Han, Confucianism was no longer the dominant intellectual force it had been earlier in the dynasty. A sort of intellectual pluralism had developed. Thinkers were more experimental, freely and widely searching a variety of sources of inspiration from the cultural tradition and drawing on different ones to satisfy different needs. Even the renowned Confucian scholar and exegete of the late Han, Ma Rong, could play the Daoist, on one occasion remarking to a friend: "Individual life is to be valued more than the entire world. Now, to sacrifice my priceless life on account of a trifling moral matter is surely not what Lao and Zhuang intended."[18] Besides writing commentaries on nearly every classic in the Confucian canon, Ma Rong also wrote commentaries on the *Laozi*, the *Huainanzi*, and the *Li Sao* (*Encountering Sorrow*).[19]

Recent scholarship has shown that by the end of the Han, those literati drawing on precedents set earlier by influential thinkers such as Zhuang Zun (59–24 B.C.E.) and his student Yang Xiong (53–18 B.C.E.) were increasingly focusing their attention on the *Book of Changes*, the *Laozi*, and the *Analects*, reading these three texts against one another. This triad of texts, to which the *Zhuangzi* was later added and which were associated with what once were thought to be incompatible intellectual schools, was now assumed by men like Xiahou Xuan (209–249), He Yan, and Wang Bi to share a coherent philosophical message. The words of the sages in these works illuminated one another and, if understood correctly, would yield a unified truth.[20]

He Yan reflects this intellectual pluralism. The dynastic history reports that "he loved the words of Lao and Zhuang and wrote the *Daode lun* [*Treatises on Way and Power*]."[21] Although the *Daode lun* is no longer extant, we learn a little about the text from contemporary references to it. The *Shishuo xinyu* says that He Yan had planned to write an interlinear commentary on the text of the *Laozi* but that, after meeting the younger, talented Wang Bi and discussing his ideas on the text with him, realized how inadequate his own draft commentary was. He thereupon abandoned his own work on it and instead wrote individual treatises on the Way and power (*Daode lun*).[22]

He's interest in the text of the *Laozi* had taken shape early in life, according to Sun Sheng (d. 373), who reported in the *Weishi chunqiu*

(*Annals of Wei*): "When He Yan was young he possessed unusual talent and was skilled in discussions of the *Book of Changes* and *Laozi*."[23] This remark is a reminder, first, that by the close of the Han, the *Book of Changes* had come to be a favored text of the literati and was routinely read against the *Laozi*, the two having become companion volumes.[24] Second, He's devotion to the words of the Daoist masters Laozi and Zhuangzi, remarked on in the dynastic history, in no manner diminished his devotion to the texts traditionally associated with Confucius: the *Book of Changes* and the *Analects*. Indeed, He Yan himself expressly argued for the ultimate compatibility of Daoist and Confucian teachings: "Laozi [in fact] was in agreement with the Sage."[25]

A few years later, Wang Bi held to a similar point of view. Wang went to visit Pei Hui (fl. 230–249), the director of the Ministry of Personnel:

> As soon as Pei saw him, he knew that this was an extraordinary person, so he asked him, "Nonbeing [*wu*] is, in truth, what the myriad things depend on for existence, yet the Sage [Confucius] was unwilling to talk about it, while Master Lao expounded upon it endlessly. Why is that?" Wang Bi replied, "The Sage embodied nonbeing, so he also knew that it could not be explained in words. Thus he did not talk about it. Master Lao, by contrast, operated on the level of being [*you*]. This is why he constantly discussed nonbeing; he had to, for what he said about it always fell short."[26]

The pluralistic attitude prevalent in the third century again is apparent. Wang Bi, one of the foremost thinkers of the *xuanxue* school (the learning of the mysterious) and one of the Chinese tradition's great commentators on the text of the *Laozi*, could defend Confucius at the same time he expressed deep admiration for his embodiment of nonbeing.[27] Indeed, in his view, the Sage had fully realized in his person what Laozi could only struggle to describe in words. Wang Bi and other thinkers in the *xuanxue* school could venerate Daoist sages and Confucian sages alike, however much they might be "rereading" some of them. This in part explains why He Yan, Wang Bi, and the great

Zhuangzi commentator Guo Xiang (d. 312), for all their interest and expertise in the texts of the *Laozi* and the *Zhuangzi*, could each write a commentary on the text of the *Analects*.[28]

It is curious that the dynastic history *Sanguo zhi* (*History of the Three Kingdoms*) speaks of He Yan's fondness for Daoism and of his authorship of the *Daode lun*, yet makes no mention of his efforts on behalf of the *Analects*. This may simply be because the court-appointed historians writing during the regime of the Sima clan despised him and wished to portray him as unconventional, personally responsible in part for the relative chaos and disorder of the Three Kingdoms period, and thus deserving of the fate that befell him at the hands of the Sima family. More simply, it may be that because the *Collected Explanations of the* Analects was a work by committee, the editors of the dynastic history did not choose to associate it with the efforts of particular individuals. In any case, although we no longer have the *Daode lun* by He's hand, we do have his coedited commentary on the *Analects*, a commentary that proved to be enormously influential in the Confucian tradition, especially until the early years of the fourteenth century when it was superseded in importance by Zhu Xi's.

In the preface to this commentary, He Yan and his colleagues provide a textual history of the *Analects* before their day. A paraphrase of this preface in its entirety gives us a sense of the state of the text as the committee inherited it and of how the committee understood its own efforts on it:[29]

> Liu Xiang said that at first there were two versions of the text, a *Lunyu* from Lu in twenty chapters compiled by the disciples of the Master and a *Lunyu* from Qi in twenty-two chapters, including a "Wen Wang" chapter and a "Zhi Dao" chapter not found in the Lu version. In the twenty chapters that the two had in common, the Lu version contained more passages. Each of these versions had its own master teachers and transmitters. In the reign of Emperor Jing of the Han (r. 157–141 B.C.E.), a third version, the *Guwen Lunyu*, was recovered from Confucius's former home in Lu as it was being demolished to make way for a palace for King Gong of Lu (r. 153–128 B.C.E.).

Like the Lu version, it did not contain the two chapters found in the Qi version. It did, however, make the "Zizhang wen" passage in the "Yao Yue" chapter into its own chapter, so that it had two "Zi Zhang" chapters and twenty-one chapters in all. Also, the order of its chapters was different from that of the Lu and Qi versions. More than a century later, Zhang Yu (d. 5 B.C.E.), marquis of Anchang (and *Lunyu* tutor to Emperor Yuan's [r. 33–7 B.C.E.] heir, the future Emperor Cheng), basing himself on the *LuLun* and simultaneously analyzing the statements in the Qi version, selected the good from them and called it the *Zhang Hou Lun*, the version that became most highly regarded. Bao Xian and a Mr. Zhou[30] issued the *zhang-ju* [commentary] on it. As for the *Guwen Lunyu*, only Kong Anguo commented on it, but it is no longer extant. Later, during the reign of Emperor Shun (125–144), the renowned scholar Ma Rong wrote a commentary on the *Zhang Hou Lun* as well. At the end of the Han dynasty, Zheng Xuan, basing himself on the chapters and passages of the *LuLun*, compared them with the Qi and *guwen* versions and then wrote a commentary. Recently, Chen Qun, Wang Su, and Zhousheng Lie all adopted this version and wrote an "explanation of its meaning." In earlier times [i.e., before Zhang Yu], although there were indeed discrepancies among the explanations of the master teachers (*shishuo*) of the *Lunyu*, no one had compiled a collection of annotations and explanations. It is only rather recently that this has been done [i.e., by Bao, Zhou, Kong, and Ma], and now they are numerous. But the views expressed in these collections differ, some being better than others. Now we have brought together in our collection the good annotations and explanations from the various schools, appending names to the comments. Occasionally, when we have not been satisfied, we have made small changes. We have entitled our text the *Lunyu jijie*. Respectfully submitted by Sun Yong, Chen Chong, Cao Xi, Xun Yi, and He Yan.[31]

The preface outlines the long process by which the different recensions of the *Analects* became fixed and especially the prominent

roles of Zhang Yu and Zheng Xuan in this process. The rash of exegetical activity on the text described in the preface by men like Bao Xian,
a Mr. Zhou, Ma Rong, and Zheng Xuan has to be understood against
the background of the excitement newly generated by the *Analects* during the Han. Scholars were eager to illuminate the significance of a
work that because of its direct association with the Master, a figure
now more revered than ever, was thought to be deeply meaningful. He
Yan and his colleagues viewed their efforts principally as rationalizing
the flurry of work done by their Han and early Wei predecessors on the
text. Based on the version of the *Analects* "fixed" by Zheng Xuan, they
brought together in the *Collected Explanations of the* Analects what they
believed to be the best and most useful annotations available for the
text, those that would give it the greatest intelligibility.

Zhu Xi and the Transformation of the Confucian Tradition

In He Yan's day, Confucianism clearly still played a central, vital role in
the lives of intellectuals like He and Wang Bi, even though it may have
competed with a variety of other beliefs. By the late third century, however, it had lost much of its vigor and appeal. Teachings associated with
texts from the Daoist canon and, even more so, Buddhism increasingly
drew the attention of Chinese intellectuals, in part no doubt because of
their timely concern with personal salvation and cosmological questions. The canonical texts of the Confucian school continued to be
read and recognized as important works in the cultural tradition, and
they continued to serve as the basis for selection into the civil service
for many of the political regimes of the day. But in general, they did
not hold the same strong attraction they had earlier for Chinese intellectuals, who were now preoccupied with broader ontological and
metaphysical concerns.[32]

In the eighth century or so, interest in the teachings of Confucianism was revived and, with it, a renewed interest in classical studies. By
the beginning of the Song dynasty, this revival in classical studies had
gained momentum, becoming what can perhaps best be described as a
sort of renaissance movement: almost all the major Song intellectual

figures—Sun Fu (992–1057), Hu Yuan (993–1059), Fan Zhongyan (989–1052), Ouyang Xiu (1007–1072), Wang Anshi (1021–1086), Sima Guang (1019–1086), Su Dongpo (1036–1101), Zhang Zai (1020–1077), Lü Ziqian (1137–1181), Cheng Hao, Cheng Yi, and of course Zhu Xi—now devoted much of their lives to studying and reflecting on the Confucian canon. To their minds, there was little question that the canon was the receptacle of the truth; the problem was that it had to be properly interpreted before the truth could be discovered. This task of revealing the truth embodied in the canonical texts became something of a mission. With the collapse of the centralized and powerful Tang empire fresh in their minds, with foreign nomads encroaching on their territory to the north, and with the "foreign" doctrine of Buddhism exercising strong influence throughout the empire, literati of the Song were fiercely dedicated to creating a strong, essentially Confucian order and were convinced that the principles in the canon could provide the basis for that order.

Here a contrast with the Wei period of He Yan is instructive. Whereas pluralism and relative intellectual openness characterized the atmosphere of the second and third centuries, a tendency toward defining a "correct" body of thought, an intellectual orthodoxy that would "save" the Chinese tradition and protect it from foreign influences, gained momentum in the Northern and Southern Song. A paring back, an attempt to define more narrowly the essential truths of the tradition, thus distinguishes the Song period. Whereas orthodoxy seems to have given way to an intellectual expansionism or pluralism in the early centuries of the Period of Disunion, in the Song period a movement to consolidate values, to return to a more narrowly and sharply articulated "orthodoxy," prevailed. The locus of literati efforts to shape such an orthodoxy was the canon of Confucian texts.

In the early years of the Song, literati intensively studied and commented on the entire canon, which by this time had grown from five texts to thirteen, although particular attention was paid to the original five.[33] In the mid-Song, their focus began to change. They singled out certain texts from among the thirteen: the *Analects* and the *Mencius*, whose text had been only recently canonized in the Northern Song; and the *Greater Learning* and the *Mean*, which were two brief chapters from the *Book of Rites*, itself one of the Five Classics. By the late Song, as a result of Zhu Xi's efforts especially, what collectively came to be called the Four Books had come to be regarded as of fundamental importance. Then in 1313, under Yuan rule, they—with Zhu Xi's commentaries—were officially recognized as the basic texts for the civil service examinations.[34]

The political situation and intellectual climate of the Northern Song were the background to this dramatic shift in classical studies. Since the early years of the tenth century, the Chinese state had been repeatedly invaded and occupied by "barbarian" neighbors to the north and northwest. Just south of the Great Wall, the Song had ceded to the Khitan people and their Liao dynasty (907–1119) sixteen prefectures of Chinese territory, and in the northwest, the Tangut had established the Xi Xia state (1038–1227), controlling much of Gansu Province and the Ordos region south of the Yellow River. The threat of "barbarian" invasion was ever present, resulting in both the buildup of the Chinese military and the frequent negotiation of peace by the Song with its neighbors, whose combined effect exacted a hefty toll on the dynasty's finances. The eleventh century, especially the reign of Emperor Renzong (r. 1023–1063), was a period of serious reform efforts, in which various measures were taken to address the most pressing political, military, and economic problems facing the Song. In the end, these attempts at reform proved largely unsuccessful. As the Northern Song came to a close, the Chinese bureaucracy was embroiled in bitter, paralyzing factionalism; the country's economy remained weak and overburdened; and to the north, China faced yet another menacing military threat in the form of the Jurchen people. Reflecting on this critical state of affairs, some Confucian thinkers concluded that simply too little attention had been given to the inner sphere, that political and social action without a strong moral foundation could lead nowhere. During Shenzong's reign (1068–1085), the failure of Wang Anshi's "new policies," perhaps the dynasty's boldest attempt at reforming the polity, merely served to confirm their conviction. Wang's efforts were well intentioned, they conceded, but they failed largely because he had not attended to the inner sphere; he had made the serious error of separating inner moral concerns from outer sociopolitical ones. Convinced now that the political and social order could not be improved by institutional and legal changes alone, these thinkers turned their attention inward to the process of moral self-perfection. Progress in the "outer" realm of political and economic affairs, they believed, depended on prior progress in the "inner" realm of self-cultivation. Accordingly, texts in the Confucian canon that focused on the "inner" realm began to receive greater attention.

Not only was there a "barbarian" presence politically, but there was a "barbarian" presence intellectually as well. The widespread popularity of Buddhism during the Tang dynasty had continued into the Song, providing additional evidence for some that the Confucian Way and way of life were at risk. The attitude of many Confucian thinkers toward Buddhism can only be described as schizophrenic. Although its very foreignness could be an affront to them and although the seductiveness of Buddhist teachings, especially those of the Chan school, remained a source of deep concern for them, these thinkers were themselves stimulated by and attracted to many of the issues that Buddhists had been directly addressing over the past few centuries: human nature, self-realization, the character of the mind, man's relation to the cosmos, and enlightenment. Since the Tang period, even though the Confucian literati might have contested the specific philosophical formulations of the Buddhists, they had come to find such issues increasingly relevant and meaningful. Indeed, dialogue between the Buddhist and Confucian schools had become commonplace and quite active in the Song: Ouyang Xiu, Wang Anshi, Su Dongpo, Zhou Dunyi, Zhang Zai, the Cheng brothers, the Chengs' disciples, and Zhu Xi, just to name a few of the great Confucians of the Song, not only numbered prominent Buddhists among their acquaintances but had themselves studied Buddhism. It is perhaps because they knew the teaching's seductiveness at first hand that many of them were so wary of the powerful influence it was exercising over the minds of Song Chinese. In any event, in their reflection on the Confucian canon, Confucians of the Song discovered texts in their own tradition that, better and more directly than the Five Classics, addressed the philosophical concerns that had come to matter most to them.

The history of the dramatic shift in classical studies during the Song is complicated and cannot be explained simply or adequately in a brief summary of the political and intellectual milieus of the period. Still, whatever the precise reasons or motivation may have been, there can be little doubt that the move at this time away from the Five Classics toward the Four Books signaled a decisive shift "inward" for the Confucian school toward texts in the canon that treated more deliberately the inner realm of human morality. To generalize, by contrast with the Five Classics—which illustrate Confucian morality using examples and lessons from history; describe how one should conduct oneself in certain, concrete objective situations; and prescribe ritualistic practices for maintaining a well-ordered society—the Four Books are concerned with the nature of man, the springs or inner source of his morality, and his relation to the larger universe. Only when such concerns became central during the Song did the age of the Five Classics come to an end, giving way to a new age, the age of the Four Books.[35] At the same time, we should note that such a move away from the lengthy, linguistically troublesome Five Classics toward the much briefer Four Books was not inconsistent with the prevailing interest of Song literati to narrow the field of philosophical inquiry and to define the core truths of the tradition more concisely than ever.

By publishing the Four Books together as a collection for the first time, Zhu Xi had an especially strong hand in inaugurating the age of the Four Books. But publication of these texts as a collection in 1190 came only after he had devoted decades to studying each of the texts and preparing commentaries on them. Zhu's serious efforts on the *Analects* began in the early 1160s. In 1163 he completed the *Lunyu yaoyi* (*Key Meaning of the* Analects) and the *Lunyu xunmeng kouyi* (*Catechism on the* Analects *for the Instruction of the Young*).[36] Nine years later, in 1172, he published the *LunMeng jingyi* (*Essential Meaning of the* Analects *and the* Mencius),[37] in which he annotated both the *Analects* and the *Mencius*. In the preface to this work, he wrote: "The *Analects* and the *Mencius* are the most important works for students pursuing the Way. . . . The words of the *Analects* are all-inclusive; what they teach is nothing but the essentials of preserving the mind and cultivating the nature."[38] Five years later, in 1177, drawing on the *LunMeng jingyi* and the *Lunyu xunmeng kouyi*, he completed the *Collected Commentaries on the* Analects *(Lunyu jizhu)*,[39] the text that became the basis of the civil service examination and the subject of this book. The completion of the *Collected Commentaries on the* Analects, however, did not end his efforts and reflection on the *Analects* text. Zhu continued to revise his reading of it throughout the remainder of his life, remarking sometime after 1194: "I have given more than forty years' attention to the *Analects*. . . . I have weighed each and every character in it without the slightest partiality. Scholars looking at my commentary ought to read through it with the greatest care."[40]

Providing confirmation—should we need any—of Zhu's untiring editorial and commentarial work on the *Analects*, as well as on the other Four Books, Huang Gan (1152–1221), his son-in law and one of his foremost disciples, wrote: "Although the Master's writings are numerous, he paid particularly great attention to the *Analects*, the *Mencius*, the *Mean*, and the *Great Learning*. As for the *Greater Learning* and the *Analects*, he revised them over and over again until he was on his deathbed."[41] Only with death, did Zhu's work on the *Analects* cease. The importance of this text to him and his Confucian vision should be clear.

Zhu Xi's life and thought are richly documented, certainly much more so than He Yan's. Zhu Xi figures prominently in the contemporary histories and, unlike He, has a lengthy biography devoted to him in the official dynastic history. More significantly, he left behind an enormous corpus of works, whose influence on the later cultural tradition can hardly be overstated. Included among them are numerous commentaries on the Confucian canon, many of which, such as those on the Four Books, served from the fourteenth century on as the basis of the civil service examinations; a host of editions and anthologies of writings and remarks by venerated predecessors; and historical studies. Zhu's collection of essays, letters, prefaces, postscripts, biographies, eulogies, tomb inscriptions, and other literary documents have been brought together in 121 chapters in the *Collected Literary Works of Master Zhu*. We are fortunate also to have a record in the voluminous 140-chapter *Conversations of Master Zhu, Arranged Topically*, of discussions between Zhu Xi and the nearly five hundred followers he attracted over the years.

Of Zhu Xi's numerous achievements, among the most heralded are the elaboration of a systematic Confucian metaphysics derived from an interpretive reading of the Four Books and a complex synthesis of ideas advanced by earlier thinkers in the Confucian school, especially the great "Neo-Confucians" of the Northern Song—Zhou Dunyi, Zhang Zai, Cheng Hao, and Cheng Yi. The metaphysical synthesis he worked out represented a new development in Chinese philosophy, an attempt to give the traditional aim of Confucian teachings—the moral cultivation of the individual—an ontological foundation. Man could become perfectly moral because the nature with which he was born was itself always moral. But his natural endowment of psychophysical stuff (*qi*) could, if it were turbid, dense, or impure enough, obscure his moral nature, and thus it had to be refined if the moral nature was to become manifest. It is this "metaphysical" reading of the Confucian tradition, systematized and promulgated by Zhu, that became both the dominant intellectual discourse and the basis of the state orthodoxy of post-Song imperial China. Zhu was interested not only in the construction of a systematic Confucian metaphysics but equally in the way this system might be taught, transmitted through a Confucian curriculum, as widely and simply as possible. Over his lifetime, Zhu Xi designed an elaborate program of learning intended to serve as the means by which man, mired in his psychophysical predicament, could refine himself and connect with his originally moral nature. This program of learning included a carefully graded curricular sequence, at the top of which was the Four Books. Students were to begin with them, for as Zhu wrote to a friend, "If we wish principle to be simple and easy to appreciate, concise and easy to grasp, there is nothing better than the *Greater Learning*, the *Analects*, the *Mencius*, and the *Mean*."[42]

In the following chapters, I have selected passages from the *Analects* that, in my judgment, deal most directly and coherently with the doctrinal issues most central to the Confucian school, and I have translated each along with He Yan's and Zhu Xi's commentaries in full.[43] My purpose is twofold: to highlight the way in which Zhu Xi dramatically transformed the meaning of this central text and to show how crucial the reading of interlinear commentary is to our understanding of the Chinese tradition. I have followed this with a lengthy and detailed analysis of the two translated commentaries, pointing out where and how Zhu Xi's reading of the canonical text diverges from what had been the standard reading up to his day. In this manner, the peculiar intellectual concerns and emphases of Zhu Xi and the twelfth century are brought into sharp focus.[44]

The passages from the *Analects* are organized into five chapters, around the key concepts of learning (*xue*), true goodness (*ren*), ritual (*li*), ruling (*zheng*), and the Way (*dao*) of the superior man (*junzi*).

This book is both a study of the commentarial genre and an intellectual history showing, through commentarial comparison, what is distinctive about Zhu Xi's understanding of the Confucian tradition. While fascinating in what it reveals about his thought, Zhu's commentary may be just as fascinating in what it reveals about his process of thinking. Zhu's construction of a Confucian vision, a vision that became the orthodoxy for much of later traditional China, as well as of Korea and Japan, emerged out of a careful engagement with canonical texts. It was a vision that developed gradually through serious and reflective dialogue with the Confucian past. The study of commentary thus enables us to observe Zhu Xi here in the very act of philosophical construction.

NOTES

1. Other studies in English that treat the role of interlinear commentary include John B. Henderson, *Scripture, Canon, and Commentary: A Comparison of Confucian and Western Exegesis* (Princeton, N.J.: Princeton University Press, 1991); Richard John Lynn, *The Classic of Changes: A New Translation of the I Ching as Interpreted by Wang Bi* (New York: Columbia University Press, 1994); Richard John Lynn, *The Classic of the Way and Virtue: A New Translation of the* Tao-te ching *of Laozi as Interpreted by Wang Bi* (New York: Columbia University Press, 1999); Steve Van Zoeren, *Poetry and Personality: Reading, Exegesis, and Hermeneutics in Traditional China* (Stanford, Calif.: Stanford University Press, 1991); and Rudolf G. Wagner, *The Craft of a Chinese Commentator: Wang Bi on the* Laozi (Albany: State University of New York Press, 2000). Japanese scholars have long been interested in the study of interlinear commentary and especially in its translation. For a very small sampling, see the two series *Zenshaku kanbun taikei* and *Shinshaku kanbun taikei*.

2. Commentaries written on many early texts in the Chinese tradition are considered in Michael Loewe, ed., *Early Chinese Texts: A Bibliographical Guide* (Berkeley: Society for the Study of Early China and Institute of East Asian Studies, University of California, 1993).

3. For instance, on this point, see John Kieschnick, "*Analects* 12.1 and the Commentarial Tradition," *Journal of the American Oriental Society* 112 (1992): 567–76.

4. John Makeham, "The Formation of *Lunyu* as a Book," *Monumenta Serica* 44 (1996): 24. Because the *QiLun* and *GuLun* recensions of the *Analects* no longer survive, their fates after the Han cannot even be reconstructed. According to Makeham, a detailed comparison of the various recensions is not possible ("The Earliest Extant Commentary on *Lunyu: Lunyu zheng shi zhu*," *T'oung Pao* 83 [1997]: 262–67). For more on these three recensions of the *Lunyu* and the work of reconciling them, see the later discussion of He Yan's "Lunyu xu," in the section in this chapter "He Yan and the *Analects* in the Third Century."

5. On the Five Classics, see Michael Nylan, *The Five "Confucian" Classics* (New Haven, Conn.: Yale University Press, 2001).

6. On the status of the *Analects* in the Han, see Tsai Yen-zen, "*Ching* and *Chuan*: Towards Defining the Confucian Scriptures in Han China (206 BCE–220 CE)" (Ph.D. diss., Harvard University, 1992), esp. 206–43. For the Seven Classics, see Tsai, "*Ching* and *Chuan*," 207–8; and Morohashi Tetsuji, *Keigaku kenkyū josetsu* (Tokyo: Meguro shoten, 1975), 40–41.

7. He's co-compilers in the *Lunyu jijie* project were Sun Yong, Zheng Chong, Cao Xi, and Xun Yi. The "Preface to the *Lunyu*" records these names—about which little is known—along with that of He Yan. For more on the preface and He Yan's role in the project, see the section in this chapter "He Yan and the *Analects* in the Third Century."

8. Both these subcommentaries circulated widely, in turn, helping ensure the prominence of the He commentary. Of course, these subcommentaries, especially the one by Huang, advance some ideas not necessarily raised by the He commentary itself. See, for instance, Dai Junren, "Huang Kan *Lunyu yishu* de neihan sixiang," in *LunMeng yanjiu lunji*, ed. Qian Mu (Taibei: Liming wenhua shiye gongsi, 1981), 141–60; and Yuet Keung Lo, "The Formulation of Early Medieval Confucian Metaphysics: Huang K'an's (488–545) Accommodation of Neo-Taoism and Buddhism," in *Imagining Boundaries: Changing Confucian Doctrines, Texts, and Hermeneutics*, ed. Kai-wing Chow, On-cho Ng, and John B. Henderson (Albany: State University of New York Press, 1999), 57–83. Indeed, Huang's subcommentary is especially interesting, as it introduces concerns associated with the *xuanxue* (learning of the mysterious) and Buddhism into its reading of the *Analects* (as the Lo article suggests).

In this study, I draw on Huang Kan's subcommentary when it helps me understand He Yan better, even though I recognize that Huang's subcommentarial reading of He is just as interpretive as He's commentarial reading of the

Analects. I make no attempt to show what influence Huang's subcommentary might have had on Zhu Xi, as my aim here is more to compare the influences of the two major commentarial traditions on the classic than to trace every source of inspiration in Zhu's reading of the text.

9. Huang Kan, *Lunyu jijie yishu*, Congshu jicheng edition, 3.

10. For a brief history of authorial attribution, see Zhuo Zhongxin, *Lunyu heshi jijie zhuzi jizhu bijiao yanjiu* (Taibei: Jiaxin shuini gongsi, 1969), 19–22.

11. *Sanguo zhi* (Beijing: Zhonghua shuju, 1959), 9.292–93. For a brief but informative sketch of He Yan and his writings, see Wang Baoxuan, *Xuanxue tonglun* (Taibei: Wunan tushu chuban gongsi, 1996), 278–92.

12. For example, see Richard Mather, trans., *Shih-shuo hsin-yü: A New Account of Tales of the World* (Minneapolis: University of Minnesota Press, 1976), 297. A similar remark is found in the *Taiping yulan* 385.3b–4a, cited in Wang Baoxuan, *Xuanxue tonglun*, 278.

13. *Sanguo zhi* 9.283.

14. *Shishuo xinyu* cites He: "Whenever I take five-mineral powder, not only does it heal any illness I might have, but I am also aware of my spirit and intelligence becoming receptive and lucid" (Mather, *Shih-shuo hsin-yü*, 36). On the nature of this drug, see Mather, *Shih-shuo hsin-yü*, 20; Jay Sailey, *The Master Who Embraces Simplicity: A Study of the Philosopher Ko Hung, A.D. 283–343* (San Francisco: Chinese Materials Center, 1978), 424–32; and Rudolph G. Wagner, "Lebensstil und Drogen im Chinesischen Mittelalter," *Toung Pao* 59 (1973): 79–178.

15. *Sanguo zhi* 9.292–293. For a brief sketch of He Yan's life and writings, see Wang Baoxuan, *Xuanxue tonglun*, 278–92.

16. Etienne Balazs, "Nihilistic Revolt or Mystical Escapism," in *Chinese Civilization and Bureaucracy: Variations on a Theme*, trans. H. M. Wright, ed. Arthur F. Wright (New Haven, Conn.: Yale University Press, 1964), 226–54.

17. For example, *Hou Han shu* (Beijing: Zhonghua shuju, 1965), 79.2547.

18. *Hou Han shu* 60.1953.

19. *Hou Han shu* 60.1972. For overviews in English of the second and third centuries, see Etienne Balazs, "Political Philosophy and Social Crisis at the End of the Han Dynasty," in *Chinese Civilization and Bureaucracy: Variations on a Theme*, trans. H. M. Wright, ed. Arthur F. Wright (New Haven, Conn.: Yale University Press, 1964), 187–225; Balazs, "Nihilistic Revolt or Mystical Escapism"; Paul Demiéville, "Philosophy and Religion from Han to Sui," in *The Cambridge History of China*, vol. 1, *The Ch'in and Han Empires, 221 B.C.–A.D. 220*, ed. Denis Twitchett and Michael Loewe (Cambridge: Cambridge University Press, 1986), 808–72; Ying-shih Yü, "Individualism and the Neo-Taoist Movement in Wei Chin China," in *Individualism and Holism: Studies in Confucian and Taoist Values*, ed. Donald J. Munro (Ann Arbor: Center for Chinese Studies, University of Michigan, 1985), 121–55; and Charles Holcombe, *In the Shadow of the Han: Literati Thought and Society at the Beginning of the Southern Dynasties* (Honolulu: University of Hawai'i Press, 1994).

20. Wang Baoxuan, *Xuanxue tonglun*, 17–26; Wang Baoxuan, *Wang Bi pingzhuan* (Guangxi: Guangxi jiaoyu chuban, 1997), 30–39; Wagner, *Craft of a Chinese Commentator*, 9–51.

21. *Sanguo zhi* 9.292.

22. Mather, *Shih-shuo hsin-yü*, 97.

23. Cited in Mather, *Shih-shuo hsin-yü*, 95.

24. Wagner, *Craft of a Chinese Commentator*, 27–51.

25. Quoted in Liu Xiaobiao's commentary on the *Shishuo xinyu* and cited in Mather, *Shih-shuo hsin-yü*, 97; and Wagner, *Craft of a Chinese Commentator*, 133.

26. From a notice on Wang Bi appended to Zhong Hui's (225–264) biography in the dynastic history, *Sanguo zhi* 28.795, cited and translated in Lynn, *Classic of Changes*, 11. This is recorded in the *Shih-shuo hsin-yü* as well (Mather, *Shih-shuo hsin-yü*, 96).

27. Wang Bi wrote the *Laozi Daodejing zhu* and also wrote what became the standard commentary on the *Zhouyi*, the *Zhouyi zhu*. Both have been translated by Lynn as *The Classic of Changes* and *The Classic of the Way and Virtue*.

28. Only He Yan's survives. Fragments from Wang's and Guo's survive in Huang Kan's (488–545) *Lunyu yishu*. According to Lo, "One of the reasons the *Analects* was so popular in the early medieval period is that Confucius was considered to be the ideal sage by early medieval thinkers in general and by the Neo-Daoists in particular. Although most people would model after Zhuangzi in their lifestyle, they did so only because the sagehood of Confucius was deemed to be too lofty and supreme for them to emulate" ("Formulation of Early Medieval Confucian Metaphysics," 61).

29. A paraphrase allows me to eliminate inessential detail and a multitude of honorific titles without encumbering the translation with ellipses.

30. The identity of this Mr. Zhou remains unknown.

31. "Lunyu xu" 1a–b. Compare Anne Cheng, "Lun yü," in *Early Chinese Texts: A Bibliographical Guide*, ed. Michael Loewe (Berkeley: Society for the Study of Early China and Institute of East Asian Studies, University of California, 1993), 313–23, esp. 315–19, although there are some inaccuracies here. For an extended, sound treatment of many of the points that He alludes to, see Makeham, "Formation of *Lunyu* as a Book."

32. Of course, some attempts were made to incorporate such metaphysical concerns into Confucian teachings, a notable one being Huang Kan's subcommentary on the *Analects*, the *Lunyu yishu* (Dai Junren, "Huang Kan *Lunyu yishu* de neihan sixiang"; Lo, "Formulation of Early Medieval Confucian Metaphysics").

33. By the mid-ninth century the canon had grown to twelve, including the *Book of Changes;* the *Book of Poetry;* the *Book of History;* the *Book of Rites* and its two companion ritual texts, the *Yili* (*Etiquette and Ritual*) and the *Zhouli* (*Rites of Zhou*); the *Spring and Autumn Annals* (with the *Zuozhuan* commentary) and its two other commentaries, the *Gongyang zhuan* and the *Guliang zhuan;*

the *Analects;* the *Classic of Filial Piety;* and the *Erya* dictionary. Toward the end of the eleventh century, the *Mencius,* the last of the Thirteen Classics, was finally added.

34. *Yüanshi* 81.2019.

35. For fuller discussions of this shift and the reasons for it, see Daniel K. Gardner, *Chu Hsi and the Ta-hsueh: Neo-Confucian Reflection on the Confucian Canon* (Cambridge, Mass.: Harvard University, Council on East Asian Studies, 1986), 5–16; and Daniel K. Gardner, *Learning to Be a Sage: Selections from the Conversations on Master Chu, Arranged Topically* (Berkeley: University of California Press, 1990), 57–80.

36. Wang Mouhong, *Zhuzi nianpu* (Taibei: Shijie shuju, 1973), 21.

37. Wang Mouhong, *Zhuzi nianpu,* 46.

38. Zhu Xi, *Hui'an xiansheng Zhu Wengong wenji,* Sibu congkan edition, 75.21a–b.

39. Wang Mouhong, *Zhuzi nianpu,* 65.

40. *Zhuzi yulei* (hereafter YL) 19.437 (*juan* 19, p. 437 of Zhonghua edition).

41. Huang Gan, *Huang Mianzhai xiansheng wenji,* Congshu jicheng edition, 186.

42. *Hui'an xiansheng Zhu Wengong wenji* 59.5a.

43. The translation is based on the He Yan commentary in *Lunyu zhushu* and the Zhu Xi commentary in *Lunyu jizhu.*

44. This sort of "historical" approach to the *Analects* is clearly less interested in understanding matters such as the "authenticity" of the analects—whether they were uttered by Confucius himself, which of them were uttered when, how they were transmitted in the various versions of the text, and the process by which the *Analects* as a collection, achieved stability and textual closure—than in understanding the meaning given to the text of the *Analects* by those in the tradition who found it meaningful. As fascinating and important as such questions are, they shed little light on how the text as received by the tradition was in fact understood by Chinese for the past two millennia.

For two recent English-language studies of such matters, see Makeham, "Formation of *Lunyu* as a Book"; and E. Bruce Brooks and A. Taeko Brooks, *The Original Analects: Sayings of Confucius and His Successors* (New York: Columbia University Press, 1998).

I

Learning

The first substantive character of the *Analects* is *xue*, "to learn." It is perhaps fitting therefore to begin our exploration into commentary on the *Analects* with a discussion of some of the passages on learning. Still more to the point is the fact that learning is a refrain for Confucius throughout the *Analects*. Disciples are exhorted repeatedly to take learning seriously as a means of refining and improving themselves. Confucius frequently describes himself to others as one who, more than anything, loves learning, suggesting that it is this love of learning that distinguishes him from others—and the superior man (*junzi*) from the little person (*xiaoren*). As this first chapter makes clear, what is meant by "learning" in the *Analects*, what makes for effective learning there, and what effect proper learning has on the learner all depend in large part on the reader's commentarial guide. Different guides lead in different directions.

Furthermore, as we shall see, concepts considered most central to Confucius's vision—true goodness, ritual, the superior man, and the Way, each of which will be taken up in subsequent chapters—are better appreciated against the background of Confucius's insistent call for learning.

I

He Yan's reading:

> The Master said, To learn and recite it in due time, is this indeed not a pleasure?

Ma [Rong] said, "*Zi* [master], a general designation for a male, refers to Kongzi [Master Kong]." Wang [Su] said, "*Shi* [in due time] means that the student recites [*songxi*] it in due time. Because he recites it in due time, the learning is never relinquished. For this reason it is a pleasure."

> To have friends come from afar, is this indeed not a delight?

Bao [Xian] said, "Fellow disciples [*tongmen*] are said to be friends [*peng*]."

> Others do not understand and yet he feels no anger, is this indeed not a superior man? (1.1 [1])[1]

Wen [to feel anger] is "anger" [*nu*]. Generally speaking, when there is that which other people do not understand, the superior man feels no anger.[2]

---

1. Analect numbers correspond to those in *Lunyu yinde* in the Harvard-Yenching Institute Sinological Index Series. The numbers in brackets refer to the passage numbers in the appendix, where the Chinese text of the analects and their commentaries is reproduced.

2. John Makeham cautions: "The traditional and continued assumption that in *LYJJ* where a commentary is not attributed to a particular commentator it should then be attributed specifically to He Yan, has yet to be justified" ("The Earliest Extant Commentary on *Lunyu: Lunyu zheng shi zhu*," *T'oung Pao* 83 [1997]: 269, n. 33). This assumption is made explicit for the first time by Huang Kan in his subcommentary on analect 1.1. As noted in the introduction, He Yan, perhaps the main contributor to the project, did indeed have collaborators, and some of the commentarial remarks likely were theirs. Thus the reference to "He Yan's reading" here and throughout the translation should be understood to be shorthand for "He Yan et al."

Zhu Xi's reading:

> The Master said, To learn and rehearse it constantly, is this indeed not a pleasure?

Xue [to learn] means "to emulate" [*xiao*]. Human nature in all cases is good, but in becoming aware of this goodness, there are those who lead and those who follow. Those who follow in becoming aware of it must emulate what those who lead in becoming aware of it do. Only then can they understand goodness and return to their original state. *Xi* is the frequent, rapid motion of a bird's wings in flight. The ceaselessness of learning is like the frequent, rapid motion of a bird's wings in flight. *Yue* means pleasure. To learn and then constantly rehearse it is to master what one has learned; the mind-and-heart thereby fills with pleasure. The progress of such a one naturally will be unceasing. Master Cheng[3] said, "*Xi* means repetition. To mull it over constantly until thoroughly imbued with it is pleasurable." He further said, "The student takes it and puts it into practice. Since he rehearses it constantly, what he learns becomes part of him. Thus, it is a pleasure." Mr. Xie [Liangzuo] said, "*Shi xi* means 'at no time does one not rehearse.' 'To sit as if personating the deceased' [*Liji* 1.8a]: in sitting at all times rehearse it. 'To stand as if sacrificing' [*Liji* 1.8a]: in standing at all times rehearse it."

> To have friends come from afar, is this indeed not a delight?

Peng [friends] means "the same kind." When they come from afar, the near-at-hand is evident. Master Cheng said, "Extend goodness to others, and those who trust and follow will be many. Hence, delightful." He also said, "'Pleasure' is in one's mind-and-heart, and 'delight' is manifested externally by the subject."

3. Zhao Shunsun (1215–1276) remarks, "The older Cheng brother is named Hao, the younger brother is named Yi. They are from Henan. Because the *Collected Commentaries* considers their schools to be alike it refers to them collectively as 'Master Cheng'" (*Lunyu zuanshu*, "LunMeng gangling" 4a). In other words, in this work, Zhu does not feel it necessary to ascribe a comment made by either Cheng to a particular brother. For a detailed discussion of Zhu's use of the term "Master Cheng," see Wing-tsit Chan, *Chu Hsi: New Studies* (Honolulu: University of Hawai'i Press, 1989), 293–97.

> Others do not know him, yet he feels no resentment, is he indeed not
> a superior man?

Wen [to feel resentment] means "to harbor anger." *Junzi* [superior man] is
the designation for a person of perfected virtue. Mr. Yin [Tun] said, "Learning rests with oneself; being known or not rests with others. How can there
be resentment?" Master Cheng said, "Although he takes delight in extending it to others, should they not appreciate this, he feels no melancholy;
such is the so-called superior man." In my humble opinion, to delight in
extending it to others is natural and easy. To be unknown and yet feel no
resentment is challenging and difficult. Thus only the person of perfected
virtue is capable of it. For virtue to become perfect depends on learning
being correct, on rehearsing being masterful, and on pleasure being profound—all without end.

Master Cheng said, "Delight follows from pleasure. One who feels no
delight is not fit to be called a superior man."

In this passage, the Master urges disciples to engage in learning.
But he is silent about what constitutes learning, so it is left to later
commentators to define and give substance to the term, which is
repeated throughout the classic. He Yan would have disciples of Confucius engage in book learning, reading and reciting texts [*song xi*]—
obviously not just any text but the proper texts—in a timely manner, so
that their understanding of them becomes deep and appreciation of
them is cause for pleasure. For Zhu Xi, learning surely would include
this sort of book learning, but the definition is far broader. "*Xue* [to
learn] means 'to emulate,'" according to the gloss with which Zhu
begins his commentary on the *Analects*. Wherever good is manifested
or expressed, whether in books, other people, or the past, disciples
need to emulate it: this is learning. Learning that does not involve
emulation of the good is not real learning. Zhu thus explicitly gives
learning a distinctly moral purpose, which is absent in He Yan's commentary. Learning is learning the good and to be good.

Herein lies another contrast between the two commentarial
readings. Zhu tries to explain why *xue*, or learning, is important, why
Confucius would admonish his disciples to devote themselves to it.

Learning makes men better. This is not to argue that He Yan does not understand moral improvement as the reason for learning; it is simply to note that any reader of the Zhu commentary cannot but take away from analect 1.1 an understanding of the pointedly moral purpose of the endeavor. Zhu, a scholar fully acquainted with the He Yan commentary—indeed, he often cites it—is no doubt taking some pains here to distance himself from what he regards as the overly scholastic bent of He Yan's reading. As committed as he may be to studying texts, especially canonical texts, Zhu nonetheless feels that students frequently lose sight of what really matters, moral learning and transformation. This, of course, is why in the conversations with his own disciples found in the *Zhuzi yulei, Conversations of Master Zhu, Arranged Topically*, he warned, "Book learning is a secondary matter for students."[4] In another conversation, about the meaning of the *Analects*, we similarly read:

> Someone asked, "To learn and rehearse it constantly," doesn't this speak of the *Book of Poetry*, the *Book of History*, the *Book of Rites*, and the *Book of Music*? He replied, No, it absolutely doesn't. Still, if there were no *Book of Poetry*, *Book of History*, *Book of Rites*, and *Book of Music*, they'd surely not get it. The learning of the sages and common learning are not the same, and it's here where there is some disagreement. Sages and worthies in teaching people to read books simply wanted them to know the Way of learning, but reading books in common learning is simply a matter of reading books and not in the least to understand how to go about the Way of learning.[5]

I suspect that Zhu Xi is implicitly taking aim at He Yan's interpretation for what he views as its narrowness, for promoting a learning that does not necessarily go beyond the mastery of the particular texts read. This disagreement with He Yan is not purely intellectual but no doubt is colored to some extent by his perspective as a Southern Song

4. YL 10.161.
5. YL 20.447.

educational critic deeply disturbed by the superficiality and careerism of contemporary learning.[6]

In this way, the reader of Zhu Xi's interlinear commentary learns that learning is fundamentally moral, and he also learns what makes learning to be moral ontologically possible. Zhu, borrowing from Mencius (fourth century B.C.E.), asserts that "human nature is in all cases good," and he then suggests that since human nature is good, learning through constant modeling and emulation to be good is nothing but the realization of one's true self. With these remarks, he is providing for his reader the assumptions that, to his mind, make Confucius's remark to his disciples intelligible. These are assumptions his reader must share if he is to understand the first passage of the *Analects* and, indeed, the rest of the classic as well.

As Zhu reads analect 1.1, the strongly moral message of the first line threads its way throughout the passage. Once a person realizes his inner goodness through the learning process, others far and wide come to follow him, taking him as their model for emulation. Whereas He Yan interprets the "friends coming from afar" to be fellow disciples interested in learning from their teacher, Zhu reads "friends" to be those attracted to the goodness this person has cultivated. And whereas He Yan understands the line to refer to the delight the teacher takes in the company of disciples who share his interests and are eager to discuss them, Zhu reads it as a reference to the good person delighting in the fact that others "trust and follow" him. Again, it is an individual's moral accomplishment that is the cause for the delight. On a few occasions, Zhu Xi's own disciples press him on his commentary on this line, wondering whether the delight the person experiences is owing to his cultivation of goodness or to the large number of people attracted to him. Although in one response he flatly says, "He delights in that those who trust and follow him are many," in others he is considerably less straightforward.[7] What remains clear, however, and to the point of our

6. Daniel K. Gardner, *Learning to Be a Sage: Selections from the* Conversations on Master Chu, Arranged Topically (Berkeley: University of California Press, 1990), 13–22.

7. YL 20.451–52.

analysis, is that it is the goodness cultivated in the process of learning that attracts others.

Finally, the last line of this opening analect is interpreted quite differently by the two commentators. For He, the superior man is the teacher implied in the previous line, and what makes him a superior man is that he feels no anger in the face of his students' failure to understand what he has taught them. The suggestion here is that the true teacher perseveres and untiringly continues with his instruction.[8] By contrast, for Zhu Xi, the superior man is a man of perfected virtue, a man who effectively engages in the learning of this first line, thereby bringing about in himself a moral transformation, and then, as in line 2, extends to others what he has discovered in himself. According to this reading, the real challenge for the morally cultivated individual comes when others are not at all moved by his goodness, when his goodness is not recognized. In Zhu's reading, it is the superior man alone who can persist in cultivating the good, in perfecting himself morally, even as worldly recognition of his accomplishment passes him by—and who feels not the slightest resentment.[9]

Zhu's commentary on the superior man has at least two important effects on the reader. First, the three lines of this opening passage of the *Analects* are given an interpretive coherence not offered by He Yan. In Zhu's reading, the Master is outlining a sequence of achievements that culminate in becoming a superior man. Thus the commentary on the final line concludes with the pointed remark that only one who learns, rehearses, and finds pleasure in it all, as prescribed in the opening line of the passage, is capable of becoming a superior man. Second, and again in a sharp and crucial difference from He's commentary, Confucius is made to be speaking to all of us. That is, we all are born

8. This reading of the line is supported by the Master's self-assessment in 7.2 and 7.34: "In teaching others I do not grow weary."

9. In his subcommentary, Huang Kan is the first to observe that the line in question is indeed open to these two quite different readings: (1) "others do not understand yet he feels no anger" and (2) "others do not know him, yet he feels no anger." The grammar of He Yan's brief commentarial remark indicates that he inclines toward the first, whereas Zhu clearly adopts the second.

with a good human nature, we have been told, and through moral learning are capable of realizing it in ourselves. To put it another way, we all are able to achieve perfect virtue. This, for Zhu Xi, is precisely the challenge the Master is issuing in the text of the *Analects*.

This point, in turn, leads to a still more general one. In his commentary, He Yan reads the text of the *Analects* mostly historically, for want of a better characterization. Through his glosses, he wants his reader to understand what Confucius was teaching his group of disciples. To be sure, He's reader might be able to extrapolate and generalize for himself from the Master's teachings to these disciples, but He Yan makes little attempt to serve as a guide. Zhu Xi, by contrast, understands Confucius to be addressing all of us and thus works in his commentary to draw out, in clear and often elaborate terms, the larger ethical and philosophical message of Confucius's teachings. Zhu's reader should appreciate not only the meaning of the *Analects*, the teachings to disciples, but also the universal applicability of the text.

2

A number of the analects take up issues suggested by analect 1.1. Confucius, perhaps persuaded that his own abilities and accomplishments have largely been unappreciated, often returns to the matter, raised in the last line of 1.1, of worldly recognition. Mostly, as passages like 1.16, 4.14, 14.30, and 15.19 suggest, he believes that winning a reputation is of no concern to a superior man. In analect 14.24, he is critical of his contemporaries because their learning, as he sees it, is aimed precisely at gaining recognition. And this, of course, is not the learning advocated in 1.1.

He Yan's reading:

> The Master said, "In ancient times, those who learned did so for the sake of themselves; nowadays those who learn do so for the sake of others." (14.24 [2])
> Kong [Anguo] said, "'For the sake of themselves' means to put it into

practice; 'for the sake of others' means merely to be able to speak about it."

Zhu Xi's reading:

> The Master said, In ancient times, those who learned did so for the sake of themselves; nowadays those who learn do so for the sake of others.
>
> Master Cheng said, "'For the sake of themselves' means that they wish to get it for themselves; 'for the sake of others' means they wish to make it known to others." Master Cheng said, "In ancient times, those who learned for the sake of themselves in the end brought other things to completion; nowadays those who learn for the sake of others, in the end, lose themselves." I would say that in discussing the boundary between success and failure in the application of the mind-and-heart, the sages and worthies offered many explanations. But none compares with this one in incisiveness. Be clear about the distinction here and examine yourself with respect to it daily and you may near the point that you are not in the dark about what to pursue.

In this analect, Confucius warns his disciples that in learning there is a choice between what is done for one's own sake and what is done for the sake of others. Learning in itself is not a virtue; rather, the kind of learning and the end to which it is put justify it. Learning whose purpose is to impress others, to win a name for oneself, is not the right sort of learning—and it is precisely this sort that Confucius finds prevalent among his contemporaries. But while He Yan and Zhu Xi agree on what constitutes "learning for the sake of others," they agree less explicitly about what Confucius means by "learning for the sake of oneself."

For He Yan, learning that does not translate into practice but remains mere words is not substantive or authentic learning. That is, for learning to be truly for one's own sake, a person must act on it. Here He no doubt has in mind the numerous analects that favor deed or action over speech (e.g., 4.22, 4.24, 12.3, and 2.13). For Zhu, real or true learning is expressly moral, just as it is in analect 1.1. If learning is not made a person's own and if it does not transform him, making him better and closer to his true self, then it is not real learning. Only real learning will enable him to extend himself to others and bring about a similar completion or self-realization in them.

In the closing lines of his commentary on this passage, Zhu speaks directly to his contemporaries—something that He Yan rarely if ever did—urging them to be mindful of the crucial distinction in learning that the Master makes here. The choice between the two, he warns, is theirs to make. Such warnings also echo throughout Zhu's conversations with his disciples in *Conversations of Master Zhu*. Convinced, as Confucius was earlier, that his contemporaries are largely engaged in the wrong kind of learning, in "learning for the sake of others," Zhu Xi exhorts them repeatedly to choose the right path over the careerist one:

> The important thing for students today is to distinguish between the paths. What's important is the boundary between "doing it for one's own sake" and "doing it for the sake of others." "To do it for one's own sake" is to grasp the essence of things and affairs firsthand in reaching an understanding of them—you want to understand them for yourself. It isn't to understand them recklessly, nor is it to understand them in a way that makes you look good, so that people will say yes, you have indeed understood. If this is how you go about it, even supposing you did understand them 100 percent accurately, they'd still have no effect on you at all.[10]

Zhu's evident disdain here for contemporary learning is clear: in his view, it is learning for the mere sake of impressing others, of winning fame and recognition, and is not anything like the learning of a superior man.

In the vision expressed in the *Analects*, as both He and Zhu understand it, gaining reputation is not the point. As Confucius stated in 15.19, "The superior man is pained by his own inabilities; he is not

10. YL 8.139.

pained by others not knowing him." Yet for all such utterances in the *Analects* to the effect that worldly reputation does not matter, occasionally an analect suggests that reputation is indeed desirable, even to be valued by the superior man, as found in analect 15.20, for example:

He Yan's reading:

> The Master said, The superior man worries lest he pass from the world without having made a name for himself. (15.20 [3])

Ji [worries] is similar to *bing* [is pained].

Zhu Xi's reading:

> The Master said, The superior man worries lest he pass from the world without having made a name for himself.

Mr. Fan [Zuyu] said, "The superior man learns for the sake of himself; his aim is not that others know him. Still, if he passes from the world without having made a name for himself, it would be clear that he had not really done good."

While He and Zhu read the passage similarly, a telling difference in their commentarial approaches becomes evident here. He Yan lets Confucius's remark stand on its own, whereas Zhu Xi, sensing an apparent contradiction with other remarks in the text, works to reconcile the different messages. Yes, he tells his reader, as Confucius asserts elsewhere, the superior man does indeed engage in learning for the sake of oneself, learning for moral improvement, and the purpose of such learning is decidedly not to impress others. But while the purpose of true learning is not to impress others and win a name for oneself, true learning naturally results in goodness, and such goodness is sure to be acknowledged by others. Thus a person intent on doing good "worries lest he pass from the world without having made a name for himself," for winning a reputation is merely evidence of his concrete achievement of good.

What is worth noting here is not whether reconciliation is really needed but that in his commentary, Zhu Xi takes it upon himself (drawing on Fan Zuyu, of course) to read the different analects side by side. Like He's commentary, Zhu's directs the reader how to understand each analect, but unlike He's, it also aids the reader in understanding the intratextual relationship of the Master's remarks. Zhu attempts to demonstrate how the text as a whole coheres, how the individual analects should be read against one another. Behind this attempt is, of course, the assumption that such coherence does in fact exist. This assumption of coherence, I would argue, is an important and distinguishing characteristic of virtually all of Zhu Xi's commentarial work. The conclusion will discuss this point at some length.

3

Throughout the *Analects*, Confucius testifies to his own personal love of learning, suggesting that it is precisely such a love of learning that accounts for what he has become. He believes that it is in the will to learn that he is truly distinguished from others. Consequently, this will to learn assumes a central place in his teachings and remains a subject of interest and concern throughout the later Confucian tradition.

The text of the *Analects* makes numerous references to the Master's own love of learning:

He Yan's reading:

> The Master said, In a hamlet of ten households, there are sure to be those who in loyalty and trustworthiness are my equal, but their love of learning will not equal mine. (5.28 [4])

Zhu Xi's reading:

> The Master said, In a hamlet of ten households, there are sure to be those who in loyalty and trustworthiness are my equal, but their love of learning will not equal mine.
> "Ten households" refers to a small hamlet. To be the equal of the Sage in loyalty and trustworthiness is to have an excellent natural constitution.

Although the Master was born knowing it [*sheng zhi*], he remained forever fond of learning. He says this, therefore, to motivate others. The passage says that an excellent constitution is easy to acquire, but the Way in its perfection is difficult to hear. Through perfect learning of it, one may become a sage. If one does not engage in learning, one cannot avoid becoming anything more than an ordinary man. Can one possibly not be motivated?

Because he provides no commentary here, He Yan seems to be reading the passage as the Master's simple autobiographical expression of his own incomparable love of learning. Zhu reads it as exhortatory, intended to motivate disciples and readers of the classic to emulate the Master and devote themselves to a similar life of true learning. Such true learning does not result merely in moral betterment, as frequently asserted elsewhere in the text; sagehood itself also is within reach, attainable through the right sort of learning. He Yan would never suggest to his readers that through learning, they might become the sage that Confucius had been. To Zhu's readers, emulation of the good, emulation of the behavior manifested by Confucius himself, grants one access to the lofty realm of the sages. Learning is thus powerful stuff, what distinguishes the sage from the common man.

Zhu Xi understands this remark by the Master against the background of Song metaphysics. People are born with different psychophysical (*qi*) endowments: those who are loyal and trustworthy are fortunate to have excellent endowments. The Master, however, his own modest assertions (e.g., 7.20) to the contrary notwithstanding, is even more fortunate, born with the best and purest endowment and thus without any need to learn. And still he devotes his life to the pursuit of learning. If this is true of the great Sage, how can others not be moved to do the same?

In alluding in the commentary here to *sheng zhi* (born knowing it), Zhu again is making intratextual connections, reminding the reader of the larger coherence to be found in the text of the classic. Analect 16.9 speaks of different grades of knowing, placing *sheng zhi* at the top: "Those born knowing it are the highest, those who through learning come to know it are next, those who learn it but with difficulty are next; and, those who because of difficulty do not learn it, these people are the lowest." Zhu, on the one hand, is making an intratextual reference to analect 16.9 when he claims here that Confucius was born knowing it, but, on the other hand, he seems to be contradicting the Master's own denial of innate knowledge in analect 7.20, in which he modestly indicates that it is only *through learning* that he has come to know it:

He Yan's reading:

> The Master said, I am not one who is born knowing it. I am one who loves antiquity and diligently pursues it. (7.20 [5])

Zheng [Xuan] said, "To say this is to exhort others to learn."

Zhu Xi's reading:

> The Master said, I am not one who is born knowing it. I am one who loves antiquity and diligently pursues it.

One who is born knowing it is of pure, clear psychophysical stuff [*qi*]; his moral principle manifests itself clearly. He knows without the need for learning. *Min* [earnestly] is *su*, "with urgency," and means *ji ji*, "eagerly."

Mr. Yin [Tun] said, "That Confucius, a sage born knowing it, always speaks of 'fondness for learning,' is not only to motivate others. It would seem that what can be known at birth is simply moral principle. As for ritual, music, names and their things, and the changing affairs past and present, these indeed must be learned, and only afterward can we test their truth."

In Zhu's reading of this passage, colored again by the *li/qi* metaphysics of the day, all human beings are born with both a human nature that is good and a particular allotment of *qi*, psychophysical stuff. Dense, turbid psychophysical stuff obstructs the realization of the inner goodness with which we are endowed. By contrast, pure, refined stuff allows the goodness to become perfectly manifest. To be born knowing it is to be born with the purest and most refined endowment of psychophysical stuff, which permits the full expression of human nature in all its moral goodness. In Zhu's mind, Confucius was indeed born with an exceptional endowment of psychophysical stuff. Thus in this sense, he was certainly born knowing (cf. 5.28), that is, knowing the moral principle that is human nature.

Citing Yin Tun, Zhu goes on to make a distinction—one that probably was intended to help reconcile his assertion that Confucius was born knowing it—from Confucius's own disclaimer here. The reader is informed that the knowing possessed innately by the Master was the moral knowing of right and wrong, not the knowing of every-day affairs and matters. These affairs—including ritual, music, and past and present events—must be learned and assessed for their truth. Learning therefore remained crucial even to a sage like Confucius if he were to conduct himself appropriately in these everyday affairs and matters. Thus Yin Tun concludes that the Master's remark in 7.20 "is not only to motivate others," as He Yan earlier argued. There was indeed real learning that the Master himself had to undertake.

In 2.4, one of the text's most often cited passages, Confucius auto-biographically recounts his lifelong pursuit of learning, which began in earnest at the age of fifteen. It was then that he first became deter-mined to learn. The general point of this influential remark is to link moral behavior directly to the pursuit of learning. In particular, it makes the Master's will or desire to learn, not the learning itself, the very foundation of his life's moral quest.

He Yan's reading:

> The Master said, At fifteen, I set my mind-and-heart on learning. At thirty, I made my stand.
> There was accomplishment.

> At forty, I had no doubts.
> Kong [Anguo] said, "He did not doubt."

> At fifty, I knew heaven's decrees. At sixty, my ears were in accord. At seventy, I followed the desires of my mind-and-heart without over-stepping right. (2.4 [6])
> Kong [Anguo] said, "He knew the decrees of heaven from beginning to

end." Zheng [Xuan] said, "His ears, upon hearing the words, would know their most subtle meaning." Ma [Rong] said, "*Ju* [right] means *fa*, 'rules.' He followed the desires of his mind-and-heart without ever going against the rules."

Zhu Xi's reading:

The Master said, At fifteen, I set my mind-and-heart on learning.
In ancient times they entered the school for greater learning at the age of fifteen. The direction of the mind-and-heart is what is meant by *zhi* [to set the mind-and-heart]. What is called learning here is the "Way of greater learning" [i.e., as found in the *Daxue*]. To set the mind-and-heart on this is to think about it all the time and to engage in it tirelessly.

At thirty, I stood on my own.
To be capable of standing on one's own is to have a secure hold on it [i.e., mind-and-heart] without having to make any effort to set it in the right direction.

At forty, I had no doubts.
With respect to affairs and things as they should be, he had no doubts at all. This being the case, he understood perfectly clearly without having to make any effort to hold on to it [the mind-and-heart].

At fifty, I knew heaven's decree.
"Heaven's decree refers to the heavenly Way spreading everywhere and imbuing all things. This is the reason that affairs and things are as they should be. To know it [heaven's decree] is knowing at its most refined—and that there would be no doubts goes without saying."

At sixty, my ears were in accord.
Sound enters, and the mind-and-heart grasps it completely and without resistance. This is to know it perfectly; it is to understand it without having to reflect.

At seventy, I followed the desires of my mind-and-heart without overstepping right.

Cong [to follow] is *sui*, "to follow or accord with." *Ju* [right] is a tool of standard measure, used for squaring. He follows the desires of his mind-and-
heart and naturally never exceeds the standard measure. He is at ease
putting them [his desires] into practice and, without any effort, hits the
mean.

Master Cheng said, "Confucius was born knowing it. Saying that it
was through learning that he brought it to perfection is to encourage
people of future generations. *Li* [to stand] is the ability to stand oneself
on this Way. *Buhuo* [to have no doubts] is to have no doubts. *Zhi tianming* [to know heaven's decree] is to probe principle and fully realize
the original human nature. *Er shun* [the ears were in accord] means that
one fully understands everything one hears. *Cong xin suo yu bu yu ju*
[to follow the desires of the mind-and-heart without overstepping right]
is to hit the mean effortlessly." He further said, "While Confucius himself
says that such was the sequence by which he advanced in virtue, this
was not necessarily the case for the Sage. He is simply establishing
here a plan that, once they fill in the holes, enables learners to move
forward and, once they complete all the steps, to achieve perfection
[*Mengzi* 4B.18 and 7A.24]." Mr. Hu [Yin][11] said, "The teachings of the
sage involve many precepts, but their essence is nothing more than to
ensure that others do not lose their original mind-and-heart. Those who
want to fulfill this mind-and-heart need merely fix it on the learning
proclaimed by the Sage, following the sequence here to move forward
until there are no blemishes and the myriad manifestations of principle
become luminous and fully realized. Only then, in the course of everyday life, will their original mind be lustrous, and in following desires, will
they always be one with principle. In this case, the mind-and-heart is
substance and the desires are function; substance is the Way and function is righteousness. One's voice becomes the law, and one's body
becomes the standard [said of the legendary ruler Yu in *Shiji* 2.51]." He

---

11. Hu Yin studied under Yang Shi, a disciple of the Cheng brothers.

further said, "The Sage says this, first, to proclaim to learners that they must immerse themselves leisurely and happily in it and must not skip any steps in going forward; second, to proclaim to learners that they must make daily advances and monthly progress [*Shijing*, Mao no. 288], never giving up halfway." In my opinion, the Sage was born knowing it [the Way] and was comfortable putting it into practice; it was certainly not a matter of gradual accumulation on his part. Yet in his own mind-and-heart, he never himself believed that he had already achieved it. In the course of everyday life, he was always mindful of his own progress, although other people could not sense it. For this reason, he claimed the general program here for himself, hoping learners would take it as their model and find motivation in it. It is not that in his mind-and-heart he really believed himself to be a sage but was being reticent because of circumstances. All later such modest remarks follow this same pattern.

The reader of Zhu Xi's commentary understands this passage as more than mere autobiography. With it, he has a practicable template he can now follow in his own moral quest. The heart of the learning program here is investigating the principle endowed in all things by heaven. That is, knowing principle, knowing why things are as they are, is to "know heaven's decree." To investigate or apprehend principle in the world is, according to Zhu Xi, precisely what is called for by the *Greater Learning*, another of the foundational texts in the Confucian tradition. According with principle is what enables one to realize one's human nature and be fully moral. Here, then, we have Zhu linking Confucius's moral autobiography to the current metaphysics of principle and psychophysical stuff, as well as linking one text in the canon, the *Analects*, to another, the *Greater Learning*. Such intertextual referencing, largely absent in He Yan's commentary, gives legitimacy to each of the texts, making each more intelligible while emphasizing their coherence and unity of message. Zhu Xi assumes here, as he does throughout all of his writing, that the canon of Confucian classics is an integrated whole in which the parts give meaning to the whole, just as the whole illuminates the parts.

As Zhu reads 2.4, Confucius predicates on the determination of the mind-and-heart (*zhi*) both the process of learning and the moral realization that is its goal. That is, only if the mind-and-heart truly "wills" it, is truly set on learning, can the student hope to understand the principle of things. And only with such understanding can there be moral perfection—that is, behavior that at all times is in perfect accord with everything and every affair the student encounters. In his writings and discussions, Zhu elaborates at great length on the concept of *zhi* introduced here. Indeed, in its meaning of "will," the component that gives the mind-and-heart its direction, *zhi* assumes a central and vital place in Zhu Xi's larger philosophical system and is an extremely popular topic of conversation with his disciples. For instance, "Students must establish their wills [*zhi*]. That people nowadays are aimless is simply because they've never taken learning seriously. In dealing with things, they're reckless simply because their wills aren't firmly established."[12] Taking his cue from the template outlined by the Master in 2.4, Zhu Xi in his Song redefinition of the Confucian tradition makes establishing the will a crucial, even a necessary, condition for success in the learning endeavor.

The Master's "autobiographical" statement in 2.4 shows why Confucius over and over expressed interest in teaching only those eager to learn, those whose will to learn equaled his, or at least what he many years later remembered it to have been. In his view, learning could not be successful if students did not bring the proper attitude, the right bent of mind-and-heart, to the process, just as he himself had done.

He Yan's reading:

> The Master said, Those not excited I do not instruct; those not eager I do not enlighten. If I raise up one corner and they do not come back with three corners, I do not continue. (7.8 [7])
> Zheng [Xuan] said, "In speaking with other people, Confucius would

12. YL 8.134; see also other comments in YL 8.

always wait for their mind-and-heart to be excited and their mouths eager, and only then would he instruct and enlighten them with explanation. This being the case, profound were their understanding and thinking. If in explanation he raised up one corner and talked about it, and the others did not think through the implications, he would not teach them again."

Zhu Xi's reading:

> The Master said, Those not anxious I do not instruct; those not eager I do not enlighten. If I raise up one corner and they do not come back with the other three, I do not continue.

Fen [anxious] has the sense of the mind-and-heart trying but not yet understanding. *Fei* [eager] is the condition of the mouth wanting to speak but being incapable. *Qi* [instruct] is to explain the idea, and *fa* [enlighten] is to convey fully the meaning of the words. A thing with four corners: hold one up and the other three can be known. *Fan* [come back with] means "to come back with corroboration." *Fu* [to repeat] is to teach them again. The preceding passage [7.7] speaks of the Sage's teaching others tirelessly. Consequently this one also is recorded in the hopes that learners will be compelled to apply themselves and to establish the groundwork for receiving instruction.

Master Cheng said, "Anxiety and eagerness are a matter of showing one's true intentions [*cheng yi*, from the *Daxue*, "Classic," par. 4] on one's face and in one's words. He waits for them to make true their intentions, and only then does he teach them. Once he has taught them, he always waits for them to understand it for themselves [*zide*, from *Mengzi* 4B.14 and *Zhongyong*, chap. 14], and only then does he continue his teaching." He further said, "If one enlightens them when they are not yet anxious and eager, their understanding may not be firm; if one enlightens them once they have become anxious and eager, their understanding will be solid."

Here again the student's psychology plays a central role in Zhu's analysis of what makes learning effective. Zhu explicitly equates the anxiety and eagerness in this analect with the outer expression of the student's intentions or bent of mind. Only the student who truly wills to learn—that is, who genuinely seeks to emulate the good [*xue*]—can understand it for himself, and only the student who understands it for himself can experience the moral progress that for Confucius, at least, resulted in "following the desires of the mind-and-heart without overstepping right" (2.4). Zhu Xi thus never seems to doubt that the *Analects* asserts the moral autonomy of the individual. But such moral autonomy carries with it a rather heavy responsibility: the individual must choose to set himself in the right direction.

In Zhu's reading of the *Analects*, Confucius repeatedly prods his followers to find the determination that will make learning successful, as in 8.17: "Learn as if you will not get there, as though you are fearful of losing it." For Zhu, only those with a mind-and-heart fearful of not getting it are properly tenacious and resolute about learning and thus likely to achieve success.

His remarks about 7.8 further illuminate the character of Zhu's commentarial style. Making both intratextual and intertextual references, he reads this passage first against the analect immediately preceding it, in which the Master remarks, "From those who have brought a bundle of dried meat on up, never have I refused instruction to anyone," and then against the texts of the *Greater Learning*, the *Mencius*, and the *Doctrine of the Mean*, the other three of the so-called Four Books. The effect of such integrating efforts is at least twofold: to lend deeper significance to the text of the *Analects* by underscoring its own coherence and demonstrating that its message is consistent with other central texts in the canon, and, at the same time, to strengthen the very canonicity of the Confucian texts, especially what were for Zhu Xi the core Four Books, by treating the message presented in them as unified and accessible to those open to hearing it.

4

In concluding this chapter on learning, we look at a passage from the *Analects* that has had great influence over the centuries, even though its meaning has remained ambiguous. Four simple characters comprise

15.39, the analect in question: *you jiao wu lei.* These four characters mean to Zhu Xi something very different from what they had meant earlier to He Yan.

He Yan's reading:

> The Master said, In instruction, there are to be no distinctions. (15.39 [8])
> Ma [Rong] said, "This is to say that with respect to receiving instruction, there are to be no distinctions in the kinds of people."

Zhu Xi's reading:

> The Master said, With instruction, there will be no distinctions.
> Human nature is in all instances good; the differences in kind of good and bad among people are the effects of psychophysical stuff and practice. For this reason, with the instruction of the superior man, everyone can return to original goodness, and never again will there be need to speak of the bad kind among people.

He Yan reads the passage in a way that emphasizes an idea apparently very much on Confucius's mind: equal access to learning. Social and economic background—with distinctions of rich and poor, noble and mean—is of no consequence in Confucius's consideration of who should be taught. Rather, it is only the eagerness that the individual brings to the learning process that distinguishes those worthy of receiving instruction from those unworthy. And, of course, He Yan's reading of this passage plays nicely off 7.7, in which the Master proudly says, "From those who have brought a bundle of dried meat on up, never have I refused instruction to anyone."

While faintly echoing He's reading, in the end Zhu's commentary goes well beyond it. Zhu also finds in this passage a call for equal educational opportunity, but of a very different sort from He's. Whether people are good or bad, owing to "the effects of the psychophysical stuff and practice," they all are entitled to receive instruction; and with instruction, each of them might be able to return to their ontologically good and true nature. Clearly, Zhu's reading is not the socioeconomic reading of He Yan but is decidedly moral in thrust: the good and the bad alike should be instructed. Furthermore, in Zhu's reading, Confucius is even more concerned with the all-important *effect* of instruction than with educational opportunity. With the superior man's instruction, all people, regardless of their psychophysical condition, will return to their original goodness. Proper instruction thus brings an end to the moral differences among people; moral equality is the outcome of good teaching. In short, to Zhu, the proper education produces good people. Thus if instruction is made available to everyone, "bad" people will no longer exist.

As he does throughout the *Analects*, Zhu Xi provides in his commentary on 15.39 the ontological and metaphysical assumptions necessary for his readers to appreciate his understanding of the passage. Learning enables us to be good because we all are born good in the first place. Learning is simply a process that, by refining our varying and unequal psychophysical endowments, returns us, one and all, to our true nature. In short, before we receive instruction, we have moral distinctions based on our individual psychophysical constitutions. But after instruction, such distinctions cease to exist.

For all its brevity, 15.39 demonstrates with great clarity, first, that different commentators find different meanings in a text. Second, and more specific to my book, Zhu Xi's understanding of what is intended by the *Analects*, as in the case here of "no distinctions," would in many instances have been utterly incomprehensible to He Yan a millennium earlier. Finally, the readers of different commentaries on a canonical text—as in the case of He Yan's and Zhu Xi's on the *Analects*—naturally take away quite different understandings of the text.

2

True Goodness

For Confucius, learning, as we saw in chapter 1, is learning to be a moral individual. To be moral is to embody virtues like sincerity, loyalty, filial piety, and trustworthiness. But the virtue that subsumes all others, the one that preoccupies the Master and his disciples throughout the *Analects*, is *ren*, translated here as "true goodness." Never does the Master provide an exhaustive definition of the term, nor does he readily describe people—including himself—as men of true goodness.[1] To be sure, there is a somewhat ineffable, indefinable quality to this supreme virtue. Still, the engaged reader of the *Analects* comes away from the text with a rough profile of the model of true goodness. For while Confucius may shy away from defining the term, he freely suggests—often through concrete examples and illustrations—the behavioral attributes that characterize it, the path that must be traveled to achieve it, and where ultimately it resides.

---

1. For example, 5.5, 5.8, 5.19, and 7.34.

I

Throughout the *Analects*, disciples relentlessly press the Master with questions: "What is true goodness?" "Is so-and-so a man of true goodness?" "Is such-and-such behavior a matter of true goodness?" and the like. The frequency with which such inquiries appear reveals an anxiety on their part as well as an eagerness to understand this paramount virtue whose full significance seems to elude them.

In responding to these many inquiries, Confucius characterizes true goodness in different ways, depending on whom and about whom he is speaking: to be slow or modest in speech (12.3); to be resolute and firm (13.27); to be possessed of courage (14.4); to be free from worry (9.29); to delight in mountains (6.23); to subdue the self and return to propriety (12.1); to be respectful, tolerant, trustworthy, diligent, and kind (17.5); and to love others (12.22). In this way, Confucius gives his followers—and readers—glimpses of various dimensions of true goodness. Nowhere, however, does he provide what might be called a comprehensive definition. Confucius seems to acknowledge that his followers are somewhat disappointed, that they are not entirely satisfied with his brief characterizations. But while they may suspect that he is withholding something from them, he assures them that he is sharing all that he knows (7.23). It thus remains for them—and us—to try to bring together these different characterizations into a more coherent, deeper understanding of this most important moral quality.

A series of exchanges between the disciple Zigong and Confucius conveys, I think, the essence of true goodness:

He Yan's reading:

> Zigong asked, Is there one word that can be practiced for the whole of one's life? The Master said, That would be "empathy" perhaps: what you do not wish yourself do not do unto others. (15.24 [9])
> This is to say, what you yourself hate do not inflict on others.

Zhu Xi's reading:

> Zigong asked, Is there one word that can be practiced for the whole of one's life? The Master said, That would be "empathy" perhaps: what you do not wish yourself do not do unto others.

Extend yourself to others, and what you do unto them will be inexhaustible. As a consequence, you will be able to practice it [empathy] for the whole of your life.

Mr. Yin [Tun] said, "In learning, we value knowing the essentials. Zigong's query can be said to be about knowing the essentials. Confucius told him the way to pursue true goodness. Extend yourself, and bring it [empathy] to perfection so that even the selflessness of a sage does not surpass it. Wouldn't it make good sense to practice this for the whole of your life?"

Here the Chinese golden rule is made the centerpiece of a Confucian life. *Shu*, "empathy," translated also as "reciprocity" or "consideration," is to treat others as one wishes to be treated oneself. It is the ability to put oneself in the place of others, to measure others and how to treat them using one's own feelings as the standard. The significance of this quality of empathy for Confucius is obvious elsewhere in the *Analects*, especially in 4.15, when in explaining to other disciples the one thread running through the Master's Way, Zengzi remarks: "The Way of our Master is doing the best one can [*zhong*] and empathy [*shu*], nothing more."

The reader of Zhu's commentary on 15.24—in contrast to the reader of He's—clearly learns that as central or essential as empathy might be, it should not be equated with true goodness. Rather, it is by means of exercising empathy in dealings with others that one may achieve true goodness. Empathy thus is a method or technique, a part of becoming truly good (cf. 12.2).

In the following passage, which likely precedes this one chronologically, Zigong, the questioner, claims to have succeeded in embodying the golden rule (however differently He and Zhu "read" the rule):

He Yan's reading:

> Zigong said, I do not wish others to mistreat me, nor do I wish to mistreat others.

Ma [Rong] said, "*Jia* [to mistreat or to inflict] means *ling*, 'to mistreat.'"

The Master said, Oh Si, you are not capable of this. (5.12 [10])
Kong [Anguo], "This is to say that he is incapable of preventing others from inflicting on him what is unrighteous."

Zhu Xi's reading:

> Zigong said, What I do not wish others to do unto me, I likewise wish not to do unto others. The Master said, Oh Si, you are not capable of this.

Zigong says that what I do not wish others to do unto me, I likewise do not wish to do unto others. This is the conduct of the truly good person and is effortless. For this reason, the Master believed it was not something Zigong was capable of.

Master Cheng said, "'What I do not wish others to do unto me, I likewise wish not to do unto others' is true goodness. 'What you do not like when done to you, likewise do not [*wu*] do unto others' is empathy [cf. *Lunyu* 15.24 and *Zhongyong*, chap. 13]. As for empathy, Zigong is perhaps capable of applying himself to it; as for true goodness, it is not something he is capable of." In my view, *wu* [not, as in "wish not"] is to be so naturally; *wu* [do not, as in "do not do unto others"] is a term of prohibition. This is the distinction between true goodness and empathy.

The Master finds Zigong's claim in the passage here to be overblown: "Oh Si, you are not capable of this." According to He Yan, in Confucius's view, although Zigong is capable of treating others well, he is not so charismatic and exemplary that others automatically treat him righteously. That is, his own lack of perfection is what explains the mistreatment of him by others, against his express wishes.

Interestingly, He Yan reads the two halves of the so-called golden rule as two grammatically independent statements, which for He have an independent semantic status as well. Zigong wishes not to mistreat others and seems to have been successful in this respect, and he wishes not to be mistreated by others, but his success here has been more limited.

For Zhu, the first half of the statement—"what I do not wish others to do unto me"—is a dependent clause that serves as the object of the wishes expressed in the second half of the statement: "I likewise wish not to do unto others." Confucius is critical because contrary to his own self-assessment, Zigong is not yet at the point that he effortlessly wishes for others what he would wish for himself. When Zhu Xi reads this passage against 15.24, he regards the previous one as an injunction forbidding one from behaving in a certain way, whereas this passage speaks of one who has successfully achieved a state of mind and being in which one "naturally"—without injunctions guiding one—behaves in this way. In sum, for Zhu Xi, a person is truly good when he *naturally* does not wish to treat others inappropriately. In contrast, he is empathetic when he consciously follows rules not to treat others inappropriately. Confucius disparages Zigong's claim here, concluding that Zigong may perhaps be capable of following "external" injunctions to be empathetic in the treatment of others but surely has not yet fully internalized the principle of empathy. Empathetic behavior is still not "natural" to him.

This commentary reflects a general preoccupation of Zhu's: internal cultivation. He Yan shows little or no interest in the issue of externality or internality. For him, goodness lies in good behavior and in the recognition of this good behavior by others. For Zhu, goodness is inherent, part of human nature, but in need of constant cultivation and refinement. In part, the goal for man is to externalize goodness through a rigorous process of cultivation. Empathy is an integral part of this process, a means of realizing in practice the goodness within and a means of manifesting that goodness in one's relations with others.

In his commentary on both this passage and 15.24, Zhu places empathy at the service of true goodness. Beyond Zigong and Confucius's response to him, the point here is that although empathetic behavior is essential to true goodness, it should not be mistaken for true goodness. It is the critical step toward cultivating it.

The golden rule may seem like a straightforward description of how to achieve true goodness, but followers of Confucius wanted to know still more. They frequently sought elaboration from him or, by way of inquiry, offered their own understanding, as in the following analect. Perhaps the Master's general reluctance to characterize others as truly good convinced them that achieving true goodness was not so straightforward as the golden rule might suggest. In analect 6.30, Zigong, having been instructed on a number of occasions about the meaning of true goodness, tries to formulate his own understanding of the virtue, only to have it dismissed by Confucius:

He Yan's reading:

> Zigong said, Suppose there was one who widely bestowed benefits on the people and was capable of bringing relief to the multitude. What would you say? Could he be called truly good? The Master said, Why just truly good? Wouldn't he surely be a sage? Even Yao and Shun would find this difficult.

Kong [Anguo] said, "Capable of bestowing benefits widely and of relieving the people from suffering—even Yao and Shun, perfect sages, would find it difficult to carry out so hard a task."

> Now, the truly good person, wishing himself to be established, establishes others; and wishing himself to achieve prominence, makes others prominent. The ability to draw analogies from what is near at hand can be called the way to true goodness. (6.30 [11])

Kong [Anguo] said, "He further explains the behavior of the truly good person for Zigong. *Fang* [way] is *dao*, 'way.' It is simply to be able to draw from oneself analogies near at hand and to be empathetic at all times, to do unto others what one desires oneself."

Zhu Xi's reading:

> Zigong said, Suppose there was one who widely bestowed benefits on the people and was capable of bringing relief to the multitude. What would you say? Could he be called truly good? The Master said, Why just truly good? Wouldn't he surely be a sage? Even Yao and Shun would find this difficult.

Bo [wide] is *guang*, "wide." "True goodness" speaks of principle [*li*], which pervades what is above and what is below. The "sage" speaks of a

position, the designation for one who reaches the utmost of true goodness. *Hu* is a term of doubt and uncertainty. *Bing* [would find difficult]
means that the mind-and-heart still has that which is not capable of it. It
says here: why just truly good? Mustn't one be a sage to be capable of
this? For even in the case of the sages Yao and Shun, their mind-and-heart
still had that which was not capable of the task. To seek true goodness in
this manner [i.e., as suggested by Zigong] is still more difficult, still more
remote.

> Now wishing himself to be established, the truly good person estab-
> lishes others; and wishing himself to achieve prominence, he makes
> others prominent.

Using oneself to approach others is the mind-and-heart of the person of
true goodness. Looking at it from this point of view, we can see that heavenly principle is all-pervasive. To sketch the substance of true goodness,
nothing comes closer than this.

> The ability to draw analogies from what is near at hand can be called
> the way to true goodness.

Pi [analogies] is *yu*, "illustration" or "metaphor." *Fang* [way] is *shu*, "technique" or "way." "Near at hand to draw" from oneself is to take what one
desires oneself and analogize it to others, understanding that what they
desire is just the same. Afterward, one approaches others extending to
them what they desire, which is a matter of empathy and the way to true
goodness. If one applies oneself here, one will possess the means of subduing the selfishness of one's human desire and preserving whole the
impartiality of heavenly principle.

Master Cheng said, "A book on medicine considers numbness of
the hands and legs to be the absence of *ren* [true goodness]. This is an
excellent description. A person of true goodness regards heaven, earth,
and the myriad things as one body. They all are his own self. If he
acknowledges them all as the self, where does he not reach? But if they
do not belong to the self, then naturally they are of no concern to the
self—which is like the absence of *ren* in the hands and legs. If one's *qi*
no longer penetrates them, none of them belongs to the self. It is for this
reason that widely bestowing benefits and bringing relief to the multi-

tude are the achievements of the sage. True goodness is extremely difficult to talk about, and so here it merely says, 'wishing himself to be established, he establishes others; and wishing himself to achieve prominence, he makes others prominent. The ability to draw analogies from what is near at hand can be called the way to true goodness.' He wished to have us understand true goodness in this way so that we could understand its substance." He further said, "The *Analects* on two occasions says, 'Even Yao and Shun would find this difficult' [cf. 14.42]. Now to bestow benefits widely is indeed what a sage desires. And yet [*Mengzi* IA.3 says that] people must be fifty to wear silk, and seventy to eat meat. In his mind-and-heart, a sage would surely want the young as well to wear silk and eat meat and would look upon such care [i.e., that advocated in *Mengzi*] as inadequate. He would find it difficult that his benefits had not been bestowed widely. Bringing relief to the multitude is indeed what a sage desires. And yet [Chinese] rule does not extend beyond the Nine Regions. A sage would surely want relief to extend beyond the Four Seas as well and would look upon the extent of such rule as limited. He would find it difficult that the relief that he had brought was not for the multitude. To extend this further: it is evident that 'to cultivate the self in order to ease the lot of the Hundred Families' [14.42] would be difficult for him, for taking self-rule as sufficient is not to be a sage."[2] Mr. Lü [Dalin][3] said, "Zigong had his mind set on true goodness, but he attended in vain to the lofty, with no understanding of the way to do it. Confucius instructed him that by drawing it from himself, he could approach and enter: this was the way to practice true goodness. Even widely bestowing benefits and bringing relief to the multitude proceed from this."

Zigong begins this passage with his own characterization of true goodness, asking Confucius what he thinks. The Master dismisses the characterization as overreaching and counters with one of his own. Finally, in concluding, he offers a technique for achieving it.

2. Compare Zhu's commentary on analect 14.42.
3. Lü Dalin (1046–1092) was a disciple of the Cheng brothers.

Similar though their general understanding of this passage may be, He's commentary is satisfied with doing little more than paraphrasing the text, whereas Zhu's goes on at great length explaining the ontological operations and assumptions that make true goodness—the topic of the analect—achievable. Because heavenly principle is all-pervasive, principle or human nature in me is the same principle or human nature in you; it is precisely this oneness of humanity that permits me to plumb my inner feelings in order to infer yours. Relying on those inner feelings is, ironically, a method of transcending my "selfish" desires and behaving in a manner consistent with my original, universal humanity. But plumbing my own feelings to judge yours—that is, to be empathetic—is not true goodness itself. Rather, true goodness is achieved when these empathetic feelings are fully actualized in my dealings with others.

For Zhu, empathy, a sensitivity to resonant or shared feelings, leads to self-perfection. And this awareness of the feelings of others serves to mute or subdue the feelings and desires that are peculiar to oneself—that is, selfish desires. When this awareness is acted upon, one is conforming to the humanity that one shares with all others, manifesting the disinterestedness of the heavenly principle with which one is born. In this manner, the contest waged in human beings between human desires, on the one hand, and heavenly principle, on the other, is decided in favor of heavenly principle, and one's inherent true goodness is realized in practice.

The person of true goodness, it is argued, can be likened to a person who regards the world around him as a biological extension of himself. Others are to him like his own hands and legs. Such a person is naturally sensitive to the needs and feelings of others, since to be insensitive to their feelings is to be insensitive to the feelings in his own body. It is to be numb to the sensations in his very own limbs. Hence, as the commentary here points outs, the medical term describing physical numbness or paralysis in the limbs, *buren*, "not *ren*," is especially felicitous.

As is characteristic of his commentary, Zhu Xi is "systematizing" this passage, reading it in light of the whole text of the *Analects* or, more accurately, his whole interpretation of it. The assumptions that make understanding it possible are presented at length. And the intertextual and intratextual references that clarify its meaning, in particular the line about Yao and Shun, are freely provided.

2

Confucius seems reticent throughout the text of the *Analects* to characterize others as truly good. But whatever his reticence and however difficult men might find it to realize the virtue of true goodness, certain passages, such as 7.30, appear to say that true goodness is in fact fairly accessible.

He Yan's reading:

> The Master said, Is true goodness indeed so far away? If I desired true goodness, true goodness would be right at hand. (7.30 [12])
> Bao [Xian] said, "The Way of true goodness is not far away; practice it and here it is."

Zhu Xi's reading:

> The Master said, Is true goodness indeed so far away? If I desired true goodness, true goodness would be right at hand.
> True goodness is a virtue of the mind-and-heart, not something on the outside. Let it go and do not pursue it, and it will seem far away. Turn within to pursue it, and there it is. It is not at all far away.
> Master Cheng said, "To be truly good springs from oneself. Desire it, and here it is. What is far away about it?"

As difficult as it might be to practice true goodness, it is not, Confucius asserts in this passage, because true goodness is remote or inaccessible. Again, the burden seems to fall on the will of the individual. If he truly desires true goodness, true goodness will result. But the Master does not explicitly say from where true goodness materializes. Instead, he reads the passage as an injunction to practice true goodness;

that is, what makes it seem distant is simply our reticence to do good. If we genuinely desire true goodness, we will find it near at hand and quite practicable. But whether true goodness is near at hand and practicable because it is encoded in our human nature or embedded in our surrounding culture—or found elsewhere—is not a matter He Yan addresses.

By contrast, Zhu's reading is clearly informed by Mencian philosophical assumptions. Mencius, one of the great early followers of the Confucian school, argued that human nature is innately good, possessing the four cardinal virtues: true goodness, righteousness, propriety, and wisdom. This position over the next millennium and a half gradually came to be widely shared and, by the Song period, had become Confucian orthodoxy. Continuing in the same ontological vein as analect 6.30, Zhu asserts here that true goodness is one of the cardinal virtues constituting man's nature, that every human being is endowed with it at birth. He reads the passage as an injunction to nurture and cultivate what is within, to devote oneself to the pursuit of an inner quality. For him, this remark is a warning not to let what is near at hand wither. As a consequence, the readers of Zhu's commentary, in contrast to the readers of He's, know both that true goodness is not far away and also where it is to be found.

As brief as the commentary to this passage is, it typifies Zhu's commentarial approach in a few important ways. First, it introduces ontological beliefs that, for Zhu, make Confucius's remark fully intelligible. After all, if true goodness were not part of human nature, how could it possibly be right at hand? The commentary thus goes beyond the text of the passage to consider what enables a person ontologically to realize the true goodness spoken of here. Second, the commentary understands the particular analect in relation to the background of the larger Confucian tradition. That is, the remark is read in light of the later Mencian view of human nature, which by Zhu's day had become orthodox. The effect here is complex: such a reconciliation of canonical passages gives deeper resonance and a more coherent meaning to this analect. But at the same time, read in this way, the analect strengthens the legitimacy and meaning of the Mencian position. In turn, the tradition reads more persuasively as a whole, and the Mencian view of our originally good nature now seems to arise quite naturally—and author-itatively—out of the teachings of Confucius himself. This all is to say that Zhu's commentary serves as a sort of broker between the passage itself and the larger Confucian tradition of which it is a part.

The difference here in the He and Zhu readings is underscored in their widely divergent readings of yet another analect, 17.2, in which Confucius himself, tersely and somewhat cryptically, raises the matter of human nature and man's behavior:

He Yan's reading:

> The Master said, By nature near together, in practice far apart. (17.2 [13])
> Kong [Anguo] said, "The superior man is very cautious about what he practices."

Zhu Xi's reading:

> The Master said, By nature near together, in practice far apart.
> What is called nature here is spoken of in combination with the psycho-physical stuff. In the psychophysical nature there are indeed differences of excellent and bad. And yet if we speak of the very beginning, people's natures are not far apart at all. It is simply that people practice good and so become good, or practice bad and so become bad. Only thus do they grow far apart.
> Master Cheng said, "This speaks of the psychophysical nature, not the original nature. If it were speaking of the original one, then nature would be identical with principle—and principle has nothing that is not good. This is what Mencius spoke of as human nature's being good. How can there be a 'near together' here?"

True to form, He Yan does little embellishing. Although Confucius says, "by nature near together," he does not elaborate on what the nature is—and neither does He Yan. As in the previous passage (7.30), his commentary emphasizes the need for *practicing* the truly good. For practicing the truly good is what makes a man truly good. Whether

Confucius intends by his remark here that people are born good but fall away from it in practice, or are born evil but, through teaching and cultivation, may become good, or are born neither good nor evil but in practice may become either—or something else altogether—is not clear. But for He Yan the real point of the passage is that it is practice that matters, practice that makes the man.

Zhu, however, reads this passage through the lens of the received tradition, which by now was clear in its assumptions about human nature. As Mencius argued, man is born good, and it is in part this original endowment that enables him to realize the goodness in practice, as Zhu's commentary on 7.30 explains. But while all men are indeed born good, surely not all realize the potentiality of that goodness. The reason is that man also is born with an endowment of *qi*, or psychophysical stuff, the quantity and quality of which varies with the person. This combines with the original nature to constitute what Zhang Zai earlier, in the Northern Song, referred to as the "psychophysical nature." This is the nature of which Confucius speaks here. It is roughly similar in all people, but because the differences in their endowments of psychophysical stuff, their behavior and practices diverge, always growing farther apart. Zhu's understanding of the analect is thus colored by developments in the tradition since the time of Confucius. Mencius spoke clearly and influentially about human nature, and men of the Northern Song strongly affirmed Mencius's position. In reading *Mencius*, these same men, especially Cheng Yi and Zhang Zai, began to distinguish between human nature and the psychophysical stuff, of which everything in the universe, including man, is constituted. Finally, in their amalgamation, human nature and psychophysical stuff came to be known as the psychophysical nature.

The He Yan commentary reads the *Analects* as exhorting man to practice true goodness. With effort he can achieve it, and by achieving it he may become a superior man. Zhu, too, understands the text to be exhorting man to practice true goodness. But Zhu's commentary frames the Master's understanding of true goodness in a systematic metaphysics developed through the centuries, beginning with Mencius. Its emphasis is more on what makes the realization of true goodness possible ontologically. The relationship here between the text of the *Analects* and the metaphysics is dynamic: the metaphysics illuminates the teachings of the *Analects*, but at the same time these teachings make meaningful the system of metaphysics. Indeed, the intertwining of the teachings of Confucius and a commentary grounded in metaphysics suggests to the reader their fundamental compatibility, which, in turn, lends to the metaphysics a "Confucian" validity and significance.

3

By saying in 7.30, "If I desired true goodness, true goodness would be right at hand," the Master seems to be suggesting to his followers that true goodness is indeed achievable, readily practicable. But because at the same time he is hesitant to acknowledge others as truly good, we—along with his followers—find ourselves stopping to consider where the difficulty lies. Our attention should turn to the first part of the statement, to the desire or devotion that must be brought to the practice of true goodness. This indeed is a subject that Confucius returns to frequently, as in 4.6:

He Yan's reading:

> The Master said, I for one have never seen a person who loved the truly good or a person who hated what is not truly good. He who loves the truly good cannot be improved upon.
> Kong [Anguo] said, "It is hard to add anything to him."

> He who hates what is not truly good practices the truly good and does not let what is not truly good get near his person.
> Kong [Anguo] said, "This is to say that he who hates what is not truly good is able to prevent those who are not truly good from inflicting on him what is unrighteous. He does not compare with one who loves the truly good and whose excellence cannot be improved upon."

Is there anyone capable for the span of a single day of devoting himself to the truly good? I for one have never seen one whose strength is not capable of it!

Kong [Anguo] said, "This is to say that people simply are not capable for the span of a single day of devoting themselves to the cultivation of true goodness. I for one have never seen one who wished to practice the truly good but whose strength was not capable of it."

I suppose there are such people, but I for one have never seen one. (4.6 [14])

Kong [Anguo] said, "Out of politeness he does not wish to slander all his contemporaries by saying that they are incapable of practicing the truly good. Therefore he says that while there exist persons capable of true goodness, I have never seen one."

Zhu Xi's reading:

The Master said, I for one have never seen a person who loved the truly good or a person who hated what is not truly good. He who loves the truly good puts nothing ahead of it, and he who hates what is not truly good practices the truly good and does not let what is not truly good get near his person.

The Master admits that he has never seen one who loved the truly good or one who hated what is not truly good. It would seem that one who loves the truly good genuinely appreciates what is to be loved about the truly good and thus puts nothing under heaven ahead of it. One who hates what is not truly good genuinely appreciates what is hateful about what is not truly good and thus in doing the truly good always is able to cut himself off from matters not truly good, thereby preventing even a small amount from reaching one's person. Both are matters of perfected virtue and, for this reason, are difficult to find.

Is there anyone capable for the span of a single day of devoting himself to the truly good? I for one have never seen one whose strength is not capable of it!

This is to say that while those who love the truly good and hate what is not truly good cannot be found, still there may be people who really are capable for the span of a single day of vigorously devoting themselves to the truly good—for never has he himself seen a person whose strength is not capable of it. It would seem that doing the truly good rests with oneself: desire it, and here it is, for where the will goes the psychophysical stuff must go [cf. *Mengzi* 2A.2]. Thus, while it is difficult to be capable of the truly good, getting to this point is quite easy.

I suppose there are such people, but I for one have never seen one. *Gai* [suppose] is an expression of doubt. "There are such people" refers to those who devote themselves to it but whose strength is not capable of it. Now, people's endowment of psychophysical stuff varies. For this reason, he suspects that there may indeed occasionally be those who, on account of serious confusion and weakness, wish to move forward but cannot; and it is only by chance that he has never met such a person. It would seem that although in the end he dares not consider it easy, at the same time he laments that people are unwilling to devote themselves to the truly good.

This chapter says that although true goodness, as perfected virtue, is difficult for men, if a learner is capable of really devoting himself to it, there is no reason that he cannot attain it. As for one who devotes oneself to it but does not get there, in his own day never has he seen such a person. This is why the Master sighs over and over in despair.

It is not that people do not have the strength to practice true goodness but that they are not devoted to its practice. They simply do not have the necessary will. He Yan and Zhu Xi understand the passage similarly, although Zhu's commentary is considerably more explicit in its emphasis on the role of the will [*zhi*]: "It would seem that doing the truly good rests with oneself: desire it, and here it is, for where the will goes the psychophysical stuff must go." For Zhu, will, ontologically, is part of the mind-and-heart, which is constituted of the most refined psychophysical stuff. When the will inclines toward true goodness, it naturally leads the mind-and-heart toward realizing true goodness, innate in human nature—and away from selfish desires that can issue from the same mind-and-heart. Here again, by reading one against the other, Zhu creates a sort of dynamic synthesis between the *Analects* and the metaphysics of ontology. Through an explanation of the operations of the will, the mind-and-heart, and human nature, the metaphysics gives deeper meaning to the words of the Master, but at the same time, the words of the Master serve as evidence that the metaphysics is an authentically Confucian construct.

The Master's deep admiration for disciple Yan Hui is better understood against the background of 4.6. For Yan Hui, we are told (6.7), could devote his mind-and-heart entirely to true goodness for the span of three months; others may have been capable of such devotion for a day, and others for even a month, but Yan Hui alone could will to true goodness for a period of three months. The difficulty of keeping to true goodness is suggested here: the will must be devoted solely to its practice. Even a moment's break, a single selfish thought, represents a parting from true goodness.

The enormity of the task of being truly good, the perseverance required, is eloquently expressed by Confucius in 8.7:

He Yan's reading:

> Zengzi said, A gentleman must be broad and resolute, for the burden is heavy and the journey is long.
> Bao [Xian] said, "*Hong* [broad] is big or great; *yi* [resolute] is to be strong and capable of decisiveness. Only if a gentleman is broad and resolute can he carry the heavy burden and go the long road."

> He takes true goodness as his burden: is that not indeed heavy?
> And only with death does he stop: is that not indeed long? (8.7 [15])
> Kong [Anguo] said, "To take true goodness as one's burden—there is nothing heavier than this. And only with death does he stop—there is nothing longer than this."

Zhu Xi's reading:

> Zengzi said, A gentleman must be broad and resolute, for the burden
> is heavy and the journey is long.

Hong [broad] means "broad" or "magnanimous"; *yi* [resolute] means "to forbear." If one is not broad, one will be incapable of bearing the heaviness; if one is not resolute, one will not have the means of going the lengthy distance.

> He takes true goodness as his burden: is that not indeed heavy?
> And only with death does he stop: is that not indeed long?

True goodness is the virtue of the mind-and-heart in its wholeness. One must try to embody it and practice it vigorously—this can indeed be called heavy. Until one's last breath, not even the slightest laxness in the will is permitted—this indeed can be called long.

Master Cheng said, "If one is broad but not resolute, one will be without compass and square and thus find it difficult to stand on one's own. If one is resolute but not broad, one will find oneself in narrow and vulgar straits and incapable of dwelling there." He further said, "Only if one is broad and resolute is one able to bear the heavy burden and go the long distance."

The uncommon man, the cultivated man of learning (*shi*), Confucius suggests, finds it a great challenge to keep to true goodness. So too—surprisingly perhaps—does the *junzi*. In 14.6, the Master laments: "Alas, there have been cases of superior men who nonetheless are not truly good." Thus no matter what one's moral status, no matter how morally conscientious one might be, keeping to true goodness is not without problems.

In his commentary on both 8.7 and 14.6, Zhu Xi is explicit where He Yan remains silent: he tells his reader *why* the cultivated man of learning and the superior man sometimes fail in their efforts to be truly good. Their will (*zhi*), Zhu remarks, grows lax and lets them down. Echoing his commentary on the preceding 8.7, Zhu in 14.6 comments: "The superior man sets his will on true goodness. But if even for the briefest of moments, his mind-and-heart is not present there, he cannot avoid practicing what is not truly good."

These passages make clear that whatever the precise role of the will, becoming a cultivated man of learning (*shi*) or a superior man (*junzi*), in Confucius's estimation, is difficult; more difficult still is becoming a person of true goodness (*renzhe*). The total embodiment of this highest virtue, *ren* or true goodness, appears to be almost beyond human reach, despite its being so near at hand (7.30).

4

For Confucius, learning to be truly good begins in the family, which is where a person is first exposed to the paradigmatic social relationships. In a model family, one comes to know how to behave in conformance with propriety as a child, as a parent, as a younger sibling, as an older sibling. Moving outside the family to the larger society, the child of such a family is sure to show proper respect and obedience to superiors; the parent is sure to treat subordinates with compassion and empathy; the younger sibling is sure to be dutiful toward elders; and the older sibling is sure to be caring and considerate toward the young. Society thus regards the family as its foundational unit; indeed, in this view, the model society depends on model families. That is, the family is the source of social virtue. The negative implication here, of course, is that wayward social behavior exhibited by an individual can likely be traced back to his family, to its wayward familial relationships. Confucius thus places a great burden on the institution of the family: it bears responsibility for the behavior of all its members both inside the family and outside it in the society at large. In analect 1.2, Youzi is obviously expressing the Master's sentiments:

He Yan's reading:

> Youzi said, One who is of filial and fraternal character but at the same time loves defying superiors is rare indeed.
> Confucius's disciple You Ruo. *Xian* [few] is *shao*, "few" or "scarce." *Shang* [superiors] refers to all those above oneself. This is to say that a filial and fraternal person will always be respectful and obedient; rare it is that he is apt to want to defy his superiors.

One who does not love defying superiors but at the same time loves sowing disorder has never existed. The superior man attends to the foundation. The foundation having been established, the Way issues forth.

Ben [foundation] is *ji*, "foundation." Only when the foundation is established can there be great accomplishment.

Filial piety and fraternal respect: are they not the foundation of true goodness? (1.2 [16])

Only if he is first capable of serving his father and older brother can he reach the Way of true goodness.

Zhu Xi's reading:

Youzi said, One who is of filial and fraternal character but at the same time loves defying superiors is rare indeed. One who does not love defying superiors but at the same time loves sowing disorder has never existed.

Youzi, a disciple of Confucius, whose personal name is Ruo. To be good at serving parents constitutes filial piety; to be good at serving older brothers and elders constitutes fraternal respect. *Fan shang* [defy superiors] means "to offend against people above one." *Xian* [rare] is *shao*, "few" or "scarce." *Zuo luan* [to sow disorder], then, is to engage in rebellion and conflict. This is to say that if a person is capable of filial piety and fraternal respect, his mind-and-heart will be obliging; rarely will he love offending against superiors, and never will he love sowing disorder.

The superior man attends to the root. The root having been established, the Way issues forth. And filial piety and fraternal respect: are they not the root of practicing true goodness?

Wu [to attend] is *zhuan li*, "to concentrate one's energy on." *Ben* [root] is *gen*, "the root." True goodness is the principle of loving, a virtue within the mind-and-heart. *Wei ren* [to practice true goodness] is the same as *xing ren*, "to practice true goodness." *Yu* [are they not] is a negative interrogative; out of humility he dare not say it flatly. This is to say that in everything the superior man concentrates his efforts on the root. Once the root is established, the Way issues forth from it. As for the filial piety and fraternal respect spoken of in the preceding passage, these are the root of practicing true goodness. If learners attend to this [root], the Way of true goodness will issue forth from it.

Master Cheng said, "To be filial and fraternal is to comply with virtue; thus, he will not love defying superiors. Can such a person ever be guilty of contravening principle or throwing norms into disorder? Virtue has its root; once the root is established, the Way grows big. Filial piety and fraternal respect are practiced in the family, and only then are true goodness and love extended to other things. This is what is meant by 'affectionate toward parents, and truly good towards people' [*Mengzi* 7A.45]. Thus practicing true goodness takes filial piety and fraternal respect as its root. From the perspective of human nature, we regard true goodness as the root of filial piety and fraternal respect." Someone asked, "Aren't filial piety and fraternal respect the root of true goodness? Isn't it by way of filial piety and fraternal respect that true goodness is reached?" Cheng replied, "No. This says that practicing true goodness begins with filial piety and fraternal respect; filial piety and fraternal respect are a matter of true goodness. It is all right to call them the root of practicing true goodness; it is not all right to call them the root of true goodness. It would seem that true goodness is human nature and that filial piety and fraternal respect are its function. Within human nature there exist true goodness, righteousness, propriety, and wisdom: these four things and nothing more. Where do filial piety and fraternal respect come in? True goodness presides over love, and in loving, there is nothing greater than loving one's parents. Therefore it says, 'Filial piety and fraternal respect: are they not the root of practicing true goodness?'"[4]

The practice of filial piety and fraternal respect is, as Confucius states here, the beginning of realizing true goodness, for it is through

---

4. The exchange here between "someone" and Master Cheng is recorded in Honan Chengshi *yishu* 18.1b.

these fundamental family virtues that one becomes accustomed to appropriately expressing one's humanity. By their extension, one may learn to express this humanity more generally to the larger society.

That is, he who learns filial piety and fraternal respect in the family will treat those people outside the family as they ideally should be treated. And thus, the analect suggests, if families were to "teach" these virtues routinely, society would become stable and harmonious, and order would prevail, without physical coercion.[5] This would be the only sort of government necessary. This would be the ideal society, one in which the Way prevailed.

The He and Zhu commentaries are at odds in their reading of this passage, notably of the line *qi wei ren zhi ben yu*, which He takes to mean, "Are they [i.e., filial piety and fraternal respect] not the foundation of true goodness?" and Zhu, "Are they not the root of practicing true goodness?" The disagreement, philological in nature, arises out of different philosophical assumptions. For Zhu, true goodness is foundational to human nature, endowed in man at birth. In this sense, filial and fraternal behavior originate in it and are an expression of it. In Zhu's view, He's reading cannot be right; filial piety and fraternal respect cannot be the foundations of true goodness because true goodness is itself ontologically foundational. Zhu's commentary suggests instead that the common character *wei* should not be read as "to constitute," as He did, but as "to practice." Thus the line means that practicing true goodness begins with the practice of filial piety and fraternal respect. In this case, consistent with Zhu's metaphysical understanding, true goodness is identical with human nature (and substance), and filial piety and fraternal respect are its function. While both the He and Zhu readings of the line are grammatically and semantically plausible, they are clearly informed by a different set of assumptions.

Two final observations on Zhu's commentary on this passage: first, as we see clearly here, contrary to the charge laid against him first by

---

5. This is why in 2.21, the Master quotes from a lost chapter of the *Book of History*: "Simply be filial to your parents, friendly toward your brothers, and you will be contributing to government."

the evidential *kaozheng* scholars of the Qing period, Zhu Xi is not un-invested philologically. For Zhu, the significance of this passage turns on the meaning of the common character *wei*. In general, Zhu pays a great deal of attention to the definition and meaning of individual words, although the glosses he provides are often drawn from earlier authorities, including even He Yan. The philological interest displayed in Zhu's commentarial remarks, not only on the *Analects* but also on the other canonical texts, relates to at least two of his concerns: to make an ancient text in which the meaning of its words and phrases is not always clear, accessible, and meaningful to his contemporaries and, through lexical and grammatical analysis, to demonstrate to his readers the rightness of his particular reading of the text, especially when that reading has been, or might be, contested.

The second observation, which relates to this first one, is that Zhu is engaging here in a sort of philosophical argumentation with earlier readings of the passage, taking He Yan, in particular, to task and attempting to convince the reader of his own textual and philosophical understanding. While He Yan is not mentioned specifically by name and while no earlier commentary—his or any of those adopting his reading (e.g., Huang Kan's *Lunyu yishu*)—is cited, every reader of the Zhu Xi commentary would know that the question posed to Cheng Yi, "Aren't filial piety and fraternal respect the root of true goodness?" is a reference to He's traditional understanding of the passage. This sort of engagement with past readings, commonly but by no means always indirect or implicit, is typical of both Zhu's commentarial style in particular and the Confucian commentarial genre more generally.

5

Analect 13.27, quite brief but well known, can serve as a sort of epilogue to this chapter. Not only does it neatly illustrate the Master's perspectival approach to "defining" true goodness, but the commentaries on it point up nicely a few of the main differences in He's and Zhu's approaches to the text of the *Analects*:

He Yan's reading:

> The Master said, "To be resolute and firm, simple and slow in
> speech, is to approach true goodness." (13.27 [17])

Wang [Su] said, "*Gang* [resolute] is to be without desire; *yi* [firm] is to be
determined and daring; *mu* [simple] is to be simple; *na* [slow in speech] is
to be slow in speech. To be possessed of these four qualities is to
approach true goodness."

Zhu Xi's reading:

> The Master said, "To be resolute and firm, simple and slow in
> speech, is to approach true goodness."

Master Cheng said, "*Mu* [simple] is to be simple; *na* [slow in speech]
is to be slow in speech. These four are characteristics that approach true
goodness." Mr. Yang [Shi] said, "Resolute and firm, one does not give in
to creaturely desire; simple and slow in speech, one does not becomes
outwardly reckless. Consequently, one approaches true goodness."

"Simple and slow in speech" becomes almost a refrain in the teachings of Confucius. For instance, in 12.3, he says, "The person of true
goodness is restrained in speech."[6] Throughout the text he repeatedly
cautions his followers not to mistake eloquence for substance, as in 1.3:
"The Master said, Artful words and a pleasing countenance have little,
indeed, to do with true goodness."[7]

Although Zhu's commentary on this brief analect, 13.27, draws
directly on He Yan's earlier commentary, it also goes well beyond it. He
simply affirms that one who is resolute and firm, and simple and slow
in speech, approaches true goodness; Zhu, by contrast, wants to understand why this is so. The answer for him is partly that restraint in
speech indicates a general self-restraint, which, in turn, indicates that

6. See also, for example, 2.13, 4.22, 4.24, and 5.4.
7. For similar remarks, see 5.4, 5.24, and 14.5.

one's original mind-and-heart, with its endowed true goodness, has been preserved and not won over by selfish desires. As Zhu says in his commentary on 12.3, "The person of true goodness is disciplined in all that he does, restrained by the dictates of his original mind-and-heart. As a consequence, the very act of speaking will naturally also be disciplined and restrained." For Zhu, words that are not simple but, rather, are "artful" (1.3) are evidence that one has become interested in "adorning oneself on the outside in an effort to please others, a matter of human desire's having grown dissolute and of the virtue of the original mind-and-heart's having become lost."

In Zhu's reading, analect 13.27 addresses what he views as the fundamental existential battle that is waged between emotions and desires in every individual, on the one hand, and the expression of the goodness of human nature, on the other. Born with such goodness, man must always be vigilant, keeping his desires in check, especially selfish desires, and restraining himself in accord with the norms of propriety. What for He Yan is simply a characterization of those traits associated with true goodness is for Zhu a statement that speaks to the critical philosophical and moral predicament confronting every human being—how to preserve intact the original mind-and-heart, with its goodness, in the face of human desires that constantly threaten to overwhelm it.

The reader of He Yan's commentary on 13.27 is given glosses of individual characters with which to make sense of the passage. Zhu's reader likewise is given glosses, but the commentary provides significantly more, fleshing out the meaning of the passage and elaborating freely on how it should be understood. Furthermore, Zhu's commentary prompts the reader to read the analect intratextually against the background of related passages in the *Analects* and their commentary, the effect of which is to enrich the meaning of 13.27, even as 13.27 might enrich them. Thus Zhu "fits" the analect into the whole of the text, making for a coherence of reading largely absent in He Yan's commentary. Finally, and again in contrast to He Yan, Zhu moves beyond the analect itself, even beyond the whole of the text itself, to "fit" the words of the Master into a larger Confucian philosophical vision, a vision that he, together with others, is in the process of shaping.

3

Ritual

If the achievement of true goodness is an unques-
tionable aim of Confucius's teachings, the relationship of *li*, translated
here as "ritual," to true goodness is more problematic. For some early
followers of the Confucian school, it was the practice of ritual that
channeled the behavior of the individual, teaching him over time to
become truly good. Ritual action is a slow but steady process of accul-
turation, a process premised on a faith in the ability of culture to help
shape a person's moral impulses and activities. Other early followers
read Confucius's message somewhat differently, understanding ritual
activity to be a means of expressing the humanity inherent in each
person. That is, ritual does not shape the moral impulses as much as
provide for their natural development. In this view, to put it somewhat
crudely, it is not society or culture in all its inherited beauty and collec-
tive wisdom that makes a person good. Rather, it is man with his inner
goodness and inner resources who gives beauty and authenticity to the
practice of ritual, thereby manifesting inner goodness outwardly and
promoting social harmony.

This unresolved relationship between true goodness and ritual resonates throughout the text of the *Analects* and led over the centuries to considerable philosophical debate within the Confucian school itself. Commentators on the *Analects*, not surprisingly, took sides in the dispute, freely disagreeing in their readings of the Master's words. In part, commentary is the locus of serious argument between commentators, frequently living centuries apart. At the same time, commentary is an attempt to reconcile with the Master himself. In a sort of dialogic exercise with the Master, interlinear commentary seeks the meaning of each of his utterances, even while it circumscribes the meaning of those utterances. The consequence for the Confucian tradition is as obvious as it is profound: the understanding that virtually every Chinese reader of the *Analects* since the Han period takes away from the text, the precise understanding of the relationship between true goodness and ritual, is dependent on the commentarial tradition accompanying it. In short, the reader's understanding of the role of ritual in Confucius's teachings is heavily mediated by his particular commentarial guide.

Analect 12.1 is a good place to begin our discussion of ritual. First, as a response to an inquiry from Yan Hui about what constitutes true goodness, this analect serves as a bridge between our discussion of true goodness in chapter 2 and our consideration of ritual. Second, this analect figures prominently in the long history of Confucian debate over the role of ritual, enlisted at various times to support almost every position in the debate. The two commentaries here are illustrative, "reading" the text of the analect differently and thus producing quite different philosophical understandings. Consequently, perhaps as well as any analect yet discussed, this one demonstrates how Confucian commentary does indeed "create" the text.

I

He Yan's reading:

Yan Yuan asked about true goodness. The Master said, To restrain the self and return to ritual constitutes true goodness.

Ma [Rong] said, "*Ke ji* [to restrain the self] is *yue shen*, 'to restrain the self.'" Kong [Anguo] said, "*Fu* [to return] is *fan*, 'to return.' If the self is able to return to ritual, this constitutes true goodness."

> If but for a single day, one restrains the self and returns to ritual, all under heaven will turn to true goodness.

Ma [Rong] said, "If within the span of one day, they might be turned, how much more if for a whole lifetime!"

> The practice of true goodness rests with oneself, not with others!

Kong [Anguo] said, "To practice goodness rests with oneself, not with others."

> Yan Yuan said, I beg to know the details.

Bao [Xian] said, "He knew that surely there were details and consequently asked about them."

> The Master said, If contrary to ritual, do not look; if contrary to ritual, do not listen; if contrary to ritual, do not speak; if contrary to ritual, do not act.

Zheng [Xuan] said, "These four items are the details of restraining the self and returning to propriety."

> Yan Yuan said, Although I, Hui, am not clever, I beg to devote myself to these words. (12.1 [18])

Wang [Su] said, "Reverently devoting himself to these words, he always put them into practice."

Zhu Xi's reading:

> Yan Yuan asked about true goodness. The Master said, To subdue the self and return to ritual constitutes true goodness. If only for a single day, someone subdues the self and returns to ritual, all under heaven will recognize his true goodness. The practice of true goodness rests with oneself, not with others!

True goodness is the virtue of the original mind-and-heart in its wholeness.

Ke [to subdue] is *sheng*, "to overcome or subdue." *Ji* [the self] refers to the selfish desires of the self [*shen zhi si yu*]. *Fu* [to return] is *fan*, "to return." *Li* [ritual] is heavenly principle in measured display. "The practice of true goodness" is the means of preserving whole the virtue of the mind-and-heart. Now, the virtue of the mind-and-heart in its wholeness is nothing but heavenly principle and thus can only be harmed by human desire. Consequently, to practice true goodness, one must have the wherewithal to subdue selfish desires and thereby return to ritual. In this case, all affairs will be a matter of heavenly principle, and the virtue of the original mind-and-heart will return to its wholeness in one's self. *Gui* [recognize] is like *yu*, "to allow or recognize." This is further to say that if for just a single day he can subdue the self and return to ritual, all people under heaven will recognize his true goodness.[1] This exaggerates the quickness and enormity of his effect. It also says that the practice of true goodness rests with oneself and is not something others are able to provide, which also indicates that the springs of action are to be found in oneself and are not difficult. If each day one subdues it [the self] and finds no difficulty in doing so, the selfish desires will be cleansed entirely and heavenly principle will prevail and one's true goodness will thereby be more than sufficient. Master Cheng said, "What is contrary to ritual is a matter of selfish intention; being selfish in intention, how can one become truly good? It is necessary to subdue entirely one's own selfishness and, in everything, return to ritual. Only then can one begin to be truly good." He further said, "If one subdues the self and returns to ritual, in all matters one will be truly good. For this reason, it says, 'all under heaven will recognize his true goodness.'" Mr. Xie [Liangzuo] said, "To subdue the self, it is necessary, following the inclinations of human nature, to subdue those places that are wayward and difficult to subdue."

> Yan Yuan said, I beg to know the details. The Master said, If contrary to ritual, do not look; if contrary to ritual, do not listen; if contrary to ritual, do not speak; if contrary to ritual, do not act. Yan Yuan said, Although I, Hui, am not clever, I beg to devote myself to these words.

1. In YL 41.1050 (cf. 41.1066), Zhu explains *gui ren* (to recognize his true goodness) as *cheng qi ren* (to commend or admire his true goodness).

Mu [details] is *tiaojian*, "items." Yan Yuan, hearing the words of the Master, is clear about the boundary between heavenly principle and human desire. Thus, having no additional questions, he bluntly asks for the details. To be "contrary to ritual" is selfishness. "Do not" is a prohibitive phrase. This is what the mind-and-heart of man takes as its ruler and is the very spring of subduing the selfish and returning to ritual. When the selfish is subdued, one's every movement will be in precise accord with ritual [*Mengzi* 7B.33], and so in daily life, heavenly principle will be sure to prevail. *Shi* [to devote] is the *shi* of the phrase *shi shi*, "to devote oneself to one's duties" [*Shangshu* 10.5b; cf. Legge, *Chinese Classics*, 3:257]. "I beg to devote myself to these words": Master Yan silently understands the principle here and, further, is aware that his own strength is capable of subduing it [the self]. Thus without any apprehension, he forthwith takes the burden upon himself.

Master Cheng said, "Master Yan asks for the details of subduing the self and returning to ritual. The Master says, 'If contrary to ritual, do not look; if contrary to ritual, do not listen; if contrary to ritual, do not speak; if contrary to ritual, do not act.' These four are the operations of one's person, arising from within in response to the external. Regulating the external is the means of nurturing what is within. By devoting himself to these words, Yan Yuan progressed toward sagehood. Those later learning to be sages should clutch them close to their breasts and not let go [*Zhongyong*, chap. 8]. Consequently, I caution myself with these admonitions: The admonition on looking says: The mind-and-heart is originally unprejudiced, responding to things without trace. There is an essence to holding it fast, which may be found in the example of looking. Clouded by contact with the outside, what is within changes. Regulate it in its dealing with the external in order to still it internally. Subdue the self and return to ritual, and in time one will become true to one's nature. The admonition on listening says: People have a constant disposition, rooted in their nature endowed by heaven. Perception beguiles it; external things alter it; and thereupon it loses its correctness. Profound are those who become aware first [cf. 1.1]; knowing where to come to rest, they become steadfast [*Daxue*, "Classic of Confucius," par. 2]. To guard against evil and preserve truthfulness, do not listen if it is contrary to propriety. The admonition on speaking says: If a person's mind-and-heart is active, he will depend on speech to express himself. If what he utters avoids the impetuous, he will remain inwardly quiet and concentrated. It is this [i.e., speaking] that is the hinge and spring, giving rise to hostilities and to friendships. Good fortune and bad luck, glory and disgrace all are called forth by it. Too casual with it and one becomes boastful; too long-winded and one becomes incoherent. Unruly in speech oneself, others become unmannerly. Utter what violates right and the reply will be contrary. The improper is not to be spoken! Be prudent in instruction and speech! The admonition on movement says: The wise man knows the incipient and remains true to it in his deliberations. The resolute gentleman acts forcefully and takes firm hold in whatever he does. Accord with principle and enjoy abundance; accord with desire and become endangered. When hurried, be capable of reflection; when trembling in fear, keep firm hold of oneself. Whether in practice perfect or perfect by nature, the sage and the worthy reach the same end."[2] In my [i.e., Zhu Xi's] humble view, the questions and replies in this chapter treat the method of transmitting the mind-and-heart and are crucially important words. If not perfectly brilliant, one is incapable of examining their subtlety; if not perfectly vigorous, one is incapable of seeing them through to their resolution. For this reason, Master Yan alone is able to hear them. Other students must make the effort. Since the admonitions of Master Cheng explain them precisely, it is particularly fitting that students ponder them seriously.

The significance of this crucial passage hinges on how one understands Confucius's brief characterization of true goodness, *ke ji fu li*. Both He and Zhu read *fu li* to mean "to return to ritual." It is in their understanding of *ke ji* and its relationship to *fu li* that a striking difference in interpretation emerges. In turn, this difference leads to differences in their understanding of ritual itself.

He Yan's brief commentary on the first line of this passage warrants close examination. He begins by citing Ma Rong's gloss of *ke ji* as *yue shen* (to restrain the self). Next he cites Kong Anguo, who glosses *fu* as *fan* (to return) and goes on to say, "If the self is able to return to

---

2. This entire passage by Cheng Yi on the four admonitions is found in *Yichuan xiansheng wenji* 4.4a–b.

ritual, this constitutes true goodness." It would seem from this that Kong understands the term *ke ji* to mean *shen neng* (if the self is able), which, while philologically plausible, is at variance with Ma's "to restrain the self." The question, of course, is what He intended by putting these two earlier remarks side by side. One possible answer is that He is showing the disagreement between two earlier authorities and allowing the disagreement to stand without resolution. But pitting one authority against another, especially without explicit comment, is not characteristic of He Yan's commentarial style. It is far more likely that He is citing Ma for his gloss on *ke ji* and then is citing Kong for his gloss on *fu li* and that he does not see a fundamental incompatibility in their respective understandings of the line as a whole. That is, for He Yan, Kong's remark, "if the self is able to return to ritual," is not basically at odds with Ma's understanding of the line "to restrain the self and return to ritual." Indeed Xing Bing's tenth-century subcommentary on the *Analects* conflates these two earlier glosses of *ke ji* by Ma and Kong, explaining it as *neng yue shen* (to be capable of restraining the self).[3] But whether the two glosses of *ke ji* in He's commentary can or should be conflated, as Xing Bing suggests, is not my point. Rather, my point is that Xing Bing concludes—as I do—that He Yan's commentary regards Ma and Kong as compatible authorities and understands the line unproblematically to mean "to restrain the self and return to ritual constitutes true goodness."

But how should He's reader understand this understanding of Confucius's response to Yan Hui? Clearly man needs to restrain himself, but why? Is it that he has innate propensities that require curbing? Or is it that some men have these innate propensities and others do not? Or is it that man has innate propensities to do good but is always at risk of going astray and so must be consciously restrained? Or is it that man is simply prone to behaving badly sometimes and thus needs to keep himself reined in? The reader cannot know. There is no hint whether human nature is at issue here; indeed, there is no emphasis at all on the inner dimension of the individual. What the reader comes

3. *Lunyu zhushu* 12.1a.

away with is an appreciation that the achievement of true goodness is the result of man's checking himself by keeping within the bounds of proper ritual. Disciplined ritual practice toward others channels man's behavior in the direction of the truly good. Look, listen, speak, and act in accord with ritual: this is to practice true goodness. That is, for He Yan, ritual—whether we understand it as social convention, mores, tradition, custom, etiquette, or prescriptions for proper behavior—is external to man; true goodness results from adhering to it.

Zhu Xi's reading of the line gives considerably more guidance to the reader, understanding the line as directly addressing the moral and metaphysical contest waging within man between human nature and selfish desires. *Ke*, he comments, is "to subdue or overcome," and *ji* refers not to the self but to one's selfish desires. He Yan's restraining the self gives way here to subduing one's selfish desires. Man is born with a nature that is truly good, but inevitably, in contact with the world around him, desires spring up in his mind-and-heart. Should these desires become excessive, he will lose the mean and behave selfishly, all but concealing his innate goodness. In Zhu's reading of 12.1, Confucius is exhorting his followers to be eternally vigilant in keeping selfish desires at bay so that true goodness, "the virtue of the original mind-and-heart in its wholeness," may be preserved. That is, overcome selfish desires, he advises them, and the originally good human nature will become manifest. With the elimination of selfish desires and the realization of one's endowed nature, one will simultaneously act in perfect accord with the dictates of ritual. In the *Conversations of Master Zhu*, Zhu explains on numerous occasions to disciples how he understands the relationship in this passage between *keji* and *fuli*. For instance, "There's not a hair's breadth of distance between 'subduing the self and returning to ritual.' To be without selfishness is to be truly good" (41.1042). A few remarks later, he says: "'Subdue the self' and ritual is spontaneously returned to. . . . It isn't that there is a separate 'returning to ritual' outside 'subduing the self'" (41.1042). In still other words, "true goodness and ritual are not two separate things" (41.1043).[4] In fact, in Zhu's view, what distinguishes the Confucian

4. Compare YL 41.1046 and 41.1049.

from the Buddhist—and a reason to criticize Buddhism—is that the Confucian who subdues selfish desires is sure to practice propriety, whereas the Buddhist who does so is certain only to "plunge into emptiness" (41.1045). Zhu, it should be clear, reverses the relationship that He's reading posits between true goodness and ritual: instead of ritual activity's producing true goodness, as it did for He, it is now produced *by* it.

This, in turn, explains Zhu's commentarial gloss of ritual (*li*) in 12.1 as "heavenly principle [*li*] in measured display," for only if man has perfected his goodness, fully realizing the principle that is his human nature, can he express principle in all matters, behaving precisely as one should. It is this behavior, this expression of the principle of his human nature, that constitutes authentic ritual activity: "heavenly principle in measured display." In this understanding, ritual is not external to man but is merely the external expression of the principle within him. In short, ritual is "natural" to man. The place of ritual in the Neo-Confucian system of thought of late imperial China is thus deeply affected by the system of metaphysics undergirding it.

Zhu Xi's commentary on 12.1 reads ritual expression to be the effect, the natural and simultaneous effect, of curbing selfish desires and manifesting true goodness. This goodness emanates from within and is expressed only when man determines to keep himself cultivated, rid of the weeds of selfish or evil desires. The process is an internal one, resulting in behavior that is truly good, truly consistent with ritual. This is why, in contrast to He Yan, who offers only a simple paraphrase of Confucius's remark, "the practice of true goodness rests with one-self," without further comment, Zhu finds in the line support for his understanding that the "springs of action are found in oneself." It is not ritual that makes man truly good, as He interprets the Master, but man who, by realizing his ontological self, practices ritual with perfection, thereby expressing true goodness and producing social harmony. Ritual activity allows man to manifest his true goodness toward others, even though it constitutes a sort of "proof" that he has indeed achieved this most prized virtue.

When Herbert Fingarette and Benjamin I. Schwartz, among others, debate today over whether the *ren*, or true goodness, that Confucius spoke of should be located in the concrete performance of a ritual act or in the inner moral life of the individual performing the ritual, they may well be drawing on a contemporary philosophical terminology. But they are still simply elaborating on and refining a disagreement in an interpretation of the *Analects* that began much earlier, in the Chinese tradition itself. Fingarette's remark that "*ren* develops only so far as *li* develops; it is the shaping of oneself in *li*. . . . Thus until *li* is learned *ren* cannot be realized,"[5] echoes He Yan's reading of this passage. When, arguing that the concept of *ren* in the *Analects* is not concerned with the language of emotions or the inner life of the individual, Fingarette says, "In the case of *ren*, we should conceive of a directed force operating in actions in public space and time, and having a person as initial point-source and a person as the terminal point on which the force impinges,"[6] He Yan might puzzle over the language but would certainly in the end find himself in agreement. Schwartz shows himself to be more sympathetic to Zhu's interpretation of the passage when he criticizes Fingarette's understanding of *ren* for ignoring what he argues is the genuine contribution of Confucius to the Chinese intellectual tradition—the emphasis on the inner life of man, the deep belief that man has "an 'inner' autonomous life as an individual" and that this inner life has an effect on social behavior.[7] This is to say that understandings of the *Analects* as divergent as Fingarette's and Schwartz's can be found in the commentarial tradition itself and that the understandings that traditional Chinese readers take away from this classic therefore can be equally divergent, depending on their commentarial authority.

It is not only in their understanding of *ke ji fu li* that He Yan and Zhu Xi disagree but also in their understanding of its broader effect, described in the next line of the text, *tianxia gui ren*. According to He,

5. Herbert Fingarette, *Confucius: The Secular as Sacred* (New York: Harper & Row, 1972), 48.
6. Fingarette, *Confucius*, 55.
7. Benjamin I. Schwartz, *The World of Thought in Ancient China* (Cambridge, Mass.: Harvard University Press, 1985), 74; for his discussion of Fingarette, see 67–85. In comments in YL on this analect, Zhu remarks emphatically: "It is simply that true goodness resides within" (41.1042).

the man who successfully restrains the self and returns to ritual will move all under heaven to do the same. To Zhu, the man who subdues selfish desires and returns to ritual will practice true goodness in everything he does and consequently will receive recognition by one and all. He's reading of the line speaks to the morally charismatic power that the man who restrains himself and returns to ritual has over others. As the later commentator Huang Kan says of He, perhaps he has in mind the ruler and the effect he has on the ruled. Zhu's reading provides a different emphasis, encouraging *all* to embark on the self-cultivation process and suggesting that while success in this process does not necessarily result in "all under heaven turning to true goodness," its external effect is so remarkable that everyone notices it. That is, no matter how private or self-oriented the process might seem, other people nonetheless readily acknowledge and commend the results. In Zhu's commentary, the powerful moral suasion that the man of true goodness naturally exercises over others yields to the universal recognition that the realization of true goodness invites.

The ambiguity in the relationship between true goodness and ritual reflected in analect 12.1 is never fully resolved in the text of the *Analects*. Other remarks by the Master that juxtapose the two central concepts of *ren* (true goodness) and *li* (ritual) do little to sort out the precise nature of the relationship, at least as he might have understood it, and thus lend themselves to interpretive differences much like those found in the commentaries on 12.1. For instance, analect 3.3:

He Yan's reading:

> The Master said, If he is a man [*ren*] but not truly good [*ren*], what has he to do with ritual? If he is a man but not truly good, what has he to do with music? (3.3 [19])

Bao [Xian] said, "This says that if he is a man but not truly good, he is absolutely incapable of practicing ritual or music."

Zhu Xi's reading:

> The Master said, If he is a man [*ren*] but not truly good [*ren*], what

does he have to do with ritual? If he is a man but not truly good, what does he have to do with music?

Mr. You [Zuo] said, "'If he is a man but not truly good,' it is that the mind-and-heart of man has been lost. 'What does he have to do with ritual or music' is to say that although he may wish to employ them, ritual and music cannot be employed by him."

Master Cheng said, "True goodness is the standard principle of all under heaven. Neglect the standard principle, and there will be no order, no harmony." Mr. Li [Yu][8] said, "Ritual and music wait for the right person, and only then are they practiced [*Zhongyong*, chap. 27]. Unless it is the right person, although jade and silk are adjoined, although bells and drums sound, what should he do? This being so, recorders [of the text] placed this passage after the 'eight rows of dancers' and 'singing the *yong* while removing the offerings' analects [3.1 and 3.2]. I suspect it was uttered for the benefit of those who usurp ritual and music."

As he does elsewhere, He Yan offers only a brief paraphrase of the passage, a punning play on the homophony of characters for "man" and "true goodness," leaving the reader to wonder what its deeper significance may be for He—and himself. After reading He's commentary, we might conclude that only a person who has fully achieved true goodness can practice ritual and music properly; or we might conclude that since it is only through the performance of ritual and music that one is led to true goodness, one who is not yet truly good has not shown oneself to be capable of practicing ritual and music. What we *should* probably conclude, however, is simply that He—unlike Zhu Xi—is not philosophically concerned here with the relationship between the two concepts, true goodness and ritual, and instead is reading the line as a matter-of-fact castigation of those unworthy nobles of Lu who in the immediately preceding analects (3.1 and 3.2) dare to usurp the ritual prerogatives of the emperor. That is, as men who rule illegitimately— and have thus shown themselves to be not truly good—they are not entitled to perform the rituals they do.

8. When Li Yu (1086–1150) was young, he studied under Yang Shi.

By citing Li Yu's remark that "ritual and music wait for the right person," Zhu is indicating that like He, he is reading the passage partly as one uttered by Confucius in response to a specific set of historical circumstances in Lu at the time. But in his commentary, Zhu goes beyond the particular historical significance of the passage to extrapolate a larger philosophical significance from it. For better or worse, in contrast to He's reader, Zhu's is not left to wonder about the deeper significance here: only the man who retains his original mind-and-heart, who cultivates the potential of the goodness endowed in him at birth, is able to perform ritual and music appropriately. Consistent with his reading of 12.1, Zhu is clearly stating here that being truly good is a matter of not losing what is innate in man; it is not primarily a matter of adhering to a set of conventional rituals and music thought to inculcate appropriate standards of behavior.

In his citation of Master Cheng, Zhu goes further to explain in ontological terms why a man who is not truly good cannot perform ritual or music. Returning to the metaphysical language of *li*, or principle, he reminds his reader that to realize true goodness is to realize principle and, conversely, to neglect true goodness is to neglect principle. Because ritual and music, like all things in the universe, are governed by principle and because principle accounts for the orderliness and harmony to be found normatively in ritual and music, a man who is not truly good, who neglects principle, may wish to practice ritual and music but cannot possibly express their orderliness or harmony. That is, if he does not "know" or realize the principle that is his human nature, he cannot "know" or realize the standard principle in anything that he does. As in 12.1, it is only by realizing the self, here associated with principle, that ritual and music come to be realized, naturally and effortlessly.

The interpretive differences over the role of ritual in the self-cultivation process and its relationship to true goodness reflected in these two analects, 12.1 and 3.3, are also revealed in the commentaries on other passages in the text. Analect 3.8 is particularly interesting, perhaps because it is rather laconic and thus permits a variety of readings. Here the process of painting serves as a metaphor for the process of self-improvement:

He Yan's reading:

> Zixia asked, What is meant by "Captivating smile, all dimpled; / lovely
> eyes, all sparkling; / the white taken for adornment"?

Ma [Rong] said, "*Qian* [all dimpled] is a smiling appearance; *pan* [all
sparkling] is an attractive appearance; *xuan* [adornment] is a decorative
or fancy appearance. The first two lines here are from the second stanza
of the 'Shiren' ode from the 'Airs of Wei' [*Shijing*, Mao no. 57]. The last line
is no longer extant."

> The Master said, Lay on color, then the white.

Zheng [Xuan] said, "*Hui* [lay on color] is to paint the decorative. In general,
when painting, one first lays on all the color and only afterward fills in with
the white in order to complete the decorative. This is a metaphor for a
beautiful woman who, even though she may have excellent qualities—all
dimpled, all sparkling—still must complete them with ritual."

> He said, Ritual comes after?

Kong [Anguo] said, "Confucius says, 'lay on the color, then the white'; Zixia
hears it and understands 'the white' to be a metaphor for ritual and consequently says, 'Ritual comes after?'"

> The Master said, Shang it is who raises me up. We can begin indeed
> to speak about the *Book of Poetry* together! (3.8 [20])

Bao [Xian] said, "*Yu* [me] is me. Confucius says, Zixia is capable of elucidating my meaning; together we can speak about the *Book of Poetry*."

Zhu Xi's reading:

> Zixia asked, What is meant by "Captivating smile, all dimpled; / lovely
> eyes, all sparkling; / the white taken for adornment"?

This is a lost poem. *Qian* [all dimpled] is nice facial expression [lit.
jawbone, or skin covering the jawbone]. *Pan* [all sparkling] means that the
white and black of the eyes are well defined. *Su* [white] is white ground,
the real substance of the painting; *xuan* [adornment] is variegated colors,

the decorative part of the painting. It says here that a person has excellent substance—all dimpled, all sparkling—and to it is added variegated decoration. This is similar to having a white background and adding variegated colors to it. Suspecting that the poem turns the matter around by taking the white for the decorative, Zixia asks about it.

> The Master said, Lay on the color after the white.

Huishi [lit. the business of laying on the color] is the business of laying color on a painting. *Hou su* [after the white] means "to follow after the white." The *Kaogong ji* [in the *Zhouli* 40.26a] says: "The business of laying color on a painting follows after the preparation of the white." This speaks of making the white background the real substance first and afterward applying the five colors. It is like a person having excellent substance and only afterward can the decorative be added.

> He said, Ritual comes after? The Master said, Shang it is who raises me up. We can begin indeed to speak about the *Book of Poetry* together!

Ritual always takes being true to one's nature [*zhong*] and true to one's word [*xin*] as the real substance. This is like when laying on color always placing the preparation of the white first. *Qi* [raises up] is similar to *fa*, "to raise." "To raise me up" is to say that he is capable of bringing out or elucidating my intention. Mr. Xie [Liangzuo] said, "Zigong came to appreciate the *Book of Poetry* from a discussion of learning [1.15], whereas Zixia came to appreciate learning from a discussion of the *Book of Poetry*. Thus both could converse with him about the *Book of Poetry*."

Mr. Yang [Shi] said, "Sweet can be blended; white can be colored; and the man who is true to himself and trustworthy can learn ritual. A person lacking such substance should not perform ritual emptily [*Liji* 24.16b; cf. Legge, *Li chi*, 1:414]. This is the meaning of 'Lay on the color after the white.' Confucius says, 'Lay on the color after the white.' When Zixia then says, 'Ritual comes after?' it is evident that he is capable of picking up the thrust. If he did not grasp the inner meaning from the outer expression, would he be capable of this? It is for this reason that Shang and Si could converse with him about the *Book of Poetry*. Getting caught

up in insignificant glossing in the interpretation of poetry leads to rigidity
and nothing more [*Mengzi* 6B.3]. What is meant by 'raises me up' is that
they [Confucius and Zixia] have been of mutual help to each other."

To appreciate their respective readings of this analect, let us
proceed line by line, closely analyzing the differences between He and
Zhu. In the first line, He understands Zixia to be asking more generally about the meaning of the entire three lines of quoted verse, and
Zhu understands him to be asking principally about the last one, "the
white taken for adornment." That is, whereas He reads the last line to
mean that the white is to be taken for adornment, Zhu finds such a reading problematic and insists in his commentary that it is because Zixia,
too, finds it problematic that he asks the Master about its meaning.

In line 2, He reads the character *hou* of the four-character phrase
huishi hou su adverbially to mean "afterward": first lay on the color,
afterward the white. Zhu reads it as a verb, "to follow," and the line to
mean laying on the color follows after the white. For He, the colors
come first, and only then is the white applied; for Zhu, the white background comes first, and then the colors are applied. Thus in He's
reading when Zixia responds in line 3, "Ritual comes after?" he is associating it with the white that is used to fill in between the decorative
portions and complete the painting. By contrast, in Zhu's reading,
Zixia is associating ritual with the color that is applied after the white
background is prepared. We can thus appreciate why He would read
the third line of verse as "the white taken for adornment." For him, the
white, albeit not colorful, is added in order to perfect the decorative
portions, which are primary to the painting. For Zhu, the white is not
adornment but should be considered the "substance" of the painting,
the background prepared first on which all else relies. Of course, it is
because Zhu is aware that he disagreeing with the traditional He Yan
commentary on the sequence about a painting that he quotes from a
section of the venerable *Rites of Zhou*, one of the Thirteen Classics,
which no doubt was intended to lend support and authority to his reading—and to undermine He's.

Because both He and Zhu agree in the end that "ritual comes
after," how are we to understand their real differences? The heart of

the issue lies in the question: Comes after what? Relying metaphori-
cally on the image of a painting, He Yan understands the painting's
colors to refer to a beautiful woman's superior qualities—her captivating smile and lovely eyes—and the white to refer to the ritual that must
adorn these superior qualities, that brings them and the beautiful
woman herself to perfection. Ritual may "come after" these superior
qualities of captivating smile and lovely eyes, but it is what produces
perfection in them.

Zhu, too, regards the painting image as a metaphor but understands the white of a painting to refer to a person's superior qualities, a
captivating smile and lovely eyes, to which decorative rituals are added.
Zhu goes further than He in his commentarial analysis, reading the
superior qualities of a captivating smile and lovely eyes themselves as
metaphors for the cardinal human virtues of *zhong*, being true to one's
nature, and *xin*, being true to one's word. This is where Zhu's understanding parts ways with He Yan's. Only when man's inner resources,
the inner potential of human nature, have been properly tended, only
when he knows how to be true to his endowed nature and trustworthy,
will ritual not be performed without meaning, to paraphrase Yang Shi.
There is no suggestion here, as there is in He's commentary, that it is
ritual that enables the person to realize perfection—indeed, is a necessary means to self-perfection. Instead, ritual activity, Zhu informs his
reader, should follow the realization of one's natural endowment. With
this analect, we are again reminded of both the traditional Xunzi/
Mencius debate and the contemporary Fingarette/Schwartz debate.
Whereas He Yan understands—and would have the reader of his
commentary understand—Confucius to mean that ritual shapes and
develops man's conduct, Zhu understands him to mean that ritual
activity is itself informed by the realization of one's inner spirit. Ritual
is the natural expression of being "true to oneself" and "true to one's
word." In fact, a close reading of He's commentary on the passage
indicates that in contrast to Zhu Xi's a millennium later, he hardly
emphasizes the inner dimension. As I have noted elsewhere, it is partly
this interiority that Zhu finds in his reading of the *Analects* that distinguishes his commentary on the text from the commentary of others,
particularly He Yan's.

2

For Zhu Xi, ritual is necessarily more than form alone. Only when the appropriate spirit is tied to the form does ritual have meaning. This is the message of Confucius's words in analect 17.9, according to Zhu, which he reads as additional evidence of the Master's interest in the interior life. As the following translation indicates, the reader of He's commentary would certainly form a different impression of the passage:

He Yan's reading:

> The Master said, "Ritual, ritual": does it mean nothing more than jade and silk?
> Zheng [Xuan] said, "Jade, as in a jade tally; silk, as in a bundle of silk. This is to say that ritual is not simply the veneration of this jade and silk. Its value lies in the value it places on putting those above at ease and bringing order to the people."

> "Music, music": does it mean nothing more than bells and drums? (17.9 [21])
> Ma [Rong] said, "The value of music lies in its transformation of custom. It is not a matter of bells and drums and nothing more."

Zhu Xi's reading:

> The Master said, "Ritual, ritual": does it mean nothing more than jade and silk? "Music, music": does it mean nothing more than bells and drums?
> Feeling reverential, he puts it into practice with jade and silk: it is this that constitutes ritual. Feeling harmonious, he issues it forth with bells and drums: it is this that constitutes music. To neglect the fundamental and concentrate only on the incidentals is surely not what is meant by ritual and music.
> Master Cheng said, "Ritual is nothing but order; music is nothing but harmony. It is just that these two characters have many meanings. Under

heaven, there is nothing that is not ritual and music. Suppose, for instance, you arrange these two chairs. If one of them is not upright, there will be no order, and if there is no order, there will be irregularity, and if there is irregularity, there will be no harmony. Take, too, the case of bandits: they do the most unprincipled things—but they still have ritual and music. It is essential that they have a leader and subordinates who obey; only then they are capable of banditry. If such is not the case, there will be uncontrolled rebellion, and they will be incapable of uniting together in banditry even for a day. There is no place that ritual and music do not reach. It is essential that students recognize this."

In Zhu's reading, ritual and music must be sustained by an inner spirit: the feeling of reverence and the feeling of harmony. It is these feelings that, in his words, are "fundamental" to the performance; that is, the performance rests on them. Indeed, the performance of them is nothing more than the outward expression of these inner feelings. The point of Confucius's remark here is obvious to Zhu Xi: the value of the performance lies not in the performance itself but in the spirit invested in the performance by the performer. The difference from He Yan's reading of the passage could hardly be more telling and is emblematic of their general interpretive differences. Reflecting on what Confucius is suggesting is the deeper significance of ritual and music, He concludes not that it is the attendant feeling, as Zhu does, but the social order and stability that result from their practice. It is not primarily that they enable one to express toward others one's inner feelings of true goodness. Instead, their purpose is to guide men in their social conduct and teach them social customs. By distinguishing the different social statuses with different ritual prerogatives, ritual and music can maintain, without force or compulsion, the normative social hierarchy, "putting those above at ease and bringing order to the people."

Citing Master Cheng, Zhu offers further commentary on the meaning of the passage, commentary that would, no doubt, seem unfamiliar to He Yan. Defining ritual as "order" and music as "harmony," Zhu asserts that since all things and events in the world have an ideal order and harmony, all things and events are really a matter of ritual and music. Our conventional view of ritual and music is much too limiting; Confucius wants his followers to appreciate that the whole of everyday life—all things, events, relationships—seeks its natural order and harmony, and thus in a sense, when properly carried out, everything is ritual and music. The implication here is that one ideally is always practicing ritual and music, not only on specially designated occasions.

In the context of this discussion, perhaps analects like 10.7 become more intelligible:

He Yan's reading:

> If a mat was not straight, he would not sit on it. In the village wine-drinking ceremony, only when those with staffs took their leave would he then leave. (10.7 [22])
> Kong [Anguo] said, "Those with staffs refer to the elderly. The village wine-drinking ceremony honors the elderly. When the ceremony is over, the elderly leave; Confucius would follow and leave after them."

Zhu Xi's reading:

> If a mat was not straight, he would not sit on it.
> Mr. Xie [Liangzuo] said, "The mind-and-heart of the sage finds contentment in the straight. Thus while a seat's not being straight may be a small matter, he does not put himself there."

As we have seen, for Zhu Xi, everything has its own order, its own harmony. Everything is a matter of ritual and music. In such a view, the simple, apparently insignificant act of sitting on a mat becomes a ritualized expression of the self. If the self is straight and true in all that it does, as is the case with the sage, unless the mat is straight and true, he dare not sit on it. To do so would represent a corruption of his mind-and-heart, which invariably would express itself in the true. But for He, sitting on a mat has no particular ritual meaning in itself, and so "if the mat was not straight, he would not sit on it" is not an especially coherent or meaningful statement on its own. Consequently, He does not offer a commentary on the line, and he determines that to have meaning, this passage must be conflated with the next line about the village wine-drinking ceremony. Furthermore, consistent with his commentary on 17.9, the previous passage, what matters to He in the conflated passage here is the precise protocol of the ceremony, as exemplified by the Master, not the state of mind or the profound feelings expressed by or invested in the ritual activity itself.

He Yan does not dwell on the role of the inner life in sustaining ritual, as Zhu Xi does. Yet it would be misleading to suggest that he does not find in the *Analects* the message that ritual must be performed with the proper feeling. Ritual activity may not be to him the natural and spontaneous expression of an endowed inner spirit, as it is for Zhu, but in He's reading, if ritual performance is not accompanied by true feeling, it is deficient. For instance, He understands analect 3.12 to be a plea by the Master to bring a "presence," physical and emotional, in the performance of ceremonies of sacrifice, to both ancestors and unrelated spirit beings. Without such a presence, the ceremony might take place, but the opportunity to "extend" the reverence that the mind-and-heart feels toward the ancestors or the spirit beings is lost, and the purpose of the sacrificial ceremony is thus not satisfactorily fulfilled.

He Yan's reading:

Sacrifice as if they were present.
Kong [Anguo] said, "This says to serve the dead as you serve the living."

Sacrifice to spirit beings as if the spirit beings were present.
Kong [Anguo] said, "This speaks of sacrificing to the hundred spirit beings."

The Master said, When I do not take part in the sacrifice, it is as if I did not offer a sacrifice. (3.12 [23])
Bao [Xian] said, "Confucius occasionally was away or ill and so did not personally sacrifice but had a replacement do it. Not extending the

reverence of his mind-and-heart was the same as not offering the sacrifice."

Although Zhu reads the first lines of this passage differently from the way that He does, regarding them not so much as principles to be practiced by anyone engaged in sacrificial rites as specific praise of the Master's exemplary behavior in sacrificial rites by his disciples, Zhu's general understanding of the passage echoes He's. For Zhu, like He, the thrust of the analect is that the performance of sacrificial rituals must be invested with the proper feeling.

Zhu Xi's reading:

> He sacrifices as if they were present; he sacrifices to the spirit beings as if the spirit beings were present.

Master Cheng said, "Sacrifice [in the first line] is to sacrifice to ancestors. Sacrifice to the spirit beings is to sacrifice to the outside spirit beings. Sacrifice to ancestors is governed by filial piety; sacrifice to the spirit beings is governed by reverence. In my view, the disciples here are recording Confucius's sincere intentions [*cheng yi*] in the performance of sacrifices."

> The Master said, When I do not take part in the sacrifice, it is as if I did not offer a sacrifice.

This further records Confucius's words in order to clarify the disciples' earlier statement. It says that sometimes he personally should have made the sacrifice but, for some reason, could not take part and so had someone replace him. In these instances, he did not extend the same "as if they were present" sincerity. Consequently, even though the sacrifice had been made, his mind-and-heart felt dissatisfied as if there had been no sacrificial offering.

Mr. Fan [Zuyu][9] said, "In the seven days of fasting and the three

9. Fan Zuyu was a scholar-statesman of the Northern Song, perhaps best known for his collaboration with Sima Guang on the *Zizhi tongjian*.

days of vigil [*Liji* 51.19a], the superior man is sure to apprehend the sacrificial object—this is sincerity in perfection. Consequently, when he performs the sacrifices to heaven, heavenly spirits arrive, and when he performs the temple sacrifices, human spirits accept the offerings. Both matters start with the self and extend to the spirits. With sincerity, the spirits come into existence; without sincerity, there are no spirits. One must be vigilant! In the saying 'When I do not take part in the sacrifice, it is as if I do not offer a sacrifice,' sincerity constitutes the solid, and ritual, the empty."

While Zhu and He generally agree on the reading of this passage, in elaborating on his understanding, Zhu introduces a couple of points that give his commentarial remarks novelty and distinguish them clearly from He's. First, he suggests in quoting Master Cheng that Confucius's sincerity in sacrificing to his ancestors is the natural expression of the cardinal virtue of filial piety. In other words, the feeling accompanying the sacrificial rituals to the ancestral dead is engendered spontaneously by the filiality innate in human nature and is the sincere or true expression of our good human nature. (Hence Zhu's use of the term *cheng yi* [sincere or true intentions] from the *Daxue*, in which it means, in his reading, to make one's intentions true to one's nature.) Zhu concludes therefore that when Confucius does not personally participate in the sacrifice, the problem is partly that this "as if they were present sincerity," a feeling that arises spontaneously out of one's humanity in response to the sacrificial object, does not arise naturally or effortlessly. This explains to him why Confucius confesses here that ceremonies have no affective value if he does not personally take part in them.

Zhu then cites Fan Zuyu, who makes a claim that is quite remarkable, one that certainly has no precedent in He Yan's commentary. Fan states that feelings of sincerity and reverence not only make the sacrificial ceremony affective and more deeply meaningful for the participant but also confer existence on the spirits themselves, guaranteeing that the sacrificial offerings will be accepted. For Fan—and Zhu—sacrificial rituals are much more than cathartic exercises. In their understanding, actual "contact" between sacrificer and spirit is possible. As Zhu puts it,

"If you are able to exercise sincerity and reverence to the utmost, there will be influence and response."[10]

Elsewhere I have discussed at length the Song beliefs in spirit beings. Suffice it here to say that Zhu Xi was particularly interested in ritual offerings to ancestral spirits, giving considerable attention to the metaphysical assumptions that lay behind them. In his view, a shared biology between ancestor and descendant—that is, a common pool of psychophysical stuff (*qi*)—makes possible a resonance or contact between ancestor and descendant. This commonality of psychophysical stuff thus explains an efficacy of ancestral sacrifice that goes well beyond cathartic expression.[11]

For He and Zhu alike, feelings are essential to the ritual performance. But whereas He, without any elaboration, tells his reader only that feelings must accompany ritual, Zhu's commentary reflects at considerable length on the source of their expression and the powerful, real effect they have on the performance itself. Indeed, Zhu is so taken with the centrality of feelings in the ritual performance that he concludes his commentary with Fan's rather bold remark that "sincerity constitutes the solid, and ritual, the empty."

Zhu's commentary on analect 3.4, where he breaks down ritual into an analysis of the traditional dyadic terms, "substance" and "ornamentation," helps illuminate this final remark. Identifying feelings with substance and ritual observances with ornamentation, he admits that while both are essential to ritual performance, substance necessarily precedes ornamentation. In this analect, Zhu's strong emphasis on feeling in ritual activity is unmistakable, especially in comparison with He Yan, who merely paraphrases the Master and gives no particular weight to the role of feelings:

10. YL 3.46. Zhu frequently repeats or paraphrases Fan's claim, as in YL: "The existence or nonexistence of the spirit depends entirely on whether or not the mind is fully sincere" (25.620).

11. In YL, Zhu remarks: "My *qi* is the *qi* of my ancestors—it's just one and the same *qi*. Thus, as soon as there's influence there's bound to be a response" (3.47). See Daniel K. Gardner, "Ghosts and Spirits in the Sung Neo-Confucian World: Chu Hsi on *Kuei-shen*," *Journal of the American Oriental Society* 115 (1995): 598–611.

He Yan's reading:

Lin Fang asked about the fundamentals of ritual.
Zheng [Xuan] said, "Lin Fang is a man from Lu."[12]

The Master said, A big question indeed. In ritual, it is better to be frugal than extravagant; in mourning rites, it is better to be sorrowful than serene. (3.4 [24])
Bao [Xian] said, "*Yi* [serene] is *heyi*, 'calm.' This says that the fundamental intention of ritual is lost in extravagance, which is not as good as frugality; and that of the mourning rites is lost in serenity, which is not as good as deep sorrow."

Zhu Xi's reading:

Lin Fang asked about the fundamentals of ritual.
Lin Fang is a man from Lu. He observes that in the performance of ritual, his age is preoccupied with elaborate ornamentation and suspects that the fundamentals are not to be found here. Consequently he raises this question.

The Master said, A big question indeed.
Confucius believed that the world at that time was chasing after inessentials and that Fang alone was determined to find the fundamentals. Consequently, he regarded this as a big question. It would seem that if one found the fundamentals, ritual in its wholeness would be present therein.

In ritual, it is better to be frugal than extravagant; in mourning rites, it is better to be sorrowful than meticulous.
Yi [meticulous] is to order well, as in *Mengzi* [7A.23], "put in order the fields of the people" [*Lau*, 186]; it means to be well versed in the ornamental details of mourning rites but without the actual feeling of grief and sadness. *Qi* is to be single-mindedly sorrowful but inadequate in the

12. This is all the information we have about Lin Fang.

ornamental details. Ritual places value on achieving a balance: extravagance and meticulousness are excessive in ornamental detail; frugality and sorrow do not go far enough [in ornamentation] but are substantive. In neither of these cases is ritual as it should be. Still, according to the principle of things in general, there must first be substance and only afterward ornamentation, which is to say that substance is the fundament of ritual.

Mr. Fan [Zuyu] said, "In sacrifices, it is better that ritual be inadequate and the feelings of reverence excessive than that the feelings of reverence be inadequate and the ritual excessive. In the mourning rites, it is better that the ritual be inadequate and the feelings of grief excessive than that the feelings of grief be inadequate and the ritual excessive. When rituals become lost in extravagance and the mourning rites become lost in meticulousness, in both cases it is because one, being incapable of returning to the fundament, follows what is inessential. In ritual, it is better to be frugal and incomplete than extravagant and complete. In the mourning rites, it is better to be sorrowful and without ornamentation than meticulous in ornamental detail. Frugality is things in their substance; sorrow is the mind-and-heart in its sincerity. Consequently, they constitute the fundament of ritual." Mr. Yang [Shi] said, "'Ceremony starts with food and drink. Therefore, they excavate the ground in the form of a jar and scoop the water into it with their two hands' [*Liji* 21.9a; cf. Legge, *Li chi*, 1:368], fashioning round and square sacrificial vessels, taller ones of bamboo and wood, and drinking cups for ornamentation. The fundament thus is nothing more than frugality. In the rites of mourning, they cannot 'give direct vent to the feeling and act it out as by a short cut' [*Liji* 9.25b; cf. Legge, *Li chi*, 1:177]; they devise practices of wearing coarse, hempen garments and of crying and leaping for the purpose of moderating the rites. The fundament thus is nothing more than sorrow. With the decline of the Zhou, the world was exterminating substance with ornamentation; Lin Fang alone was capable of asking about the fundament of ceremony. Therefore, the Master, greatly concerned, explained it to him in this way."

He Yan's commentary on 3.4 does little more than repeat Confucius's remark that in ritual, frugality is preferable to extravagance and that in mourning, ritual in particular, feelings of sorrow are preferable to feelings of detachment. Brief though the comment is, it is apparent that He understands—and would have his reader understand—that feelings do indeed play a role in rituals. But the reader of He's commentary cannot know much more than this, for like the analect itself, He's commentarial gloss is largely prescriptive, offering little explanation.

Zhu Xi's remarks are considerably more prolix, drawing out at some length the implications of the Master's brief comment and leaving the reader with little doubt about his understanding of its larger significance and, more specifically, of the "fundamental" role of feelings in the performance of ritual. In Zhu's reading, 3.4 is a condemnation by Confucius of contemporary ritual practice. Form has come to be valued over substance. Ceremony marked by indulgence and extravagance, on the one hand, and by fastidious or overscrupulous ritual observance for ritual's sake, on the other, has supplanted ceremony that more genuinely expresses human feeling. Confucius's response to Lin Fang in 3.4 is a plea to contemporaries to return to the fundamentals, or what Zhu calls the "substance" of ritual.

In his use here of the word "substance" (*zhi*), and its partner term "ornamentation" (*wen*), Zhu is making clear the intratextual references and connections to analects 6.18 and 12.8, in which it is argued that the superior man is necessarily a blend of the two. That is, man's natural substance and acquired refinement must be balanced if he is to achieve perfection. Likewise, ritual in its wholeness is composed of the same complementary qualities. Zhu equates substance with the feelings of reverence and grief that inform ritual practice, and ornamentation, with the details of ritual observance. Both feelings and observances are essential to the proper practice of ritual.

Although proper ritual practice may indeed be a composite of substance and ornamentation, substance, Zhu's commentary continues, undoubtedly comes first and thus is what is meant by the word "fundamentals" in the passage. Because the substance of ritual is found in the feelings of reverence and sorrow, it is these feelings that constitute the "fundamentals of ritual." For Zhu Xi, analect 3.4 is a call to ground ritual practice in the expression of authentic human feeling.

Zhu's understanding here of the Master's response to Lin Fang about the fundamentals of ritual is surely different from He Yan's, especially in the weight and priority it gives to feelings, and this difference partly is owing to his different reading of the characters *jian* (frugality) and *yi* (meticulous). For Zhu, as the remark by Fan Zuyu suggests, frugality implies an unadorned simplicity or plainness of ritual practice, which in turn expresses a genuine reverence; that is, Zhu reads "frugality" in the passage as a sort of shorthand for feelings of reverence. In addition, He glosses *yi* in the following phrase as "serenity" or "calm" and understands the phrase to mean that feelings of sorrow are preferable to feelings of serenity or detachment. But Zhu, citing Mencius as his authority, glosses the term as "meticulousness" and understands the phrase to mean that feelings of sorrow are preferable not to other sorts of feelings but to a meticulousness or fastidiousness in ritual observance (*yi*). For Zhu, the contrast Confucius is drawing in this line is between inner feelings of sorrow and outer display or observance of ritual.

As we have seen throughout, it is precisely this tension between ritual as an expression of human feeling and ritual as performance that Zhu Xi's commentary on ritual passages addresses. Zhu reminds his reader repeatedly that for Confucius, the significance of ritual lies not in the ritual itself but in the meaning or feeling one invests in it. Such meaning or feeling, in turn, arises naturally from within, from the human nature endowed at birth to every human being. As a consequence, Zhu's argument continues, only if one's original endowment of human nature is unobstructed or unimpeded can feelings authentic and true to one's self arise. The challenge for each person, therefore, is to keep this original endowment preserved and whole and to give it full and concrete expression in action. In short, Zhu wants his reader to understand from the *Analects* that ritual activity is a means by which one may realize and manifest in relation to others the humaneness that is one's ontological self.

Zhu Xi's commentaries on passages in the *Analects* relating to ritual, like his commentaries on those relating to learning and true goodness, tend to go on at considerable length, and commonly at greater length than the classical text itself. Like most traditional commentaries, they try to illuminate the meaning of discrete characters and phrases by providing semantic and phonological glosses. But they are more ambitious than many other commentaries and certainly more ambitious than He Yan's, attempting to piece together the parts of the elaborate system of thought undergirding the text of the *Analects*. Zhu assumes—indeed, it is almost a matter of faith for him—that the Master's individual remarks, brought together by later disciples to constitute passages in the *Analects*, are the product of a deeply coherent, meaningful vision. Equally important, Zhu assumes that this vision is fully accessible to him through the constant study and investigation of the Master's words. For Zhu, the recent argument of one scholar notwithstanding, there is nothing prophetic about his ability to arrive at a true understanding of the text.[13] Finally, Zhu believes that this vision is accessible to others as well, providing they are committed to making the effort. His commentary is an aid to them in that effort, an attempt to reveal to others the truths he feels fortunate to have found there himself.

13. Wm. Theodore de Bary speaks of a "prophetic" approach to the truth in the Cheng-Zhu school in *Neo-Confucian Orthodoxy and the Learning of the Mind-and-Heart* (New York: Columbia University Press, 1981), 9–13.

4

Ruling

When Confucius remarks in analect 12.13, "In hearing lawsuits, I am just like others. What is necessary is to see that there are no lawsuits," he is expressing both a reality and an ideal. It would appear that in the China of his day, recourse to law as a means of maintaining social order was not uncommon. And although Confucius may have been troubled by the increasingly prominent role of law, he seems to have viewed it—and the penal sanctions associated with it—as a normal part of the apparatus of government.[1] At the same time, however, his remark makes clear that Confucius would have preferred to minimize the role of law, to reduce the incidence of appeals to law to virtually nothing. Law might be essential to the governance of China, but the best government relied on it the least.

Throughout the *Analects*, the Master envisages a government that rules through ritual activity. As the expression of the ruler's virtue,

---

1. See, for example, 4.11, 13.3, and 20.2.

ritual exerts a powerful moral force over others, a power that renders physical force or legal constraints and punishments unnecessary. The people will bend to the ruler's wishes voluntarily, guided by the exemplary behavior embodied in his ritual practice. Over the centuries, scholars offered different interpretations of the locus of moral force: some suggested that the rituals themselves contained a sort of magic that worked its powers on those enmeshed in their practice; others, however, situated the charismatic force less in the rituals and more in the goodness of the perfected person performing them. These differences in emphasis were partly an extension of the interpretive differences in the relationship between ritual and true goodness considered earlier.

Whatever its source, the Master's conviction that moral force makes for good government resulted in his offering few specific policy suggestions in the *Analects*. Except for brief admonitions to enrich and teach the people, not to overtax them, and to be economical in expenditure, he says little about how the ruler is practically to administer his realm.[2] A few centuries later, by way of elaboration, Mencius argued that only if the government guarantees the people's material needs can they realize their moral propensities, and he specified the measures the government should take to guarantee those needs. The Master himself, however, did not explore specific policies, measures, or institutions in the *Analects*, offering instead a simple but profound faith in the efficacy of virtuous government by ritual alone, even once suggesting, in a vocabulary reminiscent of Daoism, that nothing but "nonaction" was required from the ruler.

Numerous remarks throughout the *Analects* address the desirability of government by virtue and ritual, but perhaps none more pithily or effectively than 2.3:

He Yan's reading:

The Master said, Lead them with tools of government,

2. See 1.5, 11.17, and 13.9.

Kong [Anguo] said, "*Zheng* [government] refers to laws and instructions."

regulate them by punishment,
Ma [Rong] said, "*Qi* [regulate] is to regulate [*zheng*] them by punishment."

and the people will avoid punishment but have no sense of shame.
Kong said, "*Mian* [evade punishment] is *goumian*, 'to avoid or escape.'"

Lead them with virtue,
Bao [Xian] said, "*De* [virtue] refers to moral virtue."

regulate them by ritual, and they will have a sense of shame and moreover set themselves right. (2.3 [25])
Ge [set right] is *zheng*, "to straighten or correct."

Zhu Xi's reading:

The Master said, Lead them with tools of government, regulate them by punishment, and the people will avoid punishment but have no sense of shame.
Dao [lead] is *yindao*, "to lead," which means "to place in front of them." *Zheng* [tools of government] refers to rules and prohibitions. *Qi* [regulate] is the means by which to bring about oneness. When you lead but they do not follow, there are punishments to bring about oneness. *Mian er wu chi* [to avoid punishment but have no sense of shame] is to say that they will avoid punishment but feel no shame. It would seem that although they dare not do evil, neither do they entirely rid themselves of the mind-and-heart for evil.

Lead them with virtue, regulate them by ritual, and they will have a sense of shame and moreover arrive at good.
Li [ritual] refers to institutions and regulated observances. *Ge* [arrive at good] is *zhi*, "to arrive or reach." This says lead them through personal conduct and the people will be deeply moved and aroused. Then through ritual, such differences among them as shallow and deep, as

substantial and insubstantial, will be reconciled, and the people will thus feel shame at not being good and, moreover, have the means of arriving at good [*zhi yu shan*]. Another explanation for *ge* [arrive] is *zheng*, "to straighten or correct," as when the *Book of History* says, "to correct the heart of wrong" [*Shangshu* 19.14b; cf. Legge, *Chinese Classics*, 3:585].

In my view, *zheng* [tools of government] are the tools of governing; punishments are statutes that assist in governing. Virtue and ritual, then, are the foundation on which to build government, and virtue, in turn, is the foundation of ritual. These are entirely mutual, and although one side is not to be favored at the expense of the other, tools of government and punishment still are capable merely of permitting people to distance themselves from punishment and nothing more, whereas the effects of virtue and ritual permit the people to move daily toward goodness without their even knowing it. Thus, in governing the people, one must not rely vainly on the inessentials; rather, one should deeply examine the fundamentals.

In their general understanding of analect 2.3, the two commentaries agree: government by virtue and ritual is preferable to government by law and punishment. It is on smaller points that disagreements, or at least different emphases, emerge. Perhaps most significant are the differences regarding the effect of good government, as Confucius characterizes it, on the governed. For He, the governed not only learn a sense of shame but correct themselves as well. What precisely He means by this, his commentary does not reveal; it merely suggests that those who come under the powerful sway of moral rule will naturally learn to comport themselves appropriately, out of self-respect or pride. Zhu Xi, typically, is considerably more explicit, reading the passage to mean that through exposure to goodness, the governed will themselves arrive at good, or as he puts it in the *Conversations of Master Zhu* (23.547), the ruler will "arouse the good mind-and-heart of the people." Zhu thus assumes a process of internalizing morality, made possible by human ontology, that is nowhere present in He's reading. Such a reading is consistent with Zhu's understanding of other analects, notably

1.1, in which he argues that realizing the good that is at the core of human existence is simply a matter of emulating those fortunate enough already to have realized it in themselves.

In this reading, government ideally influences more than just the behavior of those it governs; it affects their very mind-and-heart. Government by law and punishment may indeed keep the people in line, but it does nothing to guide them morally, to inspire the good mind-and-heart with which they are born to manifest itself and triumph over the mind-and-heart for evil—that is, the evil desires that over time develop and challenge it. As Zhu says to a disciple in a paraphrase of his commentary, "If you lead and regulate them with punishment and tools of government, you will be incapable of transforming their mind-and-heart and will merely bring about little changes" (YL 23.549). It is this transformation of the mind-and-heart, Zhu is convinced, that Confucius is aiming for in analect 2.3.

This conviction that good government transforms the very nature of those it touches may well be fueled by Zhu's reading of another, later passage in the *Analects* (13.12) that similarly treats good government. He Yan renders the passage: "The Master said, If there were a true king, it would surely be only a generation before there was truly good government," taking the final character, *ren*, to refer to *renzheng*, "truly good government." In this reading, the true king brings about good government. Zhu understands this passage quite differently: "The Master said, If there were a true king, it would surely be only a generation before all were truly good." No longer is it the government alone, led by a true king, that is made good, but all the people fortunate enough to be subject to the king's moralizing influence. Such is the stimulating resonance that can occur between beings of like nature— in this case, the good ruler and the people he governs.

Zhu Xi's ontological assumption that all human beings are endowed with goodness at birth explains, in his judgment, why mere exposure to virtue in a ruler might inspire realization of the goodness within oneself. But in recognizing that besides his endowment of human nature, man is born with different endowments of *qi*, or psycho-physical stuff, Zhu concludes in 2.3 that the presence of virtue in the ruler may not in itself be sufficient to inspire those whose endowments are especially weak or problematic. This is where government by ritual comes in. Unlike He Yan, who lumps together virtue and ritual, making little distinction between them and their effect, Zhu Xi suggests that government by virtuous leadership activates the goodness in many, but not all, people. For the rest, the concrete example of ritual practice is necessary: "In people's psychophysical stuff there exist differences of shallow and deep, substantial and insubstantial; consequently, the effect on them cannot be the same. There needs to exist ritual for regulation" (YL 23.548; cf. 23.549–50). As Zhu makes clear elsewhere, it is, of course, those of shallow and insubstantial psychophysical stuff who are in particular need of ritual (YL 23.550). It is thus in light of his ontology, his concept of *li* and *qi*, that Zhu—and the reader of his commentary—understands this passage.

There are other differences in the two commentaries. In contrast to He, Zhu acknowledges that there is indeed a place for the tools of government in ruling the people. Law and punishment may be ancillary to virtue and ritual, he asserts, but they nonetheless are necessary and should not be neglected. Whether Zhu Xi is making a realist's concession to what had become in fact routine practice in the Chinese empire or whether he understands Confucius elsewhere in the text of the *Analects* to be accommodating himself to the practice of law, he does not read 2.3 as a plea by the Master to govern by virtue and ritual exclusively. They may be the foundation of government, but law and punishment have their place as well, however subordinate. In Zhu's words, government by virtue and ritual and government by law and punishment are "entirely mutual."

Finally and briefly, lest his reader be unclear about the relationship between virtue and ritual, Zhu is emphatic where He is silent: virtue and ritual together are the foundation of good government, but virtue itself is the foundation of ritual. For Zhu Xi, ritual here, as we saw in the previous chapter, seems to be largely an expression of inner virtue, meaningless and ineffectual unless informed by this virtue.

In Zhu's reading, a number of other analects echo the message of 2.3, calling for government by ritual, but ritual that is sustained by an inner spirit. This, according to Zhu's commentary, is precisely what the Master intended in 4.13:

Zhu Xi's reading:

> The Master said, Is he is capable of governing the state with ritual
> and humility? What difficulties will he have then? If he is incapable of
> governing the state with ritual and humility, what does he have to do
> with ritual? (4.13 [26])

Humility is the substance of ritual. *He you* [what difficulties will he have] is
to say that there will be no difficulty. This passage says that if the very substance of ritual is used in governing the state, then how could there be any
difficulty? But if it is not, then while ritual may be ornamentally perfect, what
use is it, especially in governing the state?

While the final line of this analect might seem to invite consideration of the semantic relationship between ritual (*li*) and humility
(*rang*), as it does for Zhu, He Yan offers no explanation for it. The
silence probably reflects his larger commentarial attitude. He seems to
perceive his principal responsibility as a commentator to gloss or illuminate the meaning of individual characters or difficult phrases. Aided
by these glosses, the reader is expected to understand the Master's
teachings for himself. Indeed, He Yan generally is reluctant to interpret for others the significance of the Sage's revered teachings. In any
case, and whatever the reasons for its laconic style, He Yan's commentary on 4.13 evinces none of the interest in ritual's substance or inner
source that characterizes Zhu's relatively brief commentary on the
passage.

He Yan's reading:

> The Master said, Is he capable of governing the state with ritual and
> humility? What difficulties will he have then?

He you [what difficulties will he have] is to say that there will be no difficulty.

> If he is incapable of governing the state with ritual and humility, what
> does he have to do with ritual?

Bao [Xian] said, "*Ru li he* [what does he have to do with ritual] is to say that
he is incapable of using ritual."

Consistent with his commentarial remarks on ritual elsewhere, Zhu Xi here, in contrast to He Yan, underscores the difference between ritual substance and ritual form and argues that only if ritual practice is informed by an inner spirit is it authentic and, hence, effective in governing the people. Without this inner spirit, ritual, no matter how elaborate, serves no purpose. As he explains in the *Conversations of Master Zhu*, the feeling of humility, the spirit of yielding, that under-lies the authentic performance of ritual "emanates from the sincerity of the original mind-and-heart." Consequently, the humility informing the practice of ritual is capable of inspiring the mind-and-heart of others and thereby of bringing about their moral transformation (YL 26.666). In short, a sort of ontological resonance occurs between similar endowments of original mind-and-heart. Once again, Zhu returns his reader to the inner springs of ritual efficacy in governing the realm.

Ruling through ritual is a refrain repeated throughout the text of the *Analects*. It is as if the Master sensed that the people of his age, accustomed to an increasingly impersonal rule relying more and more on law, punishment, and institutions of government and less and less on the ritual duties of the person of the king, were deeply skepti-cal and in need of constant persuasion and reassurance. In 3.11, he suggests, in terms that must have struck many of his followers as hyper-bolic, the almost magical power that ritual can exercise in ruling the empire:

He Yan's reading:

> Someone asked for an explanation of the *di*, or great sacrifice. The Master said, I do not know. One who did know would deal with all under heaven as easily as pointing to this here—and he pointed to his palm. (3.11 [27])
> Kong [Anguo] said, "He answers, 'I do not know,' because the sacrifice is forbidden in Lu." Bao [Xian] said, "Confucius says to the person here that one who did know the explanation for the *di* ceremony would find dealing with all affairs under heaven to be like pointing to something in the palm of the hand, which is to say it would be easy."

Zhu Xi's reading:

> Someone asked for an explanation of the *di*, or great sacrifice. The Master said, I do not know. One who did know would deal with all under heaven as easily as looking at this here, and he pointed to his palm.

The intention of former kings to repay their ancestors with the proper sacrifices is no more ardent than in the *di* sacrifice. Unless possessed of true goodness, filial piety, truthfulness, and reverence—in perfection—one is not fit to participate in it. The particular person here is not equal to it. Furthermore, because of the law that only a ruler is to perform the *di* sacrifice, it is necessarily forbidden in Lu, and thus he responds saying he does not know. *Shi* [see] is the same as *shi*, "to see." As for "pointing to his palm": disciples are recording the Master saying this as he himself is pointing to his palm. This is to say that it is clear and easy. It seems that if a person knows the explanation for the *di* sacrifice, principle will always be clear and his truthfulness always correct. Thus he will rule all under heaven with no difficulty. Is it possible that the Sage really does not know about this matter?

He and Zhu agree on the general significance of the Master's response: one who has a true understanding of the *di* ritual is empowered to govern all under heaven. But Zhu's commentary probes considerably deeper than He's, analyzing more fully and precisely where the source of this power to govern others is located. Significantly, for Zhu, it seems not to lie in the ritual itself or in its performance. Rather, the power clearly emanates from within the individual himself. As Zhu reads the passage, one's understanding of the *di* sacrifice is evidence that one understands its principle; and having come to understand the principle here, there is no manifestation of principle anywhere in the universe that remains unclear to him. It is this apprehension of principle, which simultaneously involves realizing the principle that is one's nature and understanding the manifold things and affairs in the world, that explains the ease and success with which such a person governs the affairs under heaven. According to Zhu's reasoning, this person, by means of self-cultivation, realizes his innate capacity for goodness and naturally and effortlessly expresses it in his ritualized interaction with those around him, thereby, through ontological resonance, starting their realization of their moral nature. In this understanding, such a person governs and the people respond without the need of law or punishment or, for that matter, any other instrument of government. The moral force engendered by the full development of his innate moral endowment and expressed through ritual activity is sufficient.

It is interesting that He and Zhu offer similar explanations for Confucius's response that he does not know the *di* sacrifice. They agree that it is because the sacrifice is prohibited in the Master's native state of Lu. To this, Zhu adds that it is also because the *di* sacrifice is the prerogative of the ruler alone. But whereas He seems to take the Master's "I do not know" at face value, Zhu understands it to be largely an expression of sagely modesty, remarking: "Is it possible that the Sage really does not know about this matter?" The logic of Zhu Xi's reading of the passage—that one who knows the *di* sacrifice is simply one who knows principle in all its manifestations and is true to it in all that one does—would almost compel Zhu to conclude that the Sage must know the explanation for the sacrifice. After all, the Sage is one who fully manifests principle, fully appreciating it in all its manifestations, including its manifestation in the *di* sacrifice. It thus must be a sort of modesty—and a sense of propriety—on his part that, for Zhu, explains his admission of ignorance here.

That in this analect Zhu traces the source of the aura, the almost magical power exercised over others, to the inner dimension of one who knows the *di* sacrifice, is, as we have observed throughout, philosophically consistent with his reading of other analects. Analect 2.1, a passage we have not yet considered, argues especially effectively, in Zhu's view, for such an inner potency to attract followers and effect their transformation:

He Yan's reading:

The Master said, One who practices government by virtue may be compared to the North Star, which remains in its place while the multitude of other stars pay homage to it. (2.1 [28])

Bao [Xian] said, "The virtuous takes no action; which is similar to the North Star's not moving, and yet the multitude of stars pay homage to it."

Zhu Xi's reading:

> The Master said, One who practices government by virtue may be compared to the North Star: it remains in its place while the multitude of other stars turn toward it.

Zheng [government] is to say *zheng*, "to correct," and is that by which to correct what is incorrect in others. *De* [virtue] is to say *de*, "to get or acquire": it is to practice the Way, acquiring it in the mind-and-heart. *Beichen* [North Star] is *beiji*, the North Pole, or *tian zhishu*, the North Star. *Ju qi suo* [remains in its place] is "no movement." *Gong* [turn toward] is *xiang*, "to face toward." This to say that the multitude of other stars, in every direction, revolve around and turn toward it. He who practices government by virtue takes no action, and yet all under heaven turn toward him—such is the image. Master Cheng said, "Practice government by virtue, and only afterward is there no action." Fan [Zuyu] said, "He who practices government by virtue without moving will bring about transformation, without speaking will prove trustworthy, and without taking action will bring about completion. He holds on to utter simplicity and yet is capable of managing trouble. He dwells in utter quietude and yet is capable of controlling activity. He attends to few and yet is capable of serving all."

In opening his interlinear commentary by homophonously glossing *zheng* (to govern) as *zheng* (to correct), Zhu is drawing on the authority of the Master himself. In analect 12.17 Confucius remarks, "'To govern' [*zheng*] is 'to correct' [*zheng*]. If you lead by correctness, who will dare be incorrect?" That is, to govern others is to correct them; to correct them requires first of all that one be correct oneself. As Confucius further comments in 13.13, "If he corrects his own person, what difficulty will he have in participating in government? But if he is unable to correct his own person, what can he have to do with correcting other people?" The power that this correctness exercises over others, according to Confucius, is a moral power that operates silently and without force: "If his person is correct, he does not issue the order, yet it is carried out; if his person is incorrect, even though he issues the order, it will not be obeyed" (13.6). Zhu's intratextual reference to 12.17, "to govern [*zheng*] is to correct [*zheng*]," to open the commentary would seem to have at least one important effect: it immediately associates, in the reader's mind, the passage under discussion (2.1) with these other various remarks by Confucius and thereby lends legitimacy to Zhu's reading of the passage even as it gives greater coherence to the whole of the Master's vision.

Zhu provides a helpful and illuminating elaboration of his commentary on analect 2.1 in conversations with his disciples. He makes an especially strong case for the extraordinary power that a person with virtue has over others. In his view, this power is an attribute of the virtue itself and works effortlessly and naturally to bring about both the submission of the people and, significantly, their transformation:

> Someone asked about "One who practices government by virtue." Zhu replied, As for "one who practices government by virtue," it is not that one aims to use virtue in order to practice government; nor is it that one doltishly does absolutely nothing. It is simply that virtue becomes cultivated in the self and others naturally are stimulated and transformed. This being the case, the stimulation and transformation do not rest in the matter of government, but rather in the virtue. It would seem that to govern is the way to correct what is incorrect in others, so how could there possibly be no action? It's just that the people turn to such a person on account of his virtue and nothing more. Thus, he needn't do anything and all under heaven will turn to him, just as the multitude of other stars turn toward it. (YL 23.533–34)

For Zhu, as this passage suggests, virtue and government may be logically distinguishable but not ontologically so. Governing "biologically" derives from virtue. Explaining the analect to a disciple, he remarks: "A person who has virtue manifests it in government, just as water is something moist and fire is something hot. Once virtue exists, government exists" (YL 23.533). That is, just as water manifests itself in wetness and fire manifests itself in heat, according to Zhu Xi, virtue manifests itself in governing. The man who cultivates virtue does not take governing and transforming others as a self-conscious aim or responsibility; rather, the governing happens entirely on its own, as people are naturally inspired by him and so follow his lead. As Zhu repeatedly concludes in his conversations, the transformation of the people is not because of his governance but because of his virtue.

The character for virtue (*de*), like the character for government (*zheng*), is glossed in both the commentary and the conversations by a homophonous character, *de*, "to get" or "to acquire." With this gloss, Zhu Xi situates virtue in the mind-and-heart, explaining virtuous behavior, whether it is filial piety or true goodness, as something emanating from and reflecting what has been "got" or "acquired" within the mind-and-heart:

> Many asked about the "One who practices government by virtue" passage. Zhu replied, It rests entirely on the character *de*, virtue. The character *de* comes from the character *xin*, mind-and-heart, because one acquires [*de*] it in the mind-and-heart. For instance, to be filial is a matter of the mind-and-heart acquiring this filiality; to be truly good is a matter of the mind-and-heart acquiring this true goodness. If one is simply behaving like this on the outside but on the inside the mind-and-heart doesn't feel it, then it isn't *de*, or virtue. (YL 23.534)

To Zhu, virtue is an inner resource manifested outwardly in all activities. The occasional or sporadic acts of virtue that all of us are capable of performing are not truly virtuous, in his opinion, for they are generated more out of a sense of social duty—for outward consumption—than out of the genuine conviction residing in our own mind-and-heart. Should one bring to the governing of others the expression of such genuine inner conviction, these others will "know" it and readily follow:

> Someone asked, Your *Collected Commentaries* had said, "Virtue is to practice the Way, acquiring it in one's person." Later

"person" was changed to "mind-and-heart." Why? Zhu replied, Generally when people do good, if they simply do one or two things, it's merely because they feel compelled. It isn't that they've "acquired" it. What is meant by "acquire," is to do it with such conviction that the mind-and-heart is entirely at ease with it. If you go practice government in this way the people will submit on their own. Supposing that these days a good person were speaking; the one listening to him would naturally trust him. What is meant by "no-action" is not to dispense entirely with the various types of official documents. It's simply that when a person is possessed of this virtue others will on their own submit to him, without his forcing them to submit. (YL 23.536)

Zhu's remark in his commentary that "he who practices government by virtue takes no action" is an echo of He Yan's earlier "the virtuous takes no action." But whereas He may well have wished his reader to understand by this that in this passage Confucius was advocating a Daoist-style rulership in which things are simply left to follow their natural course, Zhu, especially in the *Conversations of Master Zhu*, is more voluble, eager to distinguish his understanding of Confucian government by nonaction from the Daoist notion of nonaction (e.g., YL 23.537). Over and over in conversation, as in the preceding exchange, Zhu acknowledges that one who rules by virtue does in fact engage in activity:

Zishan[3] asked, "Practice government by virtue and only afterward is there no action." Can the sage possibly engage in no-action at all? Zhu replied, The sage is not entirely without activity. For instance, Shun did many things. Could he possibly have been without activity? It's just that when the people in their mind-and-heart turn to the sage, it is on account of his virtue and not his activity. The considerable activity all follows from his virtue. A person without virtue who vainly turns

3. Pan Shiju was a student of Zhu's in the 1190s.

his attention to activity would become mentally vexed—and the people simply wouldn't submit. "One who practices government by virtue" is like a lamp: the oil being plentiful, the lamp is naturally bright. (YL 23.537)

Indeed, Zhu says, at times a good ruler even resorts to punishments and orders (YL 23.534). Still, he insists, it is not the ruler's activity that makes his government effective, nor is it his activity that wins over the people. Rather, it is simply the virtue of his mind-and-heart. It is the "no-action" of his virtue that results in good government.

The suggestion here in Zhu Xi's commentary on the *Analects*, made explicit in his conversations with students, is extremely interesting: he who puts virtue first need do nothing, and all under heaven will, on their own, turn to him. That is, it is his virtue that wins over the people. In his capacity as ruler, he is expected to engage in activities like issuing orders, rendering legal decisions, and deciding punishments. But because these orders, legal decisions, punishments, and the like all follow from the virtue in his mind-and-heart, they are sure to be consistent with principle and hence consistent with good government. Accordingly, the people will naturally submit to them. Indeed, so natural and appropriate is the ruler's activity that no "traces of his activity" are left behind (YL 23.537).

Zhu goes on to say rather polemically that while Laozi's nonaction is nothing but neglect—that is, doing nothing at all—Confucius's involves constant activity (YL 23.537–38). A person of Confucian virtue constantly displays sincerity and attentiveness. In turn, such sincerity and attentiveness ensure that he comprehends universal principle in its various manifestations. Comprehending it, he is bound to accord with it, the consequence being that all affairs under heaven are just as they ought to be (YL 23.537). Thus, for Zhu, "nonaction" here seems to mean no action in violation of universal principle as it should be. And activity that is one with universal principle leaves behind no discernable traces.

The understanding here is that the person of virtue needs to work to be virtuous. To apprehend the principle of things is an arduous task requiring constant attentiveness. Hence, to paraphrase Zhu, the nonaction of the virtue that makes for good government rests on constant activity. In his interlinear commentary on 2.1 and his conversations with his disciples about the analect, Zhu Xi reveals some of his most basic philosophical assumptions and concerns:

1. The source of moral human behavior is found in man.
2. Inner virtue needs cultivation and perfection.
3. There is a distinct process by which to bring about this cultivation: the apprehension of the principle in things.
4. In its capacity to be attentive, the mind of man is crucial to this process.
5. Because principle is present in all things and is knowable to the human mind, the universe and all things and affairs in it are knowable to human beings.
6. It is the understanding of universal principle in its myriad manifestations that makes for sageliness and gives one a moral power that effortlessly exerts a kind of gravitational pull on others.

If He Yan held similar assumptions and concerns, they surely were never made explicit in his commentaries.

This particular analect, 2.1, and Zhu's commentary on it, excited a great deal of discussion in the *Conversations of Master Zhu*, as we have seen. This discussion is helpful and revealing for a number of reasons. First and perhaps most important and obvious, it provides a fuller insight into Zhu Xi's reading and understanding of the *Analects*. Second, it is apparent from the discussion that commentary on the classics produces even more commentary. Students routinely inquire, even challenge, their master about the reading of the *Analects* expressed in his interlinear commentary, prompting him to reflect more deeply on the classic as well as on his commentary. It is evident that Zhu's understanding of this relatively brief classic is an ongoing, lifelong process. Third, any one doubting the seriousness with which Confucian intellectuals of the twelfth century might have regarded the canonical tradition will likely find the twenty-seven chapters of far-ranging, probing conversations in the *Conversations of Master Zhu* devoted to the text of the *Analects* ample demonstration that canonical texts, for all their antiquity, continued for millennia to be a genuine source of inspiration, instrumental in shaping and reshaping Confucian identity and community.

The conversations about analect 2.1 regarding Confucian government through nonaction frequently refer—as the preceding exchange with Zishan suggests—to the legendary ruler Shun and, in particular, to the Master's remark about him in analect 15.5. Let us look at this analect, for as brief as it is and as brief as both He's and Zhu's commentaries on it are, their different readings are especially instructive:

He Yan's reading:

> The Master said, Ruling through inactivity, is this not Shun! For what did he do? Assuming a reverential pose, he faced due south and nothing more. (15.5 [29])

This is to say that he employed others as officials and therefore ruled through inactivity.

Zhu Xi's reading:

> The Master said, Ruling through inactivity, is this not Shun! For what did he do? Assuming a reverential pose, he faced due south and nothing more.

Ruling through inactivity is a matter of the sage's virtue being of such abundance that the people are transformed without his doing anything. He singles Shun out for praise here because in succeeding Yao, he got others to fill the multitudinous offices and, as a consequence, left no traces of activity. "Assuming a reverential pose" refers to the sage's outward demeanor of reverential virtue. Because he did nothing, this is all that others saw and nothing more.

In analects 8.20, 12.22, and 8.18, Confucius remarks that by training good people to be his ministers, Shun did not personally involve himself in government. This is the message that He Yan echoes in his commentary. Zhu, while likewise offering the employ of others as the reason for Shun's inactivity, goes significantly beyond it. In his very first line of commentary, he takes the reader back to 2.1, arguing that with his abundant virtue Shun ruled effortlessly, taking no action. Furthermore—and again consistent with 2.1—he says that rule by a sage means more than simply providing order or maintaining control; it means transforming the ruled as well. Thus Zhu, in contrast to He, explicitly gives this passage, 15.5, deep moral significance, attributing the good "inactive" rule of the legendary Shun mainly to the power of an inner virtue, a virtue that naturally exerts a moral force on others, and thereby linking Shun to the North Star of analect 2.1.

Confucius's belief that sociopolitical harmony could be achieved without force, without action, is one of the cornerstones of his philosophical vision. Law and coercive punishment, while perhaps necessary evils, simply do not promote human morality effectively, nor do they create a social order based on mutual respect. Rather, an exemplary person and exemplary ritual activity are much more helpful guides. According to Confucius, without coercion of any sort they have the power to inspire in others model social behavior, born not of fear but of voluntary respect for others. In short, a man of virtue—the North Star—using ritual expression helps promote among the people a sense of shared values, creating thereby a strong communal identity, or what one scholar called "a fiduciary community based on mutual trust."[4]

In a well-known exchange with Ji Kangzi, or Jisun Fei, the minister and de facto ruler of Lu from 492 to 468 B.C.E., Confucius shows irritation with the question of whether the Way can be forcibly imposed on the people:

He Yan's reading:

> Ji Kangzi asked Confucius about government saying, Suppose I were to kill the Way-less in order to promote those possessed of the Way. What would you say?

---

4. Tu Wei-ming, *Centrality and Commonality: An Essay on Chung-yung* (Honolulu: University of Hawai'i Press, 1976), 67.

Kong [Anguo] said, "*Jiu* [to promote] is *cheng*, 'to promote or bring success to.' He wished to kill large numbers in order to bring an end to treachery."

> Confucius responded, You are governing; what need is there for killing? If you desire good, the people will be good. The virtue of the superior man is wind; the virtue of the small man is grass. When wind passes over it, grass is sure to bend. (12.19 [30])

Kong [Anguo] said, "He very much wished to have Kangzi first make himself correct. *Yan* [to bend] is *fu*, 'to lie down or bend.' Pass over the grass with wind, and there is not a blade that will not bend. It is similar to the people being transformed from above."

Zhu Xi's reading:

> Ji Kangzi asked Confucius about government saying, Suppose I were to kill the Way-less in order to promote those possessed of the Way. What would you say? Confucius responded, You are governing; what need is there for killing? If you desire good, the people will be good. The virtue of the superior man is wind; the virtue of the small man is grass. When wind passes over it, grass is sure to bend.

As for one who governs, the people look to emulate him. Why the activity of killing? Desire good, and the people will be good. *Shang* [pass over] is elsewhere written *shang*, meaning *jia*, "to add to." *Yan* [to bend] is *fu*, "to lie down or bend."

Mr. Yin [Tun] said, "Do those above really have to speak of 'killing'? Instruct them by personal example, and they will follow. Instruct them by words, and they will be litigious. How much worse is it to kill them."

Confucius's impatience here with Jisun Fei is evident. With the response, "You are governing, what need is there for killing?" Confucius is, as He Yan suggests, rather curtly reminding him that governing (*zheng*) is nothing more than correcting (*zheng*)—just as he was told in 12.17—and that correcting others necessarily finds its source in self-correction. The reprimand is harsh, as the Master admonishes Jisun Fei not to target the Way-lessness in others but in himself. Simply by addressing his own moral failings, those of the people will be addressed. There is no need to talk of killing.

He and Zhu understand the wind/grass analogy of 12.19 similarly: just as wind exerts a natural force on the grass over which it blows, so the ruler exerts a natural force over those he governs, effecting in them a powerful transformation. But Zhu's commentary subtly carries He Yan's reading a step or two farther. First, unlike He's commentary, Zhu's implies how such a transforming effect is possible. His use of the word "emulate" in the first line of commentary, "The people look to emulate the one who governs," is no doubt intended to remind the reader of Zhu's first commentarial remark on analect 1.1, in which he says, "*Xue* [to learn] means 'to emulate' [*xiao*]." The next few lines of commentary, which explain what makes emulation ontologically possible, are thus brought to the reader's mind: "Human nature is in all cases good, but in becoming aware of this goodness there are those who lead and those who follow. Those who follow in becoming aware of it must emulate what those who lead in becoming aware of it do. Only then can they understand goodness and return to their original state." That is, in Zhu's reading of 12.19, the governed are "ready" to be transformed, in that they, like the ruler, are endowed with a perfectly good nature but, unlike him, have yet to realize it. For Zhu, the emulation of the ruler by the people and his transforming effect on them are predicated on an ontological resonance that occurs *naturally* between similar endowments of human nature:[5] the goodness that the superior man manifests in ruling the people awakens the latent and unrealized goodness that is the very nature of the people, who now naturally model themselves on him.

Zhu's commentary also reinforces the notion that good government is government by nonaction. When he says in 2.1 and 15.5, "Why the *activity* of killing? Desire good, and the people will be good" (italics mine, of course), he is implicitly returning the reader to the theme of "no action" and, at the same time, is echoing the dictum of 2.3 that government by law and punishment cannot compare with

---

5. This is the reading of Zhen Dexiu (1178–1235), in *Lunyu zuanshu* 6.51b.

government by virtue and ritual. Yin Tun's remark that concludes the commentary provides corroboration and emphasis, reiterating Zhu's understanding of the Master's view of good government: law breeds litigiousness, and hence social disharmony, but still worse in its disruptive effect on the sociopolitical realm is the use of punishment. Rather, simply by expressing the goodness that is his human nature, the superior man, without needing to employ any of the common tools of government, can arouse the goodness that is innate in others and thus create a cohesive social and moral order in which all people, ruler and ruled alike, are of one mind-and-heart.

5

The Superior Man and the Way

In the text of the *Analects*, as we have it, Confucius presents an ideal of good government based on virtue and the practice of ritual. Such a government, of course, needs ideal men who themselves embrace virtue and know ritual. Indeed, the aim of the Master's teachings is largely to lead his disciples toward self-realization, enabling them to assume official positions and bring about the sort of government by moral force that he envisaged.

With this chapter's discussion of Confucius's ideal man, we have, in a sense, come full circle. Learning, the subject of chapter 1, has a clearly stated purpose: to improve the individual, permitting him to become the best human being possible. Guiding him in this process of self-cultivation are the practice of true goodness and the proper expression of ritual, the subjects of chapters 2 and 3. At the same time that they are a guide to self-improvement, practicing true goodness and practicing ritual are also the constituent expression of self-improvement. Those who diligently seek self-perfection, expressing all the various moral virtues subsumed by true goodness and conducting themselves in accord with ritual, can become *junzi*, or superior men. Indeed, it is this process of self-perfection, which begins in learning and culminates in fulfilling the Way, that Confucius outlines in his autobiographical comment in analect 2.4: "At fifteen, I set my mind-and-heart on learning. . . . At seventy, I followed the desires of my mind-and-heart without overstepping right."

As we observed in chapter 4, on ruling, this sort of perfected person, the superior man, using the powerful influence of true goodness, "corrects" (*zheng*) the people of the realm and thereby brings about the ideal of good government (*zheng*). That is, because he knows the true Way, fulfilling it and embodying it in his being, the superior man is capable of bringing it to others, almost without effort.

As scholars have frequently noted, the term *junzi* was hardly new with Confucius but had a long history before his time. Literally referring to the son or child of a ruler, *junzi* designated a person of superior birth or blood. This person was to comport himself according to a set of rituals or customs that befitted his high social status. That is, he was supposed to behave as a gentleman of his rank should behave. Confucius adopted this word in teaching his disciples, investing it more emphatically with moral significance by suggesting that it designated a moral superiority. This is not to say that the Master rejected hereditary rank. As Benjamin I. Schwartz argued, he seems in fact to have defended it, along with the aristocratic order of the day, hoping that those of superior birth and bloodline might be influenced to become true superior men. But even as Confucius defended the hereditary order, he believed—perhaps impressed by the opportunities open to men of merit for bureaucratic service—that men of all birth statuses, commoners included, could be taught to achieve true goodness and become true superior men.[1] This is precisely what Confucius, after his disappointing personal failure to find official appointment, adopted as his mission: teaching men of all social and economic stations to become morally superior human beings intent on perfecting the world around them. The *Analects* is a record of these teachings, admonishing

---

1. Benjamin I. Schwartz, *The World of Thought in Ancient China* (Cambridge, Mass.: Harvard University Press, 1985), esp. 75–117.

followers to choose the right Way to live their lives, to follow the path of moral righteousness in all that they did.

I

He Yan's reading:

> The Master said, Who can go out except by the door? Why is it that no one follows along this Way? (6.17 [31])
> Kong [Anguo] said, "This says that to establish himself and be successful, a person ought to follow the Way. It is comparable to going in and out: one must use the door."

Zhu Xi's reading:

> The Master said, Who can go out except by the door? Why is it that no one follows along this Way?
> This is to say that people cannot go out except by the door. Why is it, then, that they do not follow this Way? This is an expression of wonderment and regret.
> Mr. Hong [Xingzi][2] said, "People know that when they go out, they must go through the door, but they do not know that when they move, they must follow the Way. It is not that the Way is distant from man; it is that man distances himself from the Way."

The Master laments that there is only one proper path to follow in life, and yet people do not take it. It is not that it is not obvious; just as people know that they must use the door when going into and out of a house, so they know that to advance forward they must follow the Way. He Yan remarks in his commentary that pursuing the Way is the only means by which man can fully realize himself, leaving it to the reader to conclude why the people do not take it. Citing Hong Xingzi, Zhu provides an explanation for his reader: like true goodness (7.30), the

2. Hong Xingzi lived from 1090 to 1155.

Way is at man's very side, but man *chooses* not to take it. That is, for Zhu, although the proper path is clear and traversable, man must want to take it; he must actively decide to pursue it. This is where the Confucian learning of chapter 1 comes in, according to a remark by Zixia in analect 19.7. It guides man—and his determination—along the Way, discouraging him from taking the many other byways he encounters in life.

He Yan's reading:

> Zixia said, The hundred artisans live in the shops in order to bring their work to completion. The superior man learns in order to fulfill his Way. (19.7 [32])

Bao [Xian] said, "This says that the hundred artisans residing in their shops and bringing their work to completion is similar to the superior man learning in order to establish his Way."

Zhu Xi's reading:

> Zixia said, The hundred artisans live in the shops in order to bring their work to completion. The superior man learns in order to fulfill his Way.

Si [shops] refers to government manufactories. *Zhi* [fulfill] is *ji*, "to exhaust." If artisans do not live in the shops, they will become distracted by strange things, and their craftsmanship will not be refined. If the superior man does not learn, he will become diverted by outside enticements and lose his determination. Mr. Yin [Tun] said, "Learning is the means of fulfilling his Way. The hundred artisans living in the shops are sure to devote themselves to completing their work. In his learning, the superior man certainly knows what to devote himself to." In my opinion, these two explanations are mutually necessary; together they form a complete meaning.

This passage, like many considered earlier (e.g., 5.28, 2.4, and 7.8), exhorts students to engage in learning, for only by learning can they realize the Way and become superior men. Both He and Zhu read this analect as a reminder that devotion and determination are necessary if learning is to bear fruit. Drawing on a set of ontological assumptions, Zhu carries the implications of Zixia's words here even further. For Zhu, a preoccupation with learning itself protects against the distractions of the world, distractions that impede man's realization of the Way.

As Zhu interprets the passage, man is prone to distraction and can easily be enticed by external things and matters. This is why the artisans live in their shops, so they can maintain their focus and complete their work. In the same way, although the mind of man originally was good, through contact with the material world, it can form selfish desires and be won over to evil. Learning provides a focus and prevents the mind from going astray. To Zhu, it is not simply the content of learning that keeps the superior man on the proper path but his very attention to it. That is, the mind that is focused on or attentive to the object of learning is a mind that will not readily be distracted; and a mind that is not distracted, that is not led astray, is a mind that is preserved in its original condition, maintaining the goodness with which it was originally endowed. Attentiveness to learning, therefore, gives proper direction to man's will, with the result that he "fulfills his Way." In sum, for Zhu, the superior man is one who keeps his original condition free from harmful distractions.

As we observed in chapter 1, on learning, the Master admonished his followers to engage in what he termed learning for oneself rather than learning for the sake of others (14.24). But he never was very prescriptive—as later followers of the Confucian school were—about the particular constituents of the learning—that is, the curriculum of study. A person intent on becoming a superior man was simply instructed to "learn widely" in the literary culture. The Master broadly urged that this man undergo a sort of cultural immersion as a crucial step in the process of self-perfection:

He Yan's reading:

The Master said, The superior man who learns widely in the culture but keeps it within the bounds of ritual will surely not transgress. (6.27 [33])

Zheng [Xuan] said, "*Fu pan* [not transgress] is not to deviate from the Way."

Zhu Xi's reading:

> The superior man who learns widely in the culture and keeps to the essential through ritual will surely not transgress.
> *Yue* [keeps to the essential] is *yao*, "to keep to the essential." *Pan* [transgress] is *bei*, "to transgress or turn the back on." In learning, the superior man aims for breadth and consequently examines everything in the cultural tradition. In keeping to the important, he aims for the essential and consequently accords with ritual in whatever he does. Because he is like this, he will not turn his back on the Way.
> Master Cheng said, "To learn widely in the culture but not to keep to the essential through ritual is bound to lead to recklessness. To learn widely and, further, to be capable of keeping to ritual and of following custom is indeed not to transgress the Way."

Given the brevity of his commentarial remark, it is unclear how He understands the referent *zhi* that follows *yue* in the second phrase, *yue zhi yi li* (keeps it within the bounds of ritual). Whether he takes it to mean the wide learning of the first phrase or the person of the superior man is not known, although Huang Kan's subcommentary on He's commentary understands it as the person of the superior man, and the passage to mean, "The superior man who learns widely in the culture but keeps himself within the bounds of ritual will surely not transgress." I rendered it as I did because it appears, in the absence of any comment by He, to be syntactically the most straightforward and obvious reading. Rendered in this way, He's understanding of the passage has the Master urging his students to immerse themselves in the vast cultural tradition, the repository of all that is good, and then shape this broad learning, giving it coherence and meaning by means of ritual, so that they, as superior men, will come to recognize and keep to the true Way.

As he tells disciples in the *Conversations of Master Zhu*, Zhu Xi, reading this passage against 9.11, in which Yan Hui says of Confucius that "he broadens me with culture and restrains me with ritual," understands the *zhi*, as Huang Kan did earlier, to refer not to the broad learning but to the person (YL 33.835 and 33.837). That is, it is the superior man, not the learning, that is kept to the essential by means of ritual. In Zhu's understanding, therefore, this passage, like 9.11, is about *both* learning and self-restraint. The superior man is urged to extend his knowledge of the cultural tradition, especially the venerable classics and the six arts, and, at the same time, to keep to the essential—by means of ritual—in whatever he does. By keeping to the essential, his behavior will be as it should and thus never violate the Way. Reminding his disciples that ritual is only the outward manifestation or expression of things as they should be (i.e., principle), Zhu says: "Broadening oneself with culture involves many particulars; all of them have to be attended to. Ritual [*li*], by contrast, is just the one moral principle [*daoli*]. Looking is a matter of this ritual; listening is a matter of this ritual; speaking is a matter of this ritual; and acting is a matter of this ritual. If one broadens oneself with culture but does not keep to the essential with ritual, there will be no end to the process" (YL 33.833). Following ritual is keeping oneself to the essential; keeping to the essential is keeping to principle; and keeping to principle is keeping to the Way. The message here for Zhu is that broad mastery of the cultural tradition is important if one is to sort out right from wrong and good from bad. But only if one works to keep oneself in line with right and good, in accord with principle and by means of ritual practice, does broad learning translate into conformity with the Way. Extensive learning and mindful practice consistent with the dictates of ritual are, in Zhu's reading of the passage, mutually necessary (YL 33.832–33).

The cultural tradition of analect 6.27 is the main source of learning for those aspiring to be superior men. But it is not the only source, as we observed in chapter 1. Other people, worthy and unworthy, good and bad, can be sources of learning as well. A number of analects urge the superior man to use others to measure his own moral condition. In analect 7.22, Confucius may be talking about his own behavior, but there is little doubt that he is also describing how superior men more generally are supposed to behave:

He Yan's reading:

> The Master said, Walking in a group of three, I am sure to have teachers. I pick out the good points and follow them and the bad points and change them [in myself]. (7.22 [34])

This is to say that when walking in a group of three people, no one of whom is fundamentally wise or stupid, I pick out what is good and follow it and what is bad and change it. Consequently, I have no constant teacher.

Zhu Xi's reading:

> The Master said, Walking in a group of three, I am sure to have teachers. I pick out the good points and follow them and the bad points and change them [in myself].

Three men walk together, one of whom is me. Of the other two, supposing one is good and one is bad; I follow what is good and change what is bad. These other two are both my teachers.

Mr. Yin [Tun] said, "'When I see a worthy man, I think about equaling him; when I see an unworthy man, I look within' [4.17]. Thus good and bad are both my teachers. Advancing in goodness never comes to an end."

Understanding the two men walking with him to be a worthy man and an unworthy man, Zhu is reading this passage, 7.22, as a sort of gloss on analect 4.17: "When you see a worthy man, think about equaling him. When you see an unworthy man, look within yourself." For He, by contrast, the two with whom the Master is walking in 7.22 are fundamentally not "wise or stupid," as each offers both good and bad points to be considered in the Master's own moral development. He is thus broadening the pool of those who can serve as moral teachers beyond 4.17 to include those in the morally gray area, neither especially worthy nor especially unworthy. While I do not wish to carry the point too far, perhaps Zhu's view of human beings as innately good but sometimes caught in a psychophysical predicament from which they can choose to free themselves or not leaves less room for a morally gray area. As his one remark on this analect in the *Conversations of Master Zhu* suggests, people choose to cultivate themselves and realize their goodness and thus are worthy, or they choose not to and thus are unworthy (YL 34.892). In a sense, the worthiness lies in the choice itself.

This perhaps too is why Zhu's commentary—"I look within"—emphasizes, whereas He's is silent on, the role of inner reflection in the process of learning from others. Here—as well as in analect 4.17—Zhu reads a strong responsibility on the part of the individual aspiring to be a superior man to reflect inwardly on the state of his own moral development. Indeed, it is this inward reflection, the self-examination, that makes learning among and from others effective. In short, for Zhu, inward reflection is largely a symptom or manifestation of one's choice to become worthy, a manifestation that the will is indeed headed in the right direction.

In fact, it is because Zengzi, a renowned disciple of the Master and surely himself a *junzi*, or superior man, is given to constant self-reflection that he is singled out for such high praise in Zhu Xi's commentary on analect 1.4:

He Yan's reading:

> Zengzi said, Every day I examine my own person on three counts: in working on behalf of others, have I failed to do the best I can? In my associations with friends, have I failed to be true to my word? As for what I pass on to others, have I failed to rehearse it myself? (1.4 [35])
> This is to say that generally in matters that I pass on to others, am I able to avoid passing on what I am not fully conversant with and practiced in myself?

Zhu Xi's reading:

> Zengzi said, Every day I examine my own person on three counts: in working on behalf of others, have I failed to be true to myself? In my associations with friends, have I failed to be true to my word? As for what has been passed on to me, have I failed to rehearse it?

Zengzi is Confucius's disciple, named Can, with the *zi* of Ziyu. *Jin ji*, "to give full expression to oneself," is what is meant by *zhong* [true to myself]. *Yi shi*, "using truth," is what is meant by *xin* [true to my word]. *Chuan* [what has been transmitted to me] means "receiving it from a teacher"; *xi* [rehearse] means to make it intimately familiar to oneself. Zengzi, on these three counts, examined his own person every day, and if there was a failing, he corrected it; if there was not, he intensified his efforts. Such was his self-control, true and focused. It can be said to have served successfully as the foundation of learning. As for the sequence of these three counts, being true to one's nature and true to one's word are similarly the foundation of rehearsing what has been passed on.

Mr. Yin [Tun] said: "Zengzi kept to the essential [*Mengzi* 2A.2] and consequently in his actions always sought within his own person." Mr. Xie [Liangzuo] said, "The learning of the various disciples all issued from the Sage. The more remote from him it became, the more it lost sight of his truths. The learning of Zengzi alone focused the mind-and-heart exclusively on the internal and thus was a transmission free of corruption [of the Sage's learning], which is evident if we observe Zisi and Mencius. It is a pity that his splendid words and good conduct have not been fully transmitted to later ages. That they fortunately have been preserved and not destroyed is, of course, because students exerted themselves to the utmost."

For Zhu Xi, it is Zengzi, in his emphasis on the internal life of man, who discovered the true tradition of the Master. This is evident not only from remarks like these in the text of the *Analects* but from the ten chapters of so-called commentary in the text of the *Greater Learning* (*Daxue*), putatively in Zengzi's hand. In fact, Zhu Xi so admires the *Greater Learning* that he edited it heavily (thereby preserving Zengzi's legacy), dividing it into one chapter by Confucius and ten chapters of commentary by Zengzi, writing an extended commentary on it, and finally incorporating it into the collection known as the Four Books, together with the *Analects*, the *Mencius*, and the *Doctrine of the Mean*. From the late Song period on, these Four Books were the central inspiration in the Confucian philosophical tradition as well as the basis of the state's civil service examinations. Their influence thus was enormous. And by attributing to Zengzi the authorship—not unproblematically—of the ten chapters of the *Greater Learning*, Zhu Xi firmly fixed the disciple's place in the orthodox line of transmission of the Way, from Confucius, to Zengzi, to Zisi, to Mencius, and then to others.[3] In bringing together the Four Books as he does, Zhu is giving prominence to the interior dimension of the Confucian vision—as he does throughout his commentary of the *Analects* itself—a dimension, he believes, as is clear from the commentary here, that was largely overlooked in the tradition.

In Zhu's reading of the passage, Zengzi is especially attentive to three matters: whether he is true in his actions to the principles of his endowed good nature, true to what he says to others, and true to the learning process, studying and practicing what has been passed on to him. Being true to the principles of one's good nature is clearly the basis of all else: one who is true naturally displays benevolence, righteousness, wisdom, trustworthiness, and proper decorum, the cardinal virtues associated with the goodness of human nature. For Zhu, Zengzi's self-examination is as much vigilance over the cultivation of his own self, directed toward the realization and perfection of his endowed good nature, as it is over the expression of that nature toward others. By contrast, He Yan's reading places the focus of Zengzi's examination much more on one's behavior toward others, not on the impulse of that behavior. That is, this behavior is not explicitly, as it is in Zhu Xi's reading, the consequence of vigilance over the development of the self. This difference is reflected in the different readings of the last line of the passage: He has Zengzi holding himself responsible for teaching to others only what he truly knows himself, whereas Zhu understands Zengzi to be examining himself to ensure that whatever is taught to him by others becomes his own, part of his own self.

3. On Zhu Xi and the *Greater Learning*, see Daniel K. Gardner, *Chu Hsi and the Ta-hsueh: Neo-Confucian Reflection on the Confucian Canon* (Cambridge, Mass.: Harvard University, Council on East Asian Studies, 1986).

An analect with a similar but more hortatory message to those aspiring to become *junzi*, superior men, is 1.8. It repeats some of the points made in the other analects we are considering here, giving an opportunity to a commentator like Zhu Xi to offer further thoughts:

He Yan's reading:

> The Master said, If the superior man is not grave, he will not inspire awe, nor will his learning be solid.

Kong [Anguo] said, "*Gu* is *bi*, 'to be ignorant or dull.'" Another authority said, "This is to say that if a person is incapable of being upright and grave, he will lack awe and majesty, and furthermore, in learning, he will be incapable of solidly understanding the meaning."

> He makes it his guiding principle to do the best he can and to be true to his word. He does not befriend those who are not his equal. And when he errs, he is not reluctant to change. (1.8 [36])

Zheng [Xuan] said, "*Zhu* [makes it his guiding principle] is *qin*, 'to love or become intimate with.' *Dan* [reluctant] is *nan*, 'to find difficult.'"

Zhu Xi's reading:

> The Master said, If the superior man is not grave, he will not inspire awe, nor will his learning be solid.

Zhong [grave] is *houzhong*, "dignified." *Wei* [inspire awe] is *weiyan*, "awe and majesty." *Gu* [solid] is *jiangu*, "solid" or "firm." One who is frivolous on the outside will certainly be incapable of being solid on the inside. Therefore, if one is not grave, one will lack awe and majesty, and what one learns will indeed not be solid.

> Let him make it his guiding principle to be true to himself and true to his word.

If a person is not true to himself or true to his word, then all his affairs will be without substance. Doing evil will be easy; doing good, hard. Thus, the student must make these his guiding principle. Master Cheng said, "The human Way resides simply in being true to oneself and true to one's word: 'Without truthfulness, there is nothing' [*Zhongyong*, chap. 25]. Moreover, 'one never knows the time that it comes or goes, neither does one know the direction—this refers to the human mind-and-heart' [paraphrase of Lau, *Mencius* 6A.8, p. 165]. So if one is not true to oneself and not true to one's word, one has nothing."

Let him not befriend those who are not his equal.
Wu [let him not] is interchangeable with *wu*, "do not," a term of prohibition. Friendship is the means of promoting one's true goodness [cf. 12.24]. One who is not your equal is of no benefit and is even disadvantageous.

When he errs, let him not be reluctant to change.
Wu [let him not] is likewise a term of prohibition. *Dan* [reluctant] is *wei nan*, "to dread or fear the difficult." If one's self-control is not resolute, evil will advance daily. Therefore, if there are errors, one ought to change quickly; one must not, fearing difficulty, blithely persist. Master Cheng said, "The Way of learning is nothing but this. Know what's not good and change quickly in pursuit of the good, and that is all."

Master Cheng said, "This is just what the superior man's way of self-cultivation should be." Mr. You [Zuo] said, "The Way of the superior man regards awe and majesty as substance and learning as the means of perfecting them. The way of learning makes being true to oneself and being true to one's word the guiding principle and depends on overcoming the self for support. Yet some people, unwilling to change their erring ways, in the end have no means of entering into virtue; and those who are worthy do not necessarily find pleasure in informing them of the Way of the good. Thus, this analect ends with 'when he errs, let him not be reluctant to change.'"

Zhu's commentary makes this analect into a passage entirely about the self-cultivation of the superior man. Confucius is understood here to be calling for inner reflection, for monitoring the moral development of the endowed good nature, which leads to a grave and imposing outward demeanor. Tying this passage to another two of the Four Books, the *Doctrine of the Mean* and the *Mencius*, Zhu argues that realizing the Way begins with truthfulness to the self, which is a matter, according to Mencius, of retaining one's original mind-and-heart. This is what constitutes true or solid learning. Friends assist in this process by serving as a mirror to the superior man, reminding him that true goodness is indeed something that all men possess and that he simply has to realize. To be true to the self requires, more than anything, constant inner vigilance and a quickness in correcting whatever violates the norms of true goodness, righteousness, wisdom, and propriety.

The last line of this passage, admonishing the superior man to be quick in correcting his own errors, is echoed in analect 15.30, in which Confucius remarks, "Erring and not changing: this indeed is what is meant by erring." He Yan provided no commentary on this brief analect, but Zhu wrote, "To err but to be able to change is to return to an error-free state. Only if one does not change does the error grow until one can no longer change," implying that because of man's originally moral condition, all that is needed to keep him on the right path is a certain vigilance. If he maintains a constant check on his behavior, curbing any moral failings he might detect, he will "return" to a perfect goodness. The general point in 15.30 is therefore the same as his commentary on this passage: becoming a superior man requires that one maintain an inner vigilance at all times. The almost startling remark by You Zuo that concludes Zhu's commentary on 1.8, that "those who are worthy do not necessarily inform them [i.e., those unwilling to change their erring ways] of the Way of the good," makes clear, to any reader who still has doubts, that the burden of becoming a superior man falls completely on one's own efforts at self-examination and self-correction.

Indeed, on one occasion, the Master even "defined" the superior man as one who examined himself within and found no wrong. With this analect, the results of the strenuous process of self-examination, in which other men serve partly as a measure of one's own moral condition, as in analect 7.22, become apparent:

He Yan's reading:

> Sima Niu asked about the superior man. The Master said, The supe-
> rior man is neither anxious nor fearful.

Kong [Anguo] said, "Niu's elder brother, Huan Tui,[4] was about to stage a rebellion. Niu came from Song to study but was always anxious and fearful. It is for this reason that Confucius offered this explanation."

> He said, "Neither anxious nor fearful": Is this all that is meant by a
> superior man? The Master said, He looks within and finds nothing
> wrong. Why would he be anxious? Why would he be fearful? (12.4
> [37])

Bao [Xian] said, "*Jiu* [wrong] is *bing*, 'flaw.' He looks within and finds no evil; there is nothing to be anxious or fearful about."

Zhu Xi's reading:

> Sima Niu asked about the superior man. The Master said, The supe-
> rior man is neither anxious nor fearful.

Xiang Tui[5] was rebelling, so Niu was always anxious and fearful. It is for this reason that the Master told him this.

> He said, "Neither anxious nor fearful": Is this all that is meant by
> superior man? The Master said, He looks within and finds nothing
> wrong. Why would he be anxious? Why would he be fearful?

Niu's follow-up question is similar in meaning to the previous passage, and therefore he [Confucius] comes back with this. *Jiu* [wrong] is *bing*, "flaw."

4. According to the *Zuojuan* (Duke Ai, fourteenth year), Huan Tui, the Song minister of war, plotted rebellion against the duke. This same Huan Tui, according to the *Shiji* biography of Confucius (47.1921), also plotted to have Confucius killed when the Master was teaching in the state of Song (*Analects* 7.23).
5. The Xiang family of Song was descended from the duke of Huan; thus Xiang Tui is the same Huan Tui mentioned earlier.

This is to say that because what he does each day brings no shame to his mind-and-heart, he is able to look within and find nothing wrong and so naturally is free of anxiety and fear. He does not dismiss this as a simple matter to be disregarded.

Mr. Chao [Yuezhi] said, "To be neither anxious nor fearful results from a virtue that is complete and without wrong. Therefore, wherever he goes, he gets it for himself [*zide*] [*Zhongyong*, chap. 14]. It is not that he actually was anxious and fearful but nonetheless pushed them aside."

Two points distinguish the commentaries here: Zhu attributes the wrong or evil that one finds on self-examination to a perversion of one's natural state or condition. If one's original virtue is maintained through vigilance, if one keeps constant hold of one's original mind-and-heart, wrong or evil will have no opportunity to emerge. To put it another way, the wrong that one finds is something wrong with one's own self. He's reader is never informed what the wrong or evil is or how it emerges. The second point, related to the first, is that for Zhu, it is not simply that wrong or evil can be uncovered by the process of self-examination but that it can be prevented by it. The process of "looking within" is a process of self-examination, and the process of self-examination is nothing but the maintenance of one's original endowment. The result is moral self-realization or self-perfection. This is to become a superior man.

For the superior man, learning—whether it is from the great cultural tradition or from the example of others—is always acquired with an eye to self-improvement, with the hope of freeing oneself from moral error. As a result, what is produced by such learning is not a person with specialized knowledge or technical expertise but a person fully moral, fully compassionate and caring, and fully capable of extending himself to others. In a sense, he is omnicompetent, able through his finely honed empathetic skills to deal with the wide range of affairs confronting humankind. Confucius puts it concisely but colorfully in 2.12:

He Yan's reading:

The Master said, The superior man is not a utensil. (2.12 [38])
Bao [Xian] said, "As for utensils, each is of circumscribed usefulness.

But when it comes to the superior man, there is nothing he does not do."

Zhu Xi's reading:

> The Master said, The superior man is not a utensil.
> As for utensils, each serves its own function and is not interchangeable with others. In substance, the *shi*, or gentleman of perfect virtue, contains everything and thus in function extends everywhere. It is not that he specializes in just one talent or skill and that is all.

He and Zhu read the passage similarly, understanding the *junzi*, or superior man, to have unlimited usefulness. By identifying the superior man with the everyday *shi*, a member of what in the Song was a broad-based scholar-official class, Zhu Xi, in apparent contrast to He Yan, clearly believes that the status of *junzi*, or superior man, is reasonably widely and readily attainable. After all, these *shi*, or scholar-official elite, need only choose to maintain vigilance over their perfect virtue.

Omnicompetent though the superior man surely is, in Confucius's view, he takes considerably more satisfaction and pride in realizing true goodness, the source of his omnicompetence, than he does in achieving certain aims commonly associated with his competence, including obtaining official position:

He Yan's reading:

> The Master said, Wealth and official rank are what every man desires. If he comes by them but not by reason of the Way, he will not abide in them.
> Kong [Anguo] said, "If it is not by reason of the Way that he comes by wealth and official rank, the man of true goodness will not abide in them."

> Poverty and low station are what every man detests. If he comes by them but not by reason of the Way, he will not avoid them.
> Times being good and bad, the superior man may follow the Way and still encounter poverty and low station. This then is to come by them but

not by reason of the Way [rather, despite it]. Although they are what every man detests, he must not depart from it [the Way] in order to avoid them.

> The superior man who departs from true goodness, how can he make a name?

Kong [Anguo] said, "'How can he make a name' means he cannot make a name as a superior man."

> The superior man does not depart from true goodness for the space of a single meal. In times of haste, he keeps to it; stumbling about, he keeps to it. (4.5 [39])

Ma [Rong] said, "*Zaoci* [haste] is *jiju*, 'hurried' or 'harried.' *Dianpei* [stumbling about] is *yanfu*, 'to fall on one's back.' Whether he is in haste or stumbling about, he does not depart from true goodness."

Zhu Xi's reading:

> The Master said, Wealth and official rank are what every man desires. If he comes by them undeservedly, he will not abide in them. Poverty and low station are what every man detests. If he comes by them undeservedly, he does not avoid them.

Bu yi qi dao de zhi [should he come by them undeservedly] means *bu dang de er de zhi*, "he ought not to come by them but he does." This being the case, in regard to wealth and official rank, he does not abide in them; when it comes to poverty and low station, he does not avoid them. So it is that the superior man scrutinizes wealth and official rank and is content with poverty and low station.

> The superior man who departs from true goodness, how does he fulfill the name?

This is to say that the superior man becomes a superior man on account of his true goodness. He who covets wealth and official rank and hates poverty and low station naturally takes leave of his true goodness and so does not have the substance of a superior man. How can he fulfill its name?

The superior man does not depart from true goodness for the space of a single meal. In times of haste, he keeps to it, and in times of confusion, he keeps to it.

Zhongshi [space of a single meal] means *yifan qing*, "space of a single meal." *Zaoci* [haste] are times of haste and carelessness; *dianpei* [confusion] are occasions when he has lost his bearings. It would seem that such is the superior man's not departing from true goodness: it is not only in matters of wealth and official rank, poverty and low station, and choosing right from wrong.

This is to say that the superior man is truly good in matters of wealth and official rank, poverty and low station, and choosing right from wrong, as well as at meal times, in times of haste, and in times of confusion. At no time and in no place does he not apply himself. This being the case, as the difference between what to select and what to reject becomes clear, cultivation efforts grow more intense; and as the cultivation efforts grow more intense, the difference between what to select and what to reject becomes even clearer still.

The superior man holds on to true goodness at all costs, even at the expense of wealth and rank. For it is true goodness alone that is the mark of the superior man; thus to lose it, even for a moment, is to lose his distinction as a superior man. In the Confucian vision, to be a superior man, always according with goodness, is clearly its own reward. And in Zhu Xi's view, since man is born with this goodness, holding on to it simply means never taking leave of what he is fortunate to possesses originally, a process requiring vigilance but at the same time perhaps easier than a process requiring its appropriation from external sources.

Interesting here is the different treatment by the commentators of the character *dao*, appearing in the first two lines of the analect. He Yan reads it as *the dao*—that is, *the* Confucian Way—and understands the passage to be about the need for the superior man, in his goodness, to follow the Way, wherever it might lead and whatever the consequences. Following the Way can never be wrong. Zhu, however, reads it not as a reference to the Way but, in the lower case, to mean something like "by right," as in "by right he ought not to come by poverty and low station, but he does." The analect for him is not principally a comment about the Way and the imperative to follow it, but about holding at all times to one's true goodness, "the substance of the superior man."

Tellingly, too, the two commentators give slightly different twists to the next line, about departing from true goodness. For He, a person who chooses to depart from true goodness to avoid poverty and low station can never make a name for himself and will never earn the reputation for being a superior man. In Zhu's understanding, it is because such a person does not hold to the substance of a superior man, that as a matter of *zheng ming*, or the rectification of names, he is not deserving of the name. He's reading suggests that a superior man is one who must be acknowledged by others, for his goodness is outwardly manifest; that is, his goodness is goodness expressed in action. In Zhu's reading, since becoming a superior man is a matter of cultivating what is within, acknowledgment by others in the form of a reputation is much less at issue. Even though inner goodness, brought to realization through cultivation, is certain to be reflected in his conduct, it is the very cultivation of this goodness—and his constant attentiveness to the cultivation process—whether or not acknowledged by others, that qualifies one as a superior man.

If Confucius can say in analect 4.5 that "the superior man does not depart from true goodness for the space of a single meal," what is to be made of his apparently contradictory assertion in 14.6 that "there have been superior men who nonetheless are not truly good"?

He Yan's reading:

> The Master said, Alas, there have been superior men who nonetheless are not truly good, but never has there been a small man who nonetheless is truly good. (14.6 [40])

Kong [Anguo] said, "Although called superior men, they are still not capable of perfection."

Zhu Xi's reading:

The Master said, Alas, there have been superior men who nonetheless are not truly good, but never has there been a small man who nonetheless is truly good.

Mr. Xie [Liangzuo] said, "The superior man wills to true goodness. But if for even a moment the mind-and-heart is not present there, he cannot avoid doing what is not truly good."

The commentaries offer different explanations for the inability of superior men to be truly good. For He, some superior men are not yet entirely perfect. No reason for the lack of perfection is provided, and He seems content to let the passage stand on its own, even in the face of the last passage, 4.5. Zhu goes further, as is characteristic, explaining that even though the superior man at all times is determined to manifest true goodness, he may have occasional lapses, when despite his determination, the mind-and-heart wanders. It is during these moments, these brief lapses, that the superior man, the man of true goodness, is capable of doing "what is not truly good." There is then a reconciliation of sorts, convincing or not, with analect 4.5. Zhu's understanding seems to be that in intention and will, the superior man indeed never departs from true goodness; it is only that in taking direction from the will, his mind momentarily loses its focus, leading for a moment to what is not truly good. Echoing the commentary on analects discussed in chapter 2, on true goodness, Zhu again reminds the reader of the central importance of the individual's will—and the moral leadership that it provides to the mind—in the process of becoming truly good, of becoming a superior man.

2

The Master's regret that his contemporaries do not follow the path leading to true goodness is expressed in his lament in 6.17: "Why is it that no one follows this Way?" Indeed, his own love of learning and of teaching, reflected throughout his remarks in the analects, is born of a commitment to uncover and resuscitate this Way, which prevailed under the founding fathers of the Zhou, and to pass it on to others who might then pursue it for themselves. Confucius's ambition clearly is to create an ideal social and political order, good government and harmonious social relations—that is, to help re-create a golden age reminiscent of the early days of the Zhou period.

The passion that Confucius feels for the Way—and his hope that people of his day might realize it for themselves—is reflected in a number of remarks. Analect 4.8, however differently it may be read by He Yan and Zhu Xi, communicates perhaps more straightforwardly than any other the central place of the Way in the Confucian vision, that the Way alone gives meaning and purpose to life:

He Yan's reading:

> The Master said, In the morning if I were to hear about the Way, in the evening I would die contented. (4.8 [41])

This is to say that as he was about to die, he had yet to hear that the Way prevailed in the world.

Zhu Xi's reading:

> The Master said, In the morning, hear the Way; in the evening, die contented.

The Way is principle in affairs and things as it ought to be. If one is able to hear it, one will live prosperously and die contented, without any regrets. "Morning" and "evening" are ways of emphasizing the shortness of time.

Master Cheng said, "This is to say that people must come to understand the Way. If they are able to hear the Way, even if they die, they will be contented." He further said, "Everything is concrete principle. But for people to know and trust it is difficult. Death and life likewise are weighty matters [*Zhuangzi*, 12]. So if they do not truly understand [principle or the Way], how could they possibly be content 'in the evening to die'?"

He Yan's understanding of the passage is history specific, a lament by Confucius that as his own death approaches, there is no sign that the emergence of the Way is imminent. It is the Master's expression of deep sadness and disappointment that—all his personal efforts notwithstanding—the social and political order of the day remains far from ideal and, in any case, is unable to compare with the glorious days of the duke of Zhou. The Way simply does not prevail in the world from which he is soon to take his leave.

In Zhu's reading, 4.8 is not a personal lamentation of the Master as much as it is a moral plea to his followers to make the realization of the Way their goal. In this reading, what matters to the Master is not so much whether the Way or good order prevails in the larger state or society, as it does in He's commentary, as whether people as individuals are fortunate enough to understand or experience the Way for themselves. Zhu sees the passage as an exhortation to individuals to realize their moral potential by pursuing the Way and thereby "to live prosperously and die contented." By equating the Way with the *li* or "principle" of his metaphysical system, Zhu Xi is suggesting that theoretically, the Way is knowable, with effort, to and attainable by all.

But coming to understand the Way in practice appears to be no easy task, even for the most diligent and most gifted students. Yan Hui, the most outstanding of the Master's disciples, offers in the *Analects* a moving and sobering account of his own spiritual quest for the Way:

He Yan's reading:

Yan Yuan with a deep sigh said:
Kui [deep sigh] is a sighing sound.

I look up to it and it is ever higher; I bore into it and it is ever harder.
This is to say that it is inexhaustible.

I gaze at it to my front and suddenly it is at my back.
This is to say that because it is indistinct, it cannot assume a form.

The Master is skillful at guiding people step by step.
Xunxun [step by step] means "in a sequential manner." *You* [guiding] means "to advance or urge forward." This is to say that the Master corrects them by means of this Way of his, urging people on sequentially.

He broadens me with culture and restrains me with ritual. Even if I wish to stop, I cannot. I exhaust all my ability, yet there still seems to be something rising majestically above me. Although I wish to follow it, there is no way. (9.11 [42])

Kong [Anguo] said, "This is to say that the Master has broadened me with literature and regulated me with ritual etiquette, so that even though I wish to stop, I cannot. I exhaust all my abilities. What rises before me is majestic and unattainable. This is to say that while he himself has received the Master's expert guidance, he is still incapable of achieving what the Master sets before him."

Zhu Xi's reading:

Yan Yuan, with a deep sigh, said, I look up to it and it is ever higher; I bore into it and it is ever harder. I gaze at it to my front and suddenly it is at my back.

Kui [deep sigh] is a sighing sound. He looks up, but because it goes ever higher, he cannot reach it; he bores into it, but because it is ever harder, he cannot penetrate it. It is at his front and at his back; because it is indistinct, it has no form. It is because Yan Yuan deeply appreciates that the Way of the Master is inexhaustible and has no steady direction that he gives a sigh.

The Master is skillful at guiding people step by step. He broadens me with culture and restrains me with ritual.

Xunxun [step by step] means "in a sequential manner." *You* [guiding] is *yinjin*, "to guide or lead on." To broaden with culture and restrain with ritual is the order of instruction. This is to say that while the Master's Way is exalted, in teaching it to others he has an order. Mr. Hou [Zhongliang][6] said, "'He broadens me with culture' is 'to extend knowledge to the utmost and apprehend the principle in things' [from the *Daxue*]. He restrains me with ritual is 'to subdue the self and return to ritual' [12.1]." Master Cheng said, "This is a passage in which Yanzi praises the Sage

6. Hou Zhongliang (fl. 1100) studied under Cheng Yi and Zhou Dunyi.

most fittingly. For the Sage taught people these two matters and nothing more."

> Even if I wish to stop, I cannot. I exhaust all my ability, and it seems to be standing there right before me. But although I wish to follow it, there is no way.

Zhuo [right before me] is *limiao*, "in an erect manner." *Mo* [no] is *wu*, "no." Here Yanzi is speaking of the extent of his own learning. It would seem that the delight he takes in it is profound and that the strength he devotes to it is exhaustive. As it draws ever nearer, there is no additional effort to be made [except broadening with culture and restraining with ritual].[7] Mr. Wu Yu [d. 1154] said, "What is meant by 'right before me' is that it is even in our day-to-day matters; it is not what could be called secluded or obscure." Master Cheng said, "Once one gets to this point, the effort is especially difficult. It is really steep; brute strength cannot be used."[8] Mr. Yang [Shi] said, "From 'the desirable is called good' to 'possessing it fully and becoming great' is the product of forceful activity. 'To be great and be transformed by this greatness' is not the result of forceful activity [*Mengzi* 7B.25].[9] This is why Yanzi is 'inferior in one respect.'"[10]

Master Cheng said, "This is why Yanzi deeply appreciates Confucius and is good at learning from him." Mr. Hu [Yin] said, "Without anything precipitating it, he sighs deeply. Here, having now achieved success in

7. For this reading of the line, see YL 36.966. Zhu's conversations in YL 36.962–71 on this passage and his commentary on it were helpful in understanding the meaning of some of the commentary that follows.

8. For this reading, see the comments in YL 36.966–967.

9. The *Mengzi* passage reads: "The desirable is called 'good.' To have it in oneself is called 'true.' To possess it fully in oneself is called 'beautiful,' but to shine forth with this full possession is called 'great.' To be great and be transformed by this greatness is called 'sage'; to be sage and to transcend the understanding is called 'divine'" (D. C. Lau, *Mencius* [Harmondsworth: Penguin, 1970], 199). The point of Yang's comment is that becoming a great man is a matter of forceful activity; becoming a sage is not.

10. As Master Cheng claimed; Zhu cites Cheng's remark in his commentary on analect 6.7.

learning, Yanzi describes the reason for his earlier difficulties and the reason for his later success, attributing his achievement to the Sage. 'Higher, harder, front, and back' speak of the substance of the Way; 'looking up, boring in, gazing at, and suddenly' speak of his not yet grasping its essentials. Only when the Master had skillfully guided him step by step, first broadening him with culture so he might understand ancient and modern, penetrating the transformation of things, did he [the Master] then restrain him with ritual so that he might honor what he had heard and put into practice what he had come to know—just as [naturally as] a traveler goes home or an eater fills his stomach. Thus, even though he may have wished to stop, he could not. Exhausting his mind-and-heart and all his strength, he did not rest even for a moment. Only then did he appreciate the loftiness of where the Master stood. Although he wished to follow him, there was no way. Now, it was not that he was lazy about following him, for he was quite determined to reach the lofty spot. The sigh here perhaps came after his 'I beg to devote myself to these words' [12.1], during 'the three-month period when he did not depart from true goodness' [6.7]."

How do our two commentators understand this passage? They seem to agree on a number of basic points: the Way is formless and inexhaustible. In teaching it to others, the Master follows an established order, and Yan Hui concludes that despite his best efforts, there is no clear means to achieve the Way of the Master. It is here that their shared understanding of the passage ends.

Both commentators explain to their readers that the Master teaches his Way sequentially. But He characteristically limits his remark to a paraphrase of the text of the analect, glossing "step by step" as "in a sequential manner" and then commenting that "the Master corrects them by means of this Way of his, urging people forward sequentially." For He, in this passage Yan Hui is praising the instruction of the Master for being orderly and coherent but is not explaining what in particular makes it orderly and coherent.

By contrast, Zhu reads Yan Hui to be telling his audience what the particular sequence is and ties his explanation to the next line of text: "He broadens me with culture and restrains me with ritual," a line that

He Yan reads independently. For Zhu, the first step in the order of instruction is broadening the student with culture, which here he explicitly associates with the key concepts of apprehending the principle in things (*ge wu*) and extending knowledge (*zhi zhi*), from another of the Four Books, the *Greater Learning*. According to the text of the *Greater Learning*, these are the first steps in the process of self-cultivation. Only after the student has broadened himself with culture and extended his understanding of principle is he next taught self-restraint, that is, to subdue his selfish desires and accord with ritual, as the opening line of analect 12.1 recommends. In this reading of the analect, the Master's teaching is grounded firmly in the investigation and apprehension of principle in the things and affairs out there. A resonance is thereby struck in Zhu's commentary both with the larger Confucian tradition and its canon of texts, especially the Four Books, and with the contemporary metaphysics that regards the Way as nothing but the manifestation of "principle in affairs and things as it ought to be," as Zhu himself reminds the reader in analect 4.8, immediately before.

Although Yan Hui receives expert instruction from the Master, his progress along the path, in his own assessment at least, is not without problems: "Although I wish to follow it, there is no way." The commentaries provide different explanations of this line, resulting in somewhat different understandings of the Way, as well perhaps as different understandings of the disciple Yan Hui. In He's reading, as much as Yan Hui might wish to fulfill the Way, as much as he might exhaust himself in its pursuit, in the end he finds it unattainably lofty ("There still seems to be something rising majestically above me"). And for He Yan, that one so gifted and dedicated as Yan Hui is incapable of achieving the Way is confirmation of the Way's unbounded vastness and majesty.

Zhu Xi's reading of the line, in contrast, seems to place much of the burden for not achieving the Way on Yan Hui himself. In Zhu's understanding, the Way is to be found right in front of us, "even in our day-to-day matters." It is immanent in all things and, with the effort of "broadening with culture" and "restraining with ritual," its essentials can be apprehended, as Hu Yin's remark suggests. The Way may be great and inexhaustible but is shrouded here in none of the inexpressible mystery suggested by He's commentary. Thus for Zhu, the inability in this passage to achieve it rests principally not on the quality of the Way itself but on Yan Hui's own efforts and capabilities. Yan Hui falls short, it seems, because he does not understand that at a certain point in the pursuit of the Way, strenuous effort is no longer desirable. As one approaches the Way, neither "forceful activity" nor "brute strength" is what is needed. This is, Zhu suggests here in citing Yang Shi and elsewhere argues more fully (YL 36.968), where Yan Hui is "inferior" to the Master himself. Confucius, after setting his mind-and-heart on learning at an early age and expending considerable effort to bring this learning to perfection, reached the stage later in life at which he understood, without need for reflection and sustained effort: "At sixty, my ears were in accord, and at seventy, I followed the desires of my mind-and-heart without overstepping right" (2.4). The point of this observation, as well as numerous others found in the *Conversations of Master Zhu* (36.962–71), is that Yan Hui, unlike Confucius, does not appreciate that once exhaustive and strenuous effort is spent on "broadening oneself with culture" and "restraining oneself with ritual," following the Way (i.e., principle as it ought to be) proceeds almost without force or effort.

If Yan Hui, the most exemplary of disciples, confesses to finding true understanding of the Way to be something of a struggle—for whatever reason—those less capable are sure to find it at least as challenging. Although the Master is optimistic that by means of proper teaching, rituals, music, punishments, and the like, people can be led along the right path, he acknowledges that bringing to them a genuine understanding of it is more problematic:

He Yan's reading:

> The Master said, The people can be made to follow it, but they cannot be made to understand it. (8.9 [43])
> *You* [to follow] is *yong*, "to use." That they can be made to use it but cannot be made to understand it means that the common people [*baixing*] are capable of using it daily but incapable of understanding it.

Zhu Xi's reading:

> The Master said, The people can be made to follow it, but they cannot be made to understand it.

The people can be made to follow this principle as it should be, but they cannot be made to understand why it is as it is.

Master Cheng said, "In establishing his teaching, it was not that the Sage was not hopeful that it would be widely understood by the people. Yet the people could not be made to understand it. They could be made only to follow it. If we were to say that the Sage did not enable people to understand it, this would be the 'four in the morning, three in the evening' deception of later ages [*Zhuangzi*, 5; cf. Watson, *Chuang Tzu*, 36]. How could this possibly be the mind-and-heart of the Sage?"

Teaching people to follow the Way is not the same as teaching them to understand the Way. But the explanations offered by He and Zhu for why people cannot be made to understand are at variance. He tells his reader that what Confucius means here by *min* is the common people (*baixing*) and that the common people simply are not capable of understanding it. By implication, since they are incapable of achieving understanding, there is no hope of making them understand, but merely of channeling their behavior into conformity with the Way.

Zhu, by contrast, seems not to interpret *min* here in the more narrow sense of the common people, but as a general term for people. The Master believes that people can be taught to accord with the Way, to do what they should do to be consistent with principle in things and affairs. That is, through example, ritual, music, punishment, and instruction, they can be made to behave in a filial manner, or in the manner of a subject, or in the manner of a younger brother, and so forth (YL 35.936). But unlike He Yan's reading, Zhu assumes that the Master also believes that people are indeed capable of understanding the reason for the principle governing such behavior. This is why, in Master Cheng's words, "In establishing his teaching, it was not that the Sage was not hopeful that it would become widely understood by the people." The significance of 8.9, as Zhu reads it, is that the Master, assuming that people are capable of understanding the Way or princi-ple, tries to elucidate it for them through his teaching, only to discover that they cannot be *made* to understand it. They can indeed be made to comply with it, but understanding it, the possibility of which he believes is open to them, is more their own doing. As Zhu puts it suc-cinctly elsewhere: "To be incapable of *making* them understand it is not the same as not having them understand it" (italics obviously mine).[11] He offers further elaboration in the *Conversations of Master Zhu*: "Someone asked about 'the people can be made to follow it, but they cannot be made to understand it.' Zhu replied, The Sage merely made others filial and that was sufficient; he made others fraternal and that was sufficient. There was no way, however, that he could visit them and explain one by one the reasons why we ought to be filial and the reasons why we ought to be fraternal. Naturally there was no way he could do this" (YL 35.936). In Zhu Xi's reading of the passage, one at odds with He Yan's, the Master would indeed have people (*min*) come to understand the Way—or principle as it ought to be—but sug-gests that the effort must be theirs, as it is not likely that this more abstract understanding could be readily provided by others. In this reading, the limitations of "making them understand it" are related more to the difficulty of communicating the Way or principle in its abstractness to others than to the incapability of people, common or other, to achieve understanding. Understanding it—or not—rests with them: those who will it, those who are dedicated and make the effort, can perhaps hope to achieve real understanding.

Whatever the reasons for, or the precise meaning of, this observa-tion that people "cannot be made to understand it," Confucius contin-ues his efforts to elucidate the Way throughout the text of the *Analects*. Aware perhaps, however, that his many and various characterizations of the Way tend to be "perspectival" (dependent to a considerable degree on the disciple or disciples with whom he is speaking) and rather dis-parate (dependent on the particular subject at hand) and aware, too, that even brilliant disciples like Yan Hui find its pursuit a challenge, the

---

11. *Lunyu zuanshu* 4.40a.

Master reminds those gathered around him one day that there is indeed a fundamental coherence in his Way:

He Yan's reading:

> The Master said, Shen! My Way has one thread running through it. Zengzi said, Yes, of course.

Kong [Anguo] said, "He understood immediately, without any questioning. Thus he responded with *wei*, 'yes, of course.'"

> The Master left and his disciples asked, What did he mean? Zengzi said, The Way of our Master is doing the best one can and empathy, nothing more. (4.15 [44])

Zhu Xi's reading:

> The Master said, Shen! My Way has one thread running through it. Zengzi said, Yes, of course.

Shen hu means that he cried out Zengzi's personal name to tell him this. *Guan* [running through] is *tong*, "to penetrate or run through." *Wei* [yes, of course] is "to assent immediately, with no uncertainty." The mind-and-heart of the Sage is everywhere of one principle. Yet being broadly responsive and minutely sensitive in its function, it differs in accord with the situation. With respect to this function aspect, Zengzi, it seems, examines each circumstance carefully and then energetically acts. But he simply does not yet appreciate the oneness of substance here. The Master knows that if he truly exerts himself over a long period of time, he will understand it and thus cries out to tell him this. Zengzi actually is silently able to grasp the gist here and so assents immediately and without hesitation.

> The Master left and his disciples asked, What did he mean? Zengzi said, The Way of our Master is to be true to oneself and empathetic toward others, nothing more.

"To give full expression to oneself" [*jin ji*] is what is meant by *zhong*; "to extend oneself" is what is meant by *shu*. "Nothing more" is a phrase meaning "exhaustive," nothing else. That the one principle of our Master is everywhere and yet is broadly responsive and minutely sensitive is comparable to heaven and earth being perfectly true [*cheng*] and unceasing even as each of the myriad things attains its own place [*Zhongyong*, chap. 26]. There really is no rule beyond this—nor is there any need to look further. Zengzi had some understanding of it yet found it difficult to speak about. Therefore he drew on the main point, that the learner give full expression to himself and extend himself to others, and explicated its meaning, for he wanted others to understand it readily. It seems that "to be perfectly true and unceasing" is the substance of the Way and the reason for the one foundation among the myriad differences. "Each of the myriad things attaining its own place" is the function of the Way and the reason for the myriad differences in the one foundation. From this point of view, the truth of "one thread running through it" is evident. Someone said, "*Zhong*, 'center,' and *xin*, 'mind-and-heart,' constitute the character *zhong* [to be true to oneself]; *ru* 'like,' and *xin*, 'mind-and-heart,' constitute the character *shu* [empathetic toward others]." This indeed gets at their meaning.

Master Cheng said, "Using oneself to approach other things is *ren*, 'true goodness.' Extending oneself to other things is *shu*, 'empathy.' This is to be 'not far from the Way' [*Zhongyong*, chap. 13]. To be true to oneself and empathetic toward others is the one thread running through it. Being true to oneself is the Way of heaven; being empathetic toward others is the Way of man. Being true to oneself is to be without falsehood; being empathetic toward others is the means by which to put being true to oneself into actual practice. Being true to oneself is substance; being empathetic toward others is function: these are the great foundation and the universal Way [*Zhongyong*, chap. 1]. This is even rarer than not being far from the Way and is something only heaven can inspire." He again said, "'The decree of heaven / how deep and unintermitting' [*Shijing*, Mao no. 267; cf. Legge, *Chinese Classics*, 4:570] is to be true to oneself. 'The change and transformation of the Way of *qian* in each instance keep the nature and destiny of things correct' [*Zhouyi*, 1; cf. Lynn, *Classic of Changes*, 129) is to be empathetic toward others." He further said, "In teaching other men, the Sage accorded with their abilities. 'My Way has one thread running through it': Zengzi alone was capable of understanding this, which is why Confucius told it to him. Zengzi told the disciples, 'The Way of our Master is to be true to oneself and empathetic toward others, nothing more,' which is similar to what the Master told Zengzi. What is said in the *Zhongyong*, 'To be true to oneself and empathetic toward others is to be not far from the Way': this then is the meaning of 'study low to penetrate high' [14.35]."

This seems a particularly fitting analect with which to close this chapter, for a few reasons. First, it is effective in its intention to offer a meaningful and synoptic characterization of the Way, one that is both reasonably accessible and practicable for those eager to hear it. The discursive treatment of the Confucian Way offered in the twenty chapters of text is reduced here to a manageable essence, encouraging followers of the Confucian school—and us as well perhaps—to take away from a reading of the text the impression that the nature of the composition and of the argumentation of the *Analects* notwithstanding, a doctrinal unity, a strong coherence, underlies the vision of the Master. With this remark, the reader is reminded that the very practice of empathy, the ability to put oneself in the place of others, using one's own appropriate feelings as a measure of how to treat those others appropriately, is to embark on the path of the Way. Consequently, the Way is not something distant or remote but can be found near at hand, in taking stock of one's own self and feelings in one's dealings with fellow human beings. This ability "to draw analogies from what is near at hand" (6.30), in turn, is what guarantees that one will uphold the Chinese golden rule: "What you do not wish yourself, do not do unto others" (15.24). One who without interruption practices empathy toward others and who thereby unfailingly upholds the golden rule is recognized as a person of true goodness. The empathetic treatment of others, the role of self in the analogizing process, the ideal of the golden rule, and the paramount virtue of true goodness all are conceptual strands that come together here in the "one thread running through it."

This is also a passage that allows us to draw some summary comparisons between the two commentaries, with respect to both style and content. While He is brief in the extreme, offering no commentary on Zengzi's remark and only a brief gloss on the first line by the Master, Zhu goes on at great length, considerably greater length than the text of the classic itself. He Yan seems to believe that the meaning of the analect is straightforward and can, or should, stand on its own. By contrast, Zhu's extended commentary suggests a number of points: that the passage is of great importance and warrants the sort of consideration he gives it; that he, at least, is confident that he grasps its essential meaning, whereas others might not; and that others reading the text need the guidance of an extended commentary if they are to be sure of understanding the text as they should.

Also obvious from this one passage is that Zhu Xi places his understanding of the text of the *Analects* in a much larger context. We find him reading this analect against the background of the entire tradition, both canonical and philosophical. He cites passages from the *Doctrine of the Mean*, the *Book of Poetry*, the *Book of Changes*, and the *Analects* itself in order to give greater significance to the remark here. Popular concepts from the contemporary Confucian metaphysics—most notably principle, substance, and function—lend relevance and meaning to the text for the contemporary reader. But the effects of such "contextualization" are multiple and complex. To be sure, such citations do illuminate the base text, the *Analects*, and make it intelligible, which no doubt is the principal motive behind the very act of commentarial writing itself. But the effects go beyond elucidation of the particular passage in question. As we noted earlier, by attempting to show that the message in the *Analects* is consistent with that found in other parts of the canon, the commentary makes a strong argument, even if only implicitly, that the larger tradition is coherent and unified and that the *Analects* indeed is a rightful and legitimate part of it. At the same time, by attempting to show that the words of the Master echo the message of other canonical texts, it in turn deepens the significance of these other texts and enhances their canonical legitimacy. Similarly, while the text of the *Analects* here is given a contemporary metaphysical relevance and perhaps consequently is made more meaningful to the reader of Zhu's commentary, the effect works in the other direction as well: a metaphysics that can be read meaningfully against the words of the Master becomes a distinctively Confucian metaphysics, an organic and seemingly natural product of the very tradition it illuminates. Its legitimacy is thereby enormously strengthened and its significance greatly enhanced.

Finally, and related to the previous point, Zhu Xi brings to bear in his commentarial writing a host of ontological and metaphysical assumptions, which He Yan earlier seemed not to have shared. Zhu's reader, by contrast, must accept these assumptions if he is to understand the text as Zhu does. Perhaps the most important among them, on which so many others seem to rest, is the belief that principle inheres in all things in the universe and that ultimately, in all its manifestations, principle is one. In human beings, this principle is identified with human nature, which, as Mencius argued early on, is good, encoded as it is with the cardinal virtues of Confucianism. The challenge for man thus is to learn how to realize this innate endowment—that is, how to be unfailingly true to one's original self, one's original mind-and-heart. By expressing one's true self in all one's dealings with others, one may become truly good. Indeed, one may become the ideal person, the superior man.

Conclusion

Reading the *Analects* with commentary by Zhu Xi is a different intellectual experience from reading the *Analects* with commentary by He Yan and, in turn, produces a rather different understanding of both the classic itself and the larger Confucian tradition of which it is a part. What makes the experience different—for us today as well as the typical Chinese reader through the early twentieth century—is that Zhu brings to the commentarial task a different set of intellectual assumptions and beliefs that color his reading of the text and, by extension, the reader's. Equally important, Zhu brings to the task a different conception of the commentator's role itself—that is, a different sense of what the commentator does, of the commentator's role in relation to both the text and his reader.

In my conclusion, therefore, I would like to make some general observations about, first, how Zhu Xi perceived his role and purpose as commentator and, second, how Zhu's reshaping and redefining of the *Analects* was informed by the intellectual assumptions and beliefs he brings to the text. As he has throughout, He Yan provides an instructive basis of comparison.

On the Role of the Commentator

He Yan's and Zhu Xi's different conceptions of the role of commentator are revealed in their distinctive commentarial styles and approaches. For instance, He's commentaries tend to be brief, philological and semantic, limited to the particular passage at hand, and bound closely to the readings of earlier authorities. Zhu's, by comparison, tend to be much longer, more interpretive and philosophical, intratextually and intertextually sensitive, and, while clearly indebted to earlier readings, freer of them. Of course, such differences in style and approach reflect different stages in the genre's historical development. He and Zhu, after all, were operating according to two different sets of generic conventions, one from the third century and the other from the twelfth century. But even though it is historically conditioned, a commentary's style and approach shed light on how the commentator at that particular time understands his role—that is, how he understands his relationship to the text, the tradition, and the reader.

Consider how He Yan and Zhu Xi treat the earlier authorities they cite and what this reveals about their assumptions concerning what a commentator is supposed to do. Both, of course, draw heavily on remarks by others, but they do so to a quite different effect. He Yan cites Bao Xian, Ma Rong, Zheng Xuan, Wang Su, and others, usually permitting their remarks to stand on their own; their voices command full authority, unmediated by his. By contrast, Zhu generally begins his commentary on each line with his own remarks and only then cites those of others: the Cheng brothers, Xie Liangzuo, and Fan Zuyu. Although he cites them as authorities, they are authorities who largely support Zhu's own views. Never does his own voice recede in his commentary on the *Analects*. Rather, he positions himself at the center of a number of ongoing dialogues: between himself and the classic, between himself and earlier authorities in the tradition, and between himself and the reader of his commentary.

Serving as an active agent between the text and the tradition of commentary on it, Zhu Xi has a greater, more autonomous presence and identity in his commentary than He Yan does in his. By simply citing authorities like Ma Rong, He Yan seems to be trying to transmit to his reader the understanding of the text that those in the tradition themselves have reached. Zhu, however, plays a considerably more prominent role than He does, actively shaping his understanding of the text. It is his voice, in his own words, that responds to each passage of the text, followed by voices that support or embellish his own. The understanding of the *Analects* that Zhu's reader is expected to reach is the one that he personally has labored to negotiate. In short, Zhu makes no effort to minimize his authorial hand in the commentarial project.

Why do He and Zhu take such different approaches? And why does He keep the commentary relatively short, limiting it to glosses on characters and phrases, while Zhu carries on at great length, overwhelming the text itself?

He Yan seems to believe that the reader can understand the meaning of the *Analects* with the aid of simple glossing and that the reader can—indeed, should—confront the words of the Master with a minimum of mediation. Perhaps He was confident that given the flurry of commentarial activity on the text during the second century and the high status recently accorded to it, the elite would already be reasonably familiar with its teachings and the tradition of understanding surrounding them. His glosses are often little more than reminders of a textual understanding he presumed to be generally shared. Viewed in this light, He Yan's commentaries on the *Analects* are just passing on a tradition developed by Ma Rong, Zheng Xuan, Wang Su, and others, which in the second and third centuries was quite well understood and little contested.

If He Yan were writing in the third century, when reflective and engaged literati, more pluralistic than ever in their philosophical interests, were re-turning their attention to the Daoist texts—as I suggested in the introduction—the brevity of He's commentaries might simply indicate a commitment to the text of the *Analects* less passionate than that of Zhu Xi almost a millennium later. Contemporary sources comment on He's abiding interest in the writings of Laozi and Zhuangzi but do not mention an interest in or commentary on the *Analects*. I do not mean to suggest that He Yan's commitment to the text of the *Analects* was not genuine or deep, only that his interest was not so single-minded as Zhu Xi's or so driven by the same intense conviction. He seems to have regarded the *Analects* as one among a variety of texts from a variety of philosophical traditions of equal claim, whereas Zhu appears to have considered the tradition founded by Confucius as unchallenged in its claim to truth.

Zhu Xi's more elaborate treatment of the *Analects* may partly relate to his feeling that the great length of time separating the composition of the text from the Song necessitated a fuller commentary in order for contemporary readers to understand its meaning. But no doubt in larger part, it relates to his proselytizing attitude and efforts on behalf of the Confucian tradition. Zhu Xi was "making a case" in his commentary on the *Analects* for Confucian teachings and principles, trying to demonstrate their relevance and applicability to his contemporaries, many of whom remained doubtful. His commentary reads as a sort of polemic, an expression of his sense that the Confucian Way was under threat—indeed, in crisis—during the Song, as evidenced by the "barbarian" presence to the north, the continued widespread popularity of Buddhism, and the factionalism and strife in government. If Zhu's life can be understood as being devoted to restoring the Way, to resuscitating those truths transmitted by the great sages of Chinese antiquity, his commentaries on texts like the *Analects* must be understood as a central part of that effort.[1]

Zhu was defending not only the larger Confucian tradition and its Way, but also, more narrowly, the *Analects* itself. It was Zhu Xi, after all, who was the first to argue systematically that the *Analects*—together with the *Greater Learning*, the *Mencius*, and the *Doctrine of the Mean*—were the core texts in the Confucian tradition, the texts to be read before all others, including the previously authoritative and venerated Five Classics. Through his commentaries, he was thus attempting to convince the readers of the *Analects* not just that Confucian truths were relevant but that those truths were best expressed in the Four Books.

This deep, almost religious commitment to the text of the *Analects* clearly accounts for Zhu's strenuous commentarial efforts. The preface to his commentary is instructive here. Whereas He's preface, as we have seen, is devoted entirely to a history of editions and commentaries on the text of the *Analects* and to situating He's own commentary within this history, Zhu's is an anthology of remarks from the *Shiji*, He Yan, and Cheng Yi, the principal purpose of which was to praise Confucius the Sage and elevate the status of the *Analects*. The following remarks by Cheng Yi, with which Zhu Xi concludes his preface, speak eloquently to Zhu's (and, of course, to Cheng Yi's as well) affection for and faith in the text:

> Master Cheng said, "In reading the *Analects*, there are those who read it and are utterly unaffected by it. There are those who read it, understand only a line or two, and are happy. There are those who read it and know that they love it. Then there are those who read it and right away, without even knowing it, are dancing with their hands and feet."
>
> Master Cheng said, "People nowadays don't know how to read. If in reading the *Analects*, someone is the same person when he's finished reading as when he began, he hasn't really read it."
>
> Master Cheng said, "Since the age of seventeen or eighteen, I've been reading the *Analects*. Already then I understood its meaning. But only by reading it more and more have I come to realize how profound and far-reaching its significance is."

For Zhu Xi, the *Analects* is not merely profound in its significance but profoundly transforming. The true reader will find himself spiritually moved and uplifted by it, his very life and very being changed by the reading experience. No doubt it was this sort of faith in the power and efficacy of the text that motivated Zhu's own lifelong work on it. And no doubt it was his hope that his commentary would help make this power and efficacy apparent and available to others as well.

Once we understand that Zhu assumed that his task as commentator was not simply to explicate a text but to defend it and the tradition of which it was a part, other general distinguishing features of his commentarial style and approach become more understandable. For if his commentary was written in part as an apologetic, trying to convince the reader, first, that the Confucian tradition was still vital and relevant in the Song and, second, that the *Analects* and the other Four Books captured the essence of that tradition better than the authoritative Five Classics did, the intertextuality that characterizes his commentary should not be surprising. That is, if in fact Zhu was arguing on behalf of the larger Confucian tradition, his referring to this larger tradition and its body of texts would be natural. And if in fact he was arguing that the *Analects* was one of the four foundational texts in this tradition, more central than the Five Classics themselves, showing that the text coheres especially well with the rest of the canon and that it reflects the canon's message especially richly and resonantly also would be natural. Similarly, Zhu's intertextual references to the *Greater Learning*, the *Mencius*, and the *Doctrine of the Mean* would be natural, too, if he was reading these four books as a privileged collection of texts expressing the fundamental truth of the Confucian tradition.

He Yan, as we have noted, does not have such singular devotion to the Confucian tradition or its texts. More philosophically pluralistic, He was not nearly so intent on defending or privileging any one school or any particular set of texts. It is this difference from Zhu's approach that may help explain why his commentary does not exhibit comparable intertextual tendencies.

Another, related contrast in the two men's commentarial approaches and styles, implicit perhaps in the discussion thus far, deserves some explicit comment. Throughout his commentaries, He Yan demonstrates an interest in clarifying and making intelligible the meaning of the *Analects*, the meaning traditionally given to the text by men like Ma Rong and Zheng Xuan. For He, commentary is largely a vehicle for passing on this tradition of meaning, from his predecessors to his contemporaries and those who follow. Its purpose is to preserve and maintain the tradition of meaning as he receives it, acknowledging that this act, of course, involves selection and personal interpretation.

Like He Yan, Zhu Xi is drawing on his commentarial predecessors but is more actively shaping the meaning of the *Analects* text. Zhu regards commentary as necessary to negotiate between the words of the canonical text and a community of believers whose set of assumptions, whose worldview, is dramatically different from that of the author(s) and compiler(s) of the *Analects*. For Zhu, commentary is an opportunity to shape the analects into a tradition that will have meaning to a contemporary audience (hence his introduction of the goodness of human nature in his commentary on the very first passage of the text, as well as his frequent references throughout to the metaphysics of *li* and *qi*). This task is especially important if that audience is thought to be skeptical and needing convincing that Confucian teachings are relevant to their world.

Zhu's rather aggressive shaping of the tradition, particularly his introduction of an elaborate metaphysics into a reading of the classical texts, has long been questioned by Chinese scholars themselves. Evidential, or *kaozheng*, scholars of the *Qing* were especially harsh in their criticism of what they viewed as Zhu's philosophical interventionism in the canonical texts of Confucianism, especially in the Four Books.[2] The issue for us, as students of intellectual history—who necessarily approach the canonical texts in a different spirit from that of those living in the tradition and embracing these texts as sacred—is to consider not so much the appropriateness of Zhu's creative reading of the *Analects* (even though we might acknowledge the legitimacy of the *kaozheng* position) as the explanation for his creativity. Our main interest is in tracing the changes in the reading and understanding of those canonical texts, in trying to explain these changes, and in finding the larger influence that such changes might have had.

We noted earlier that the status of the Confucian tradition in the third century and that in the twelfth century were quite different and that this difference might partly account for Zhu Xi's bolder, more aggressive commentarial approach. Such an approach might also reflect the commentator's confidence that whatever the differences in time or philosophical assumptions, he was able to apprehend the true intentions of the Sage. Zhu was convinced, for instance, that while the Sage may not have explicitly raised the matter of the goodness of human nature in the *Analects*, he did assume that human nature was good. Zhu could have pointed to the tradition immediately following Confucius to explain some of his readings, as he might have for human nature. But when he introduces in his commentary ideas about the mind, principle, psychophysical stuff, psychophysical nature, and so forth, the Confucian tradition—and certainly the pre-Song Confucian tradition—provided little interpretive guidance and justification.[3]

If Zhu's commentarial boldness relates to confidence, where does the confidence come from? Considered in the larger context of the ontological and epistemological beliefs commonly shared in the Song by Buddhists, Daoists, and Confucians alike and certainly by Zhu Xi— beliefs that certainly would have had no place in He Yan's world— Zhu's commentarial approach becomes clearer. In sum, during the Song, it was believed that all human beings are born with the same good nature and same good mind. The nature and mind of the person on the street are ontologically no different from the nature and mind of sages past. This person on the street, however, must work to maintain the goodness of his original nature and mind. This is where self-cultivation comes in. Every mind has the epistemological capability of shedding its distractions, selfish desires, and the like and, in turn, realizing the good, thereby recovering or returning to its pure and perfected state.

Zhu Xi was confident that his mind had become one with the mind of the sages. Through serious investigation of the tradition and particularly through conscientious reflection on the canon, he had indeed achieved total understanding of principle and had "enter[ed] the realm of the sages and worthies."[4] The intentions of these sages of the past were now perfectly clear to him. If they were not, how could he presume to add to the text of the *Greater Learning*, another of the influential Four Books, his own "reconstructed" chapter on *ge wu/zhi zhi*, claiming simply that he was "filling in the lacunae" in a sacred classic?[5] Zhu's understanding of the sages' intentions was of course aided, he himself would argue, by the efforts of his Northern Song predecessors, especially the Cheng brothers, who had rediscovered the Way of the sages of the past and "continued the line of transmission, which for a thousand years had not been handed down."[6] Like himself, having perfectly cultivated their minds, they had come to appreciate the intentions of the sages. Their appreciation, in turn, mediated Zhu Xi's own reading and understanding of the canonical tradition. By bringing together in a collection of commentaries his reading of the *Analects* with earlier readings that similarly apprehended the intentions of the great Sage, Zhu Xi hoped to help make those intentions clear to others.

Intellectual Assumptions and Commentary

It is, of course, quite apparent that the intentions of the Sage for Zhu Xi, and hence for readers of the text with his commentary, were not the same as they were for He Yan and for readers of the text with his commentary. This is where the two commentators' different philosophical assumptions and beliefs, regardless of how the two might have conceived their role as commentator, come into play. For such differences in philosophical assumptions and beliefs derived from different intellectual contexts profoundly shaped the two commentators' readings, producing, in turn, quite different understandings of the *Analects*.

Perhaps most noticeable in this respect is the system of metaphysics expressed in Zhu Xi's commentary on the *Analects*. It was a metaphysics, Zhu believed, that emerged naturally out of serious reflection on the canonical tradition. Cheng Yi and others before him had done much to demonstrate how the language of human nature (*xing*), mind-and-heart (*xin*), psychophysical stuff (*qi*), and principle (*li*) not only was consistent with the teachings of the tradition but also illuminated and deepened their meaning. Inheriting from these recent thinkers a tradition now metaphysically charged, Zhu Xi continued to shape and develop it, convinced that it was a tradition implied by the Sage, consistent with his intentions.

The different commentarial readings of the *Analects* are, to a considerable degree, the product of historical context. Zhu Xi's twelfth-century treatment of the text would have been unlikely—indeed, impossible—in the third century, for it was itself the product of the tradition as it had evolved over the many centuries between the Wei period and the Southern Song. This, of course, is not to say that the commentary was entirely "historically determined." It was, after all, given particular shape by a particular person with a particular understanding of the tradition and the larger world, even if such understanding was colored by historical context and the current state of the tradition.

An interesting process was thus at work: the commentator's understanding of the tradition mediated his understanding of the text; the commentary produced through such mediation, in turn, (re-)shaped the understanding of the tradition; and the tradition, now reshaped by commentary, itself mediated later commentaries. Consider how Zhu Xi's commentary on the *Analects* and the other Four Books dominated the understanding of Confucian intellectual tradition for centuries. Wang Yangming's philosophical program, as distinctive as it was, as combative as it frequently was with Zhu Xi's philosophical understanding, would surely not have emerged without his mediation, which Wang inherited through the tradition and with which he carried on a dialogue.

It is not only in a metaphysics that Zhu Xi's commentary differs from that of He Yan. The two differ in interpretation and emphasis of matters as central to Confucian doctrine as the nature of learning, the process of self-cultivation, the realization of true goodness, the source of this true goodness, and the practice and effect of ritual. Of these many differences, the defining one, the one on which so many of the others depended, was the two men's understanding of the Way. According to Zhu, since the Way is knowable by man, man can actively cultivate himself in accord with it and thereby achieve moral perfection. Because he did not share this confidence in the Way's knowability, He did not propose, as Zhu did, a comprehensive program by which man could hope to learn it.

He Yan appeared to understand the Way in terms likely inspired by the teachings of Laozi and Zhuangzi. To He, the Way was inexhaustible, without form or bounds (9.11); "profound and abstruse," not readily open to human comprehension or easily attainable (5.12 and 9.11). Thus when the disciple Yan Hui laments the difficulty of the spiritual quest he has undertaken with the Master, He Yan identifies the main source of the difficulty as the challenge posed by the Way itself (9.11). (Zhu relates the difficulty more to Yan Hui's own inadequate efforts.) And when Confucius in analect 7.6 admonishes, "Set your mind-and-heart on the Way," He glosses *zhi* (to set the mind-and-heart on) as *mu* (to long for) and explains: "Because the Way cannot be embodied, one may long for it and nothing more." It is to this wondrous, ineffable quality of the Way that He's commentary speaks, over and over reminding his reader that it cannot be easily described or defined.

Viewing the Way as finally unknowable, not fully open to human comprehension, He Yan offers no program for learning it. From the few disparate remarks he makes in his commentary, we can begin to piece together his understanding of realizing or experiencing the Way. It is an understanding with rather strong affinities to the teachings of classical Daoism. For instance, when it is said of the Master in analect 9.4 that he refused to be egotistical (*wu wo*, lit. without self), He glosses *wo* as *shen* (the self or person or body) and writes, "It is the Way alone that he follows, and consequently there is no such thing as his self."[7] With this, He Yan hints that the Sage was successful in merging with the Way only by giving up his sense of individuated person or self. Here the *xuanxue* admiration for Confucius, especially for his embodiment of nonbeing, which a few years later Wang Bi expressed, is apparent.

Analect 11.18 produces a similar explanation by He, in a commentary that is interesting because it clearly shows a philosophical pluralism—that is, a willingness to draw simultaneously from both the classical Confucian and Daoist traditions. An example is the seven-character passage describing the Master's beloved disciple, Yan Hui: *Hui ye qi shu hu lü kong* (lit. Hui comes near to it. He is frequently empty). This is one of the rare instances in his entire commentary in which He Yan offers two entirely different explanations of the same passage. Making no explicit attempt to reconcile the two, he first states, "Hui comes near to the Way of a sage. Although he frequently is in straits, he nonetheless remains joyful therein," taking the character *kong* (lit. empty) to mean *kongkui* (poor) and understanding the passage to mean that despite the awful material conditions in which Yan Hui finds himself, he is not the least bit distracted from his pursuit of and affection for the Way. This became the standard reading of the description of Yan Hui in 11.18 adopted by the Confucian tradition, including Zhu Xi in his Song commentary. But He's commentary goes on to add: "Another authority has said, '*Lü* [frequently] is similar to *mei*, 'always.' *Kong* [lit. empty] is similar to *xu zhong*, 'to empty out what is within.' . . . Of those who are almost always able to empty out what is within, Hui alone cherishes the Way, profound and far-reaching. If one does not empty the mind, one is incapable of knowing the Way." In this reading of the passage, we find the view of Yan Hui often presented in Zhuangzi's writings, of a sage capable of fasting his mind, emptying himself of intellection, gathering in emptiness, and thereby becoming one with the Way. As in 9.4 on *wu wo*, the characterization here of sageliness and of the path to realizing the Way is compatible with descriptions found in the teachings of classical Daoism.

I am not, of course, saying that He Yan should be characterized as "Daoist." What it meant in the third century to be "Daoist"—or, for that matter, "Confucian" (or Ru) or a student of *xuanxue*—is not yet especially clear. A commentary like He's suggests that categorizing third-century thinkers into the conventional schools of thought does not take us very far. It also, and more significantly, suggests how the genre of commentary can deepen students' appreciation of the commentator's philosophical orientation and lead to a fuller, more nuanced understanding of developments in Chinese intellectual history. From He's commentary, a complicated but intelligible picture of a body of beliefs begins to take shape: the Way is inexpressible; man is hardpressed to experience or achieve it; man's mind is itself an obstruction to its achievement; and, consequently, learning is of limited efficacy in guiding man toward it. Ritual, unlike the Way, is knowable to man, and to learn and practice it results in good behavior. Thus ritual in its articulated form, not the ineffable Way, provides a ready model for order in the world.

The strong suggestion in He's commentary is that while man cannot directly access the Way through his mind, he can hope to harmonize his actions with it through ritual practice, to align himself with its orderly pattern. According to He, ritual provides an answer to the problem of how, in a world in which the Way itself is unknowable, order and coherence can be established. By restraining human beings and their untoward impulses and encouraging proper behavior, especially toward others (12.1 and 17.9), ritual offers the possibility that the way of man might approach the Way of the universe, and also the possibility that some relief might be brought to the prevalent social and political disorder of the day.

Ritual likely had additional significance for He. Because of the newly instituted so-called nine-rank system, which ranked individuals for official service primarily on the basis of class, culture, and character, the knowledge and practice of ritual had become especially important to members of the medieval elite wishing to separate themselves from the rest of society.[8] The *Analects* and its code of ritual could be enormously helpful in this endeavor. In He Yan's commentary on 17.9, "'Ritual, ritual'—does it mean nothing more than jade and silk?" he concluded: "This is to say that ritual is not simply the veneration of this jade and silk. Its value lies in the value it places on putting those above at ease and bringing order to the people."

This analysis is very much an extrapolation of He Yan's rather unsystematic views. He is never very explicit or comprehensive in presenting an understanding of the Way, of the capabilities of man and his mind, and of ritual as a guide to human behavior in a morally mysterious universe; and certainly he never explicitly shapes these views into a coherent body of thought. It is at the risk of imposing order where there is little or none that I have tried to construct a systematic philosophical argument from a series of discrete comments on the Master's own series of discrete comments.

Zhu Xi, however, does this work for the reader, imposing his own coherent order on the text, by forging a system of understanding from its verses and chapters. To Zhu, Confucius is not offering merely a collection of significant insights or pithy teachings but a profound and unified vision, a message whose individual parts neatly form a comprehensive whole. The aim of Zhu's commentary is to bring this coherence into sharper focus, by showing explicitly and in detail how the various insights and teachings of the Master and his disciples presented in the text can be integrated into a system of understanding.

For Zhu Xi, in contrast with He Yan, the Way expounded by the Master can be defined and should be understood as "principle in affairs and things as it ought to be" (4.8). A neat, short elaboration of this understanding is provided in an exchange in the *Conversations of Master Zhu*:

> Someone asked how the Way and principle are to be distinguished. Zhu said: The Way is the path. Principle is the pattern. Like the grain in wood? Yes, Zhu replied. In that case,

the questioner said, they seem to be alike. Zhu said: The word Way is all-embracing. Principle refers to the many veins within the Way. He also said: The word Way refers to the whole, principle to the details. (YL 6.99)

A few extremely important and related implications proceed from this understanding, implications that set Zhu's understanding of the concept of the Way—and, in the end, of the *Analects* more generally—rather far apart from He Yan's. First, there is a pattern or coherence in the Way; second, because it is principle in its all-embracing manifestation, the Way is knowable; and finally, in its knowability the Way and sagehood itself are attainable by all, through a rigorous process of learning and cultivation (19.7). Thus, in his commentary on 5.28, Zhu remarks: "The Way in its perfection is difficult to hear. Through perfect learning of it one may become a sage. If one does not engage in learning, one cannot avoid becoming anything more than an ordinary man."

Through a process of self-cultivation, man learns to express his true self, the potential for empathy and humaneness endowed in him at birth. It is thus precisely the full development of self—rather than its abnegation, as He Yan suggested—that Zhu Xi requires in order to apprehend the Way and achieve sagehood. For example, Zhu differed with He in his understanding of analect 9.4 regarding the Master's refusal to be egotistical. By explaining the phrase *wu wo* (without self) to mean that the Master kept himself free of selfish thoughts, Zhu understands the passage to be calling not to give up the self, as He had, but to rid oneself of thoughts and desires that concealed one's true self. For Zhu, *wu wo* means bringing to perfection the self with which one is born, fully developing one's identity as a human being endowed with the four cardinal virtues. Only with this is realization of the Way genuinely possible.

As a consequence of his view of the Way as knowable to man, Zhu Xi is considerably more explicit and more programmatic than He Yan about how one can realize it. Indeed, whereas He understands the mind to be highly problematic in one's quest for the Way, an impediment to realization, Zhu predicates the entire process of realization on the mind's inherent capability to arrive at true understanding. Thus whereas He explains 7.6, "set your mind-and-heart on the Way," to mean "because the Way cannot be embodied, one may long for it and nothing more," Zhu Xi reads it as a plea to fix one's will or determination on learning the Way: "*Zhi* [to set the mind-and-heart on] is the term meaning the direction that the mind-and-heart takes. As to the Way, it lies in what ought to be practiced in daily human relations. Understanding this, the mind-and-heart is bound to head toward it and so will arrive at the right place, without conflicting doubts." The Way is apprehensible, but self-cultivation, a rigorous process of learning by the mind-and-heart, is required; and fixing or establishing the will or determination is the starting point in such a process. The central importance played by the will in "the learning proclaimed by the sage" is, as we have seen, a prominent leitmotif running throughout Zhu Xi's commentary—a theme given no particular attention or importance in He Yan's commentary.

This general understanding that the Way is knowable and accessible to people who make the right sort of effort explains much of what is distinctive about Zhu Xi's commentarial interpretation. Its preoccupation with the will as well as the roles of human nature and the mind-and-heart in achieving true goodness and the Way; with man's psychophysical endowment, which can obstruct the realization of original goodness and the practice of the Way; with the selfish desires that lead the mind-and-heart astray; and with a program of learning that prescribes both a process—*ge wu* and *zhi zhi*, the apprehension of principle and the extension of knowledge—and a curriculum of texts centering on the Four Books is tied to Zhu's view that humankind is capable of achieving a sort of universal understanding and fully realizing the all-embracing Way.

If the Way is knowable, the challenge is finding the proper course of human action that will result in true knowledge of it. The particular course of action proposed by Zhu, as we have seen, is grounded in a systematic process of self-cultivation, which takes as its first substantive step the investigation and apprehension of the universal principle underlying each thing in the world. Books, like all else, manifest this principle. Those written by the sages and worthies manifest it particularly clearly, and thus reading them, in Zhu's view, is an especially effective means of cultivating the self. When the process of self-cultivation is successful, when its efforts lead to the full apprehension of the universal principle, nothing distinguishes the minds of sages past—who were sages precisely because they had fully realized this principle in all that they did—from the perfected mind of the self-cultivated student. When he has achieved the mind of a sage, the student himself has become a sage. Indeed, as the case of Zhu Xi illustrates, sagehood in the twelfth century, in contrast to that in the third century, is an articulated, realizable goal for thinkers of the Confucian school. Their philosophical reflection was focusing more than ever before on its practical achievement.

Given that each man has perfection within him, self-cultivation, the realization of the perfection, is the means by which man learns—indeed, embodies—the Way. He Yan, with his considerably less optimistic view of the accessibility and knowability of the Way, seems to assume that ritual practice is the only means by which man might give autonomous expression to his action and still accord with the order of the Way. He lacks Zhu's assurance that man is innately good, originally possessed of principle—that is, has a moral human nature—and thus is linked ontologically to the Way. What value could self-realization have for him? In light of He's assumptions, it is not surprising that ritual—for him, an external guide to ordering behavior—is the answer provided by his commentary to the problem of actualizing the Way in human society. Nor is it surprising, in light of his ontological and epistemological assumptions, that Zhu Xi would regard ritual as largely incidental to realizing the Way in oneself through self-cultivation. As a means of external restraint, ritual is largely unnecessary in this sort of internal process.

In Zhu's commentarial reading of the *Analects*, ritual is not the ordering instrument that it is for He Yan. It simply does not have the same sort of agency. Instead, as we have seen throughout, ritual is more a natural expression or manifestation of the ontological goodness, a realization of the potential humaneness that every human being has at birth. The individual who brings this potential to perfection will manifest humaneness in all that he does, expressing it through exemplary behavior—that is, behavior in perfect harmony with the norms of *li*, or ritual. In short, he will become a sage. And it is this sage—not ritual itself—who embodies the power to order the world around him, to transform society into the community that it ideally should be.

The *Analects* with the twelfth-century commentary by Zhu Xi clearly is not the *Analects* with the third-century commentary by He Yan and his colleagues. But if different interlinear commentary informs the reading of the text differently, lending different meaning to the text, as I have suggested, the question remains: What does this single classic, the *Analects*, really mean? In fact, it has no one real meaning. As I also suggested, the true meaning of the *Analects* is the actual meaning that actual readers, to whom the text is meaningful, discover in it. This actual meaning evolves over time and place. Even as the *Analects* nourishes the tradition that holds it sacred, the tradition in its constant reinterpretation and reinvigoration of its own identity, in turn, nourishes the reading and understanding of the *Analects*. The study of commentary then is invaluable in shedding light on the actual meaning of canonical texts. But just as significant, commentary also serves as a window of understanding on the changing shape of the tradition, on the dynamic relationship between the canon and the tradition, and on how different thinkers at different times and in different places think differently about the canon and the tradition.

Zhu Xi's *Collected Commentaries on the* Analects offers Zhu Xi's understanding of the classic. Because this commentary quickly became the standard one, required reading not only for examination candidates but also for anyone aspiring to claims of literacy, it shaped and conditioned how others in the tradition understood the text. The *Analects* in particular, and the Confucian tradition more generally, are thus invested through Zhu's commentary with new significance and meaning: a language of metaphysics—principle (*li*), psychophysical stuff (*qi*), and human nature (*xing*)—became linked to Confucian doctrine, even if only to provide a context for the school's more traditional anthropocentric concerns. The mind, capable of apprehending the Way but at risk of losing its equilibrium, assumes new, critical importance; sageliness, as the perfect expression of a human nature thought to be ontologically good, moves within closer reach than ever before; and thus the constituents of the proper program of learning, the program by which such sageliness might be best realized, become the subject of intense interest and debate.

NOTES

1. Daniel K. Gardner, *Learning to Be a Sage: Selections from the* Conversations on Master Chu, Arranged Topically (Berkeley: University of California Press, 1990), 10–34.

2. See, for instance, Benjamin Elman, *From Philosophy to Philology: Intellectual and Social Aspects of Change in Late Imperial China* (Cambridge, Mass.: Harvard University, Council on East Asian Studies, 1984), chaps. 1 and 2; and Michael Nylan, *The Five "Confucian" Classics* (New Haven, Conn.: Yale University Press, 2001), 51–59.

3. The writings of thinkers like Wang Bi, Huang Kan, and Li Ao (772–841)—to the extent that these men can be said to be of the Confucian tradition—represent some pre-Song exceptions.

4. *Hui'an xiansheng Zhu Wengong wenji* 82.26a.

5. Daniel K. Gardner, *Chu Hsi and the Ta-hsueh: Neo-Confucian Reflection on the Confucian Canon* (Cambridge, Mass.: Harvard University, Council on East Asian Studies, 1986), esp. 46–59.

6. Zhu Xi, "Zhongyong zhangju xu," in *Sishu jizhu*, Sibu beiyao edition, 2b.

7. The second part of He's short comment strongly echoes *Zhuangzi*, chap. 5, p. 15.

8. Charles Holcombe, *In the Shadow of the Han: Literati Thought and Society at the Beginning of the Southern Dynasties* (Honolulu: University of Hawai'i Press, 1994), 78–84.

Appendix

I

[何]子曰學而時習之不亦說乎_{馬曰子者男子之通稱謂孔子也}王曰時者學者以時誦習之誦習以時學無廢業所以爲說懌有朋自遠方來不亦樂乎_{包曰同門曰朋}人不知而不慍不亦君子乎_{慍怒也凡人有所不知君子不怒}

[朱]子曰。學而時習之。不亦說乎. _{學之為言效也.人}性皆善.而覺有先後.後覺者.必效先覺之所為.乃可以明善而復其初也.習.鳥數飛也.學之不已.如鳥數飛也.說.喜意也.既學.而又時時習之.則所學者熟.而中心喜說.其進自不能已矣.程子曰.習.重習也.時復思繹.浹洽於中.則說也.又曰.學者將以行之也.時習之.則所學者在我.故說.謝氏曰.時習者.無時而不習.坐如尸.坐時習也.立如齊.立時習也.有朋自遠方來。不亦樂乎. _{朋.同類也.自遠方來.則近}者可知.程子曰.以善及人.而信從者眾.故可樂.又曰.說在心.樂主發散在外.人不知而不慍。不亦君子乎. _{慍.含怒意.君子成德}

之名.尹氏曰.學在己.知不知在人.何慍之有.程子曰.雖樂於及人.不
見是而無悶.乃所謂君子.愚謂及人而樂者順而易.不知而不慍者逆而
難.故惟成德者能之.然德之所以成.亦曰學之正.習之熟.說之深.而
不已焉耳.○程子曰.樂由說而後得.非樂不足以語君子.

2

[何]子曰古之學者為己今之學者爲人_{孔曰為己履而行之}
爲人徒能言之

[朱]子曰.古之學者為己.今之學者爲人. 程子曰.為
己.欲得之於己也.爲人.欲見知於人也.○程子曰.古之學者為己.其
終至於成物.今之學者爲人.其終至於喪己.愚按聖賢論學者用心得失
之際.其說多矣.然未有如此言之切而要者.於此明辨而日省之.則庶
乎其不昧於所從矣.

3

[何]子曰君子疾沒世而名不稱焉_{疾猶病也}

[朱]子曰.君子疾沒世而名不稱焉. 范氏曰.君子學以爲
己.不求人知.然沒世而名不稱焉.則無爲善之實可知矣.

4

[何]子曰十室之邑必有忠信如丘者焉不如丘之好學
也

[朱]子曰.十室之邑.必有忠信如丘者焉.不如丘
之好學也。十室.小邑也.忠信如聖人.生質之美者也.夫子生知.而
未嘗不好學.故言此以勉人.言美質易得.至道難聞.學之至.則可以為聖
人.不學.則不免為鄉人而已.可不勉哉.

5

[何]子曰我非生而知之者好古敏以求之者也鄭曰言此
者勸人學

[朱]子曰。我非生而知之者。好古敏以求之者也。
生而知之者．氣質清明．義理昭著．不待學而知也．敏．速也．謂汲汲也．〇
尹氏曰．孔子以生知之聖．每云好學者．非惟勉人也．蓋生而可知者義理
爾．若夫禮樂名物．古今事變．亦必待學．而後有以驗其實也．

6

[何]子曰吾十有五而志于學三十而立有所成也四十而
不惑孔曰不疑惑五十而知天命孔曰知天命之終始六十而耳
順鄭曰耳聞其言而知其微旨七十而從心所欲不踰矩馬曰矩法
也從心所欲無非法

[朱]子曰。吾十有五而志于學。古者十五而入大學．心之
所之謂之志．此所謂學．即大學之道也．志乎此．則念念在此．而為之不
厭矣． 三十而立。有以自立．則守之固．而無所事志矣。四十而
不惑。於事物之所當然．皆無所疑．則知之明．而無所事守矣。五十
而知天命。天命．即天道之流行．而賦於物者．乃事物所以當然之
故也．知此．則知極其精．而不惑又不足言矣。六十而耳順。聲入
心通．無所違逆．知之至．不思而得也。七十而從心所欲。不
踰矩。從．隨也．矩．法度之器．所以為方者也．隨其心之所欲．而自
不過於法度．安而行之． 不勉而中也。〇程子曰．孔子生而知之也．言
亦由學而至．所以勉進後人也．立．能自立於斯道也．不惑．則無所疑
矣．知天命．窮理盡性也．耳順．所聞皆通也．從心所欲．不踰矩． 則不
勉而中矣．又曰．孔子自言其進德之序如此者．聖人未必然．但為學者
立法．使之盈科而後進．成章而後達耳．胡氏曰．聖人之教亦多術．然
其要．使人不失其本心而已．欲得此心者．惟志乎聖人所示之學．循其
序而進焉．至於一疵不存．萬理明盡之後．則其日用之間．本心瑩然隨
所意欲．莫非至理．蓋心即體．欲即用．體即道．用即義．聲為律．而身
為度矣．又曰．聖人言此．一以示學者當優游涵泳．不可躐等而進．二以

示學者當日就月將.不可半塗而廢也.愚謂聖人生知安行.固無積累之漸.然其心未嘗自謂已至此也.是其日用之閒.必有獨覺其進.而人不及知者.故因其近似以自名.欲學者以是為則而自勉.非心實自聖.而姑為是退託也.後凡言謙辭之屬.意皆放此.

7

[何]子曰不憤不啓不悱不發舉一隅不以三隅反則不復也鄭曰孔子與人言必待其人心憤憤口悱悱乃後啓發為說之如此則識思之深也說則舉一隅以語之其人不思其類則不復重教之

[朱]子曰。不憤不啟。不悱不發。舉一隅。不以三隅反。則不復也。憤者.心求通而未得之意.悱者.口欲言而未能之貌.啟.謂開其意.發.謂達其辭.物之有四隅者.舉一可知其三.反者.還以相證之義.復.再告也.上章已言聖人誨人不倦之意.因并記此.欲學者勉於用力.以為受教之地也.○程子曰.憤悱.誠意之見於色辭者也.待其誠意而後告之.既告之.又必待其自得.乃復告爾.又曰.不待憤悱而發.則知之不能堅固.待其憤悱而後發.則沛然矣.

8

[何]子曰有教無類馬曰言人所在見教無有種類

[朱]子曰。有教無類。人性皆善.而其類有善惡之殊者.氣習之染也.故君子有教.則人皆可以復於善.而不當復論其類之惡矣.

9

[何]子貢問曰有一言而可以終身行之者乎子曰其恕乎己所不欲勿施於人言己之所惡勿加施於人

[朱]子貢問曰。有一言而可以終身行之者乎。子曰。其恕乎。己所不欲。勿施於人。推己及物.其施不窮.故可以終身行之.○尹氏曰.學貴於知要.子貢之問.可謂知要矣.孔子告以求仁之方也.推而極之.雖聖人之無我.不出乎此.終身行之.不亦宜乎.

10

[何]子貢曰我不欲人之加諸我也吾亦欲無加諸人焉曰加陵也子曰賜也非爾所及也孔曰言不能止人使不加非義於己

[朱]子貢曰。我不欲人之加諸我也。吾亦欲無加諸人。子曰。賜也。非爾所及也。子貢言我所不欲人加於我之事。我亦不欲以此加之於人。此仁者之事。不待勉強。故夫子以爲非子貢所及。○程子曰。我不欲人之加諸我。吾亦欲無加諸人。仁也。施諸己而不願。亦勿施於人。恕也。恕則子貢或能勉之。仁則非所及矣。愚謂無者自然而然。勿者禁止之謂。此所以爲仁恕之別。

11

[何]子貢曰如有博施於民而能濟眾何如可謂仁乎子曰何事於仁必也聖乎堯舜其猶病諸孔曰君能廣施恩惠濟民於患難堯舜至聖猶病其難夫仁者己欲立而立人己欲達而達人能近取譬可謂仁之方也已孔曰更爲子貢說仁者之行方道也但能進取譬於己皆恕己所欲而施之於人.

[朱]子貢曰。如有博施於民。而能濟眾。何如。可謂仁乎。子曰。何事於仁。必也聖乎。堯舜其猶病諸。博。廣也。仁以理言。通乎上下。聖以地言。則造其極之名也。乎者。疑而未定之辭。病。心有所不足也。言此何止於仁。必也聖人能之乎。則雖堯舜之聖。其心猶有所不足於此也。以是求仁。愈難而愈遠矣。夫仁者。己欲立而立人。己欲達而達人。以己及人。仁者之心也。於此觀之。可以見天理之周流而無閒矣。狀仁之體。莫切於此。能近取譬。可謂仁之方也已。譬。喻也。方。術也。近取諸身。以己所欲。譬之他人。知其所欲。亦猶是也。然後推其所欲以及於人。則恕之事而仁之術也。於此勉焉。則有以勝其人欲之私。而全其天理之公矣。○程子曰。醫書以手足痿痹爲不仁。此言最善名狀。仁者以天地萬物爲一體。莫非己也。認得爲己。何所不至。若不屬己。自與己不相干。如手足之不仁。氣已不貫。皆不屬己。故博施濟眾。乃聖人之功用。仁至難言。故止曰。己欲立而立人。己欲達而達人。能近取譬。可謂仁之方也已。欲令如是觀仁。可以得仁之

體.又曰.論語言堯舜其猶病諸者二.夫博施者.豈非聖人之所欲.然必
五十乃衣帛.七十乃食肉.聖人之心.非不欲少者亦衣帛食肉也.顧其
養有所不贍爾.此病其施之不博也.濟眾者.豈非聖人之所欲.然治不
過九州.聖人非不欲四海之外亦兼濟也.顧其治有所不及爾.此病其濟
之不眾也.推此以求.脩己以安百姓.則為病可知.苟以吾治已足.則便
不是聖人.呂氏曰.子貢有志於仁.徒事高遠.未知其方.孔子教以於己
取之.庶近而可入.是乃為仁之方.雖博施濟眾.亦由此進.

12

[何]子曰仁遠乎哉我欲人斯仁至矣包曰仁道不遠行之卽
是

[朱]子曰.仁遠乎哉.我欲仁.斯仁至矣.仁者.心之
德.非在外也.放而不求.故有以爲遠者.反而求之.則卽此而在矣.夫其
遠哉.○程子曰.為仁由己.欲之則至.何遠之有.

13

[何]子曰性相近也習相遠也孔曰君子慎所習

[朱]子曰.性相近也.習相遠也.此所謂性.兼氣質而
言者也.氣質之性.固有美惡之不同矣.然以其初而言.則皆不甚相遠
也.但習於善則善.習於惡則惡.於是始相遠耳.○程子曰.此言氣質之
性.非言性之本也.若言其本.則性卽是理.理無不善.孟子之言性善是
也.何相近之有哉.

14

[何]子曰我未見好仁者惡不仁者好仁者無以尚之孔曰
難復加也惡不仁者其為仁矣不使不仁者加乎其身孔曰言惡
不仁者能使不仁者不加非義於己不如好仁者無以尚之為優有能一日
用其力於仁矣乎我未見力不足者孔曰言人無能一日用其力脩
仁者耳我未見欲為仁而力不足者蓋有之矣我未之見也孔曰謙不
欲盡誣時人言不能為仁故云為能有爾我未之見也.

[朱]子曰。我未見好仁者。惡不仁者。好仁者。無以尚之。惡不仁者。其為仁矣。不使不仁者加乎其身。夫子自言未見好仁者.惡不仁者.蓋好仁者.真知仁之可好.故天下之物.無以加之.惡不仁者.真知不仁之可惡.故其所以為仁者.必能絕去不仁之事.而不使少有及於其身.此皆成德之事.故難得而見之也.有能一日用其力於仁矣乎。我未見力不足者。言好仁惡不仁者.雖不可見.然或有人果能一旦奮然用力於仁.則我又未見其力有不足者.蓋為仁在己.欲之則是.而志之所至.氣必至焉.故仁雖難能.而至之亦易也.蓋有之矣。我未之見也。蓋.疑辭.有之.謂有用力而力不足者.蓋人之氣質不同.故疑亦容或有此昏弱之甚.欲進而不能者.但我偶未之見耳.蓋不敢終以為易.而又歎人之莫肯用力於仁也.○此章言仁之成德.雖難其人.然學者苟能實用其力.則亦無不可至之理.但用力而不至者.今亦未見其人焉.此夫子所以反覆而歎息之也.

15

[何]曾子曰士不可以不弘毅任重而道遠包曰弘大也毅強而能斷也士弘毅然後能負重任致遠路仁以為己任不亦重乎死而後已不亦遠乎孔曰以仁為己任重莫重焉死而後已遠莫遠焉

[朱]曾子曰。士不可以不弘毅。任重而道遠。弘.寬廣也.毅.強忍也.非弘不能勝其重.非毅無以致其遠.仁以為己任。不亦重乎。死而後已。不亦遠乎。仁者.人心之全德.而必欲以身體而力行之.可謂重矣.一息尚存.此志不容少懈.可謂遠矣.○程子曰.弘而不毅.則無規矩而難立.毅而不弘.則隘陋而無以居之.又曰.弘大剛毅.然後能勝重任而遠到.

16

[何]有子曰孔子弟子有若其為人也孝弟而好犯上者鮮矣鮮少也上謂凡在己上者言孝弟之人必恭順好欲犯其上者少也不好犯上而好作亂者未之有也君子務本本立而道生本基也基立而後可大成孝弟也者其為仁之本與先能事父兄然後仁道可大成

［朱］有子曰。其爲人也孝弟。而好犯上者鮮矣。不好犯上。而好作亂者。未之有也。有子.孔子弟子.名若.善事父母為孝.善事兄長為弟.犯上.謂干犯在上之人.鮮.少也.作亂.則為悖逆爭鬪之事矣.此言人能孝弟.則其心和順.少好犯上.必不好作亂也.君子務本。本立而道生。孝弟也者。其爲仁之本與。.本立則其道充大孝務.專力也.本.猶根也.仁者.愛之.理.心之德也.為仁.猶曰行仁.與者.疑辭.謙退不敢質言也.言君子凡事專用力於根本.根本既立.則其道自生.若上文所謂孝弟.乃是爲仁之本.學者務此.則仁道自此而生也.○程子曰.孝弟.順德也.故不好犯上.豈復有逆理亂常之事.德有本弟行於家.而後仁愛及於物.所謂親親而仁民也.故為人以孝弟為本.論性.則以仁為孝弟之本.或問孝弟為仁之本.此是由孝弟可以至仁否.曰.非也.謂行仁自孝弟始.孝弟是仁之一事.謂之行仁之本則可.謂是仁之本則不可.蓋仁.是性也.孝弟.是用也.性中只有箇仁義禮智四者而已.曷嘗有孝弟來.然仁主於愛.愛莫大於愛親.故曰.孝弟也者.其為仁之本與.

17

［何］子曰剛毅木訥近仁王曰剛無欲毅果敢木質樸訥遲鈍有斯四者近於仁

［朱］子曰。剛毅木訥。近仁。程子曰.木者質樸.訥者遲鈍.四者質之近乎仁者也.楊氏曰.剛毅.則不屈於物欲.木訥.則不至於外馳.故近仁.

18

［何］顏淵問仁子曰克己復禮為仁馬曰克己約身孔曰復反也身能反禮則為仁矣一日克己復禮天下歸仁焉馬曰一日猶見歸況終身乎為仁由己而由人乎哉孔曰行善在己不在人也顏淵曰請問其目包曰知其必有條目故請問之子曰非禮勿視非禮勿聽非禮勿言非禮勿動鄭曰此四者克己復禮之目顏淵曰回雖不敏請事斯語矣王曰敬事此語必行之

［朱］顏淵問仁。子曰。克己復禮為仁。一日克己復禮。天下歸仁焉。為仁由己。而由人乎哉。仁者.本心之全德.克.勝也.己.謂身之私欲也.復.反也.禮者.天理之節文也.為仁者.所以全其心之德也.蓋心之全德.莫非天理.而亦不能不壞於人欲.故為仁者.必有以勝私欲而復於禮.則事皆天理.而本心之德.復全於我矣.歸.猶與也.又言一日克己復禮.則天下之人.皆與其仁.極言其效之甚速而至大也.又言為仁由己.而非他人所能預.又見其機之在我而無難也.日日克之.不以為難.則私欲淨盡.天理流行.而仁不可勝用矣.程子曰.非禮處便是私意.既是私意.如何得仁.須是克盡己私.皆歸於禮.方始是仁.又曰.克己復禮.則事事皆仁.故曰.天下歸仁.謝氏曰.克己.須從性偏難克處克將去。顏淵曰。請問其目。子曰。非禮勿視。非禮勿聽。非禮勿言。非禮勿動。顏淵曰。回雖不敏。請事斯語矣。目.條件也.顏淵聞夫子之言.則於天理人欲之際.已判然矣.故不復有所疑問.而直請其條目也.非禮者.己之私也.勿者.禁止之辭.是人心之所以為主.而勝私復禮之機也.私勝.則動容周旋.無不中禮.而日用之間.莫非天理之流行矣.事.如事事之事.請事斯語.顏子默識其理.又自知其力有以勝之.故直以為己任而不疑也.〇程子曰.顏子問克己復禮之目.子曰.非禮勿視.非禮勿聽.非禮勿言.非禮勿動.四者.身之用也.由乎中而應乎外.制於外.所以養其中也.顏淵事斯語.所以進於聖人.後之學聖人者.宜服膺而勿失也.因箴以自警.其視箴曰.心兮本虛.應物無迹.操之有要.視為之則.蔽交於前.其中則遷.制之於外.以安其內.克己復禮.久 而誠矣.其聽箴曰.人有秉彝.本乎天性.知誘物化.遂亡其正.卓彼先覺.知止有定.閑邪存誠.非禮勿廳.其言箴曰.人心之動.因言以宣.發禁躁妄.內斯靜專.矧是樞機.興戎出好.吉凶榮辱.惟其所召.傷易則誕.傷煩則支.己肆物忤.出悖來違.非法不道.欽哉訓辭.其動箴曰.哲人知幾.誠之於思.志士勵行.守之於為.順理則裕.從欲惟危.造次克念.戰兢自持.習與性成.聖賢同歸.愚按此章問答.乃傳授心法切要之言.非至明不能察其幾.非至健不能致其決.故惟顏子得聞之.而凡學者亦不可以不勉也.程子之箴.發明親切.學者尤宜深玩.

19

［何］子曰人而不仁如禮何人而不仁如樂何_{包曰言人而}
不仁必不能行禮樂

［朱］子曰。人而不仁。如禮何。人而不仁。如樂何。
游氏曰。人而不仁。則人心亡矣。其如禮樂何哉。言雖欲用之。而禮樂不
為之用也。○程子曰。仁者。天下之正理。失正理。則無序而不和。李氏
曰。禮樂待人而後行。苟非其人。則雖玉帛交錯。鐘鼓鏗鏘。亦將如之何
哉。然記者序此於八佾雍徹之後。疑其為僭禮樂者發也。

20

［何］子夏問曰巧笑倩兮美目盼兮素以爲絢兮何謂也_馬
_{曰倩笑貌盼動目貌絢文貌此上二句在衞風碩人之二章其下一句逸也}子
曰繪事後素_{鄭曰繪畫文也凡繪畫先布重色然後以素分布其間以成其}
_{文喻美女雖有倩盼美質亦須禮以成之曰禮後乎孔曰孔子言繪事後素子}
_{夏聞而解知以素喻禮故曰禮後乎}子曰起予者商也始可與言詩
已矣_{包曰予我也孔子言子夏能發明我意可與共言詩}

［朱］子夏問曰。巧笑倩兮。美目盼兮。素以爲絢兮。
何謂也。此逸詩也。倩。好口輔也。盼。目黑白分也。素。粉地。畫之質
也。絢。采色。畫之飾也。言人有此倩盼之美質。而又加以華采之飾。如
有素地而加采色也。子夏疑其反謂以素為飾。故問之。子曰。繪事
後素。繪事。繪畫之事也。後素。後於素也。考工記曰。繪畫之事後素
功。謂先以粉地為質。而後施五采。猶人有美質。然後可加文飾。曰。
禮後乎。子曰。起予者商也。始可與言詩已矣。禮
必以忠信為質。猶繪事必以粉素為先。起。猶發也。起予。言能起發我
之志意。謝氏曰。子貢因論學而知詩。子夏因論詩而知學。故皆可與言
詩。○楊氏曰。甘受和。白受采。忠信之人。可以學禮。苟無其質。禮不
虛行。此繪事後素之說也。孔子曰。繪事後素。而子夏曰。禮後乎。可謂
能繼其志矣。非得之言意之表者能之乎。商賜可與言詩者以此。若夫玩
心於章句之末。則其為詩也固而已矣。所謂起予。則亦相長之義也。

21

[何]子曰禮云禮云玉帛云乎哉鄭曰玉圭璋之屬帛束帛之屬
言禮非但崇此玉帛而已所貴者乃貴其安上治民樂云樂云鐘鼓
乎哉馬曰樂之所貴者移風易俗非謂鐘鼓而已

[朱]子曰。禮云禮云。玉帛云乎哉。樂云樂云。鐘鼓
云乎哉。敬而將之以玉帛.則為禮.和而發之以鐘鼓.則為樂.遺其
本而專事其末.則豈禮樂之謂哉.○程子曰.禮只是一箇序.樂只是
一箇和.只此兩字.含蓄多少義理.天下無一物無禮樂.且如置此兩椅.一
不正.便是無序.無序便乖.乖便不和.又如盜賊至為不道.然亦有禮
樂.蓋必有總屬.必相聽順.乃能爲盜.不然.則叛亂無統.不能一日相
聚而為盜也.禮樂無處無之.學者須要識得.

22

[何]席不正不坐鄉人飲酒杖者出斯出矣孔曰杖者老人也
鄉人飲酒之禮主於老者老者禮畢出孔子從而後出

[朱]席不正。不坐。謝氏曰.聖人心安於正.故於位之不正者.
雖小不處.

23

[何]祭如在孔曰言事死如事生祭神如神在孔曰謂祭白神子
曰吾不與祭如不祭包曰孔子或出或病而不自親祭使攝者為之不
致肅敬於心與不祭同

[朱]祭如在。祭神如神在。程子曰.祭.祭先祖也.祭神.祭
外神也.祭先主於孝.祭神主於敬.愚謂此門人記孔子祭祀之誠意.子
曰。吾不與祭。如不祭。又記孔子之言以明之.言己當祭之
時.或有故不得與.而使他人攝之.則不得致其如在之誠.故雖已祭.而
此心缺然.如未嘗祭也.○范氏曰.君子之祭.七日戒.三日齊.必見所
祭者.誠之至也.是故.郊則天神格.廟則人鬼享.皆由己以致之也.有

其誠則有其神．無其誠則無其神．可不謹乎．吾不與祭如不祭．誠為實．
禮為虛也．

24

[何] 林放問禮之本鄭曰林放魯人子曰大哉問禮與其奢也
寧儉喪與其易也寧戚包曰易和易也言禮之本意失於奢不如儉喪
失於和易不如哀戚

[朱] 林放問禮之本．林放．魯人．見世之為禮者．專事繁文．而
疑其本之不在是也．故以爲問．子曰．大哉問．孔子以時方逐
末．而放獨有志於本．故大其問．蓋得其本．則禮之全體．無不在其中
矣．禮．與其奢也．寧儉．喪．與其易也．寧戚．易．
治也．孟子曰．易其田疇．在喪禮．則節文習熟．而吾哀痛慘怛之實者
也．戚則一於哀而文不足耳．禮貴得中．奢易．則過於文．儉戚．則不及
而質．二者皆未合禮．然凡物之理．必先有質而後有文．則質乃禮之本
也．○范氏曰．夫祭．與其敬不足而禮有餘也．不若禮不足而敬有餘也．
喪．與其哀不足而禮有餘也．不若禮不足而哀有餘也．禮失之奢．喪失之
易．皆不能反本．而隨其末故也．禮奢而備．不若儉而不備之愈也．喪易而
文．不若戚而不文之愈也．儉者．物之質．戚者．心之誠．故為禮之本．
楊氏曰．禮始諸飲食．故汙尊而抔飲．為之簠簋籩豆罍爵之飾．所以文
之也．則其本儉而已．喪不可以徑情而直行．為之衰麻哭踊之數．所以
節之也．則其本戚而已．周衰．世方以文滅質．而林放獨能問禮之本．故
夫子大之．而告之以此．

25

[何] 子曰道之以政孔曰政謂法教齊之以刑馬曰齊整之以刑
罰民免而無恥孔曰免苟免道之以德包曰德謂道德齊之以禮
有恥且格格正也

[朱] 子曰．道之以政．齊之以刑．民免而無恥．道．猶
引導．謂先之也．政．謂法制禁令也．齊．所以一之也．道之而不從者．有
刑以一之也．免而無恥．謂苟免刑罰．而無所羞愧．蓋雖不敢為惡．而為惡

之心．未嘗忘也．道之以德。齊之以禮。有恥且格。禮．謂制度品節也．格．至也．言躬行以率之．則民固有所觀感而興起矣．而其淺深厚薄之不一者．又有禮以一之．則民恥於不善．而又有以至於善也．一說．格．正也．書曰．格其非心．○愚謂政者．為治之具．刑者．輔治之法．德禮．則所以出治之本．而德又禮之本也．此其相為終始．雖不可以偏廢．然政刑能使民遠罪而已．德禮之效．則有以使民日遷善而不自知．故治民者．不可徒恃其末．又當深探其本也．

26

[何]子曰能以禮讓為國乎何有_{何有者言不難}不能以禮讓為國如禮何_{包曰如禮何者言不能用禮}

[朱]子曰。能以禮讓為國乎。何有。不能以禮讓為國。如禮何。讓者．禮之實也．何有．言不難也．言有禮之實以為國．則何難之有．不然．則其禮文雖具．亦且無如之何矣．而況於為國乎．

27

[何]或問禘之說子曰不知也_{孔曰荅以不知者為魯諱}知其說者之於天下也其如示諸斯乎指其掌_{包曰孔子謂或人言知禘禮之說者於天下之事如指示掌中之物言其易了}

[朱]或問禘之說。子曰。不知也。知其說者之於天下也。其如示諸斯乎。指其掌。先王報本追遠之意．莫深於禘．非仁孝誠敬之至．不足以與此．非或人之所及也．而不王不禘之法．又魯之所當諱者．故以不知答之．示．與視同．指其掌．弟子記夫子言此而自指其掌．言其明且易也．蓋知禘之說．則理無不明．誠無不格．而治天下不難矣．聖人於此．豈真有所不知也哉．

28

[何]子曰為政以德譬如北辰居其所而眾星共之_{包曰德者無為猶北辰之不移而眾星共之}

[朱]子曰。為政以德。譬如北辰。居其所。而眾星共之。政之為言正也。所以正人之不正也。德之為言得也。行道而有得於心也。北辰．北極．天之樞也．居其所．不動也．共．向也．言眾星四面旋繞而歸向之也．為政以德．則無為而天下歸之．其象如此．程子曰．為政以德．然後無為．范氏曰．為政以德．則不動而化．不言而信．無為而成．所守者至簡．而能御煩．所處者至靜．而能制動．所務者至寡．而能服眾．

29

[何]子曰無爲而治者其舜也與夫何為哉恭己正南面而已矣言任官得其人故無爲而治

[朱]子曰。無爲而治者。其舜也與。夫何為哉。恭己正南面而已矣。無爲而治者．聖人德盛而民化．不待其有所作爲也．獨稱舜者．紹堯之後．而又得人以任眾職．故尤不見其有爲之迹也．恭己者．聖人敬德之容．既無所為．則人之所見如此而已．

30

[何]季康子問政於孔子曰如殺無道以就有道何如孔曰就成也欲多殺以止姦孔子對曰子為政焉用殺子欲善而民善矣君子之德風小人之德草草上之風必偃孔曰亦欲令康子先自正偃仆也加草以風無不仆者猶民之化於上

[朱]季康子問政於孔子曰。如殺無道。以就有道。何如。孔子對曰。子為政。焉用殺。子欲善。而民善矣。君子之德風。小人之德草。草上之風。必偃。為政者．民所視效．何以殺為．欲善．則民善矣．上．一作尚．加也．偃．仆也．○尹氏曰．殺之為言．豈為人上之語哉．以身教者從．以言教者訟．而況於殺乎．

31

[何]子曰誰能出不由戶何莫由斯道也孔曰言人立身成功當由道譬猶出入要當從戶

[朱]子曰。誰能出不由戶。何莫由斯道也。言人不能出不由戶. 何故乃不由此道邪. 怪而歎之之辭. ○洪氏曰. 人知出必由戶. 而不知行必由道. 非道遠人. 人自遠爾.

32

[何]子夏曰百工居肆以成其事君子學以致其道 包曰言百工處其肆則事成猶君子學以致其道

[朱]子夏曰。百工居肆以成其事。君子學以致其道。肆. 謂官府造作之處. 致. 極也. 工不居肆. 則遷於異物而業不精. 君子不學. 則奪於外誘而志不篤. 尹氏曰. 學所以致其道也. 百工居肆. 必務成其事. 君子之於學. 可不知所務哉. 愚按二說相須. 其意始備.

33

[何]子曰君子博學於文約之以禮亦可以弗畔矣夫 鄭曰弗畔不違道

[朱]子曰。君子博學於文。約之以禮。亦可以弗畔矣夫。約. 要也. 畔. 背也. 君子學欲其博. 故於文無不考. 守欲其要. 故其動必以禮. 如此則可以不背於道矣. ○程子曰. 博學於文. 而不約之以禮. 必至於汗漫. 博學矣. 又能守禮而由於規矩. 則亦可以不畔道矣.

34

[何]子曰三人行必有我師焉擇其善者而從之其不善者而改之 言我三人行本無賢愚擇善從之不善改之故無常師

[朱]子曰。三人行。必有我師焉。擇其善者而從之。其不善者而改之。三人同行. 其一我也. 彼二人者. 一善一惡. 則我從其善而改其惡焉. 是二人者. 皆我師也. ○尹氏曰. 見賢思齊. 見不賢而內自省. 則善惡皆我之師. 進善其有窮乎.

35

［何］曾子曰馬曰弟子曾參吾日三省吾身為人謀而不忠乎
與朋友交而不信乎傳不習乎言凡所傳之事得無素不講習而
傳之

［朱］曾子曰。吾日三省吾身。為人謀。而不忠乎。與
朋友交。而不信乎。傳不習乎。曾子．孔子弟子．名參．字子
輿．盡己之謂忠．以實之謂信．傳．謂受之於師．習．謂熟之於己．曾子以
此三者．日省其身．有則改之．無則加勉．其自治誠切如此．可謂得為學之
本矣．而三者之序．則又以忠信為傳習之本也．○尹氏曰．曾子守約．故動
必求諸身．謝氏曰．諸子之學．皆出於聖人．其後愈遠而愈失其真．獨曾子
之學．專用心於內．故傳之無弊．觀於子思孟子可見矣．惜乎其嘉言善行．
不盡傳於世也．其幸存而未泯者．學者其可不盡心乎．

36

［何］子曰君子不重則不威學則不固孔曰固蔽也一曰言人不
能敦重既無威嚴學又不能堅固識其義理主忠信無友不如己者過
則勿憚改鄭曰主親也憚難也

［朱］子曰。君子不重則不威。學則不固。重，厚重．威．
威嚴．固．堅固也．輕乎外者．必不能堅乎內．故不厚重．則無威嚴．而
所學亦不堅固也．主忠信。人不忠信．則事皆無實．為惡則易．為善
則難．故學者必以是爲主焉．程子曰．人道惟在忠信．不誠則無物．且出
入無時．莫知其鄉者．人心也．若無忠信．豈復有物乎．無友不如己
者。無．毋通．禁止辭也．友所以輔仁．不如己．則無益而有損．過則
勿憚改。勿．亦禁止之辭．憚．畏難也．自治不勇．則惡日長．故有過
則當速改．不可畏難而苟安也．程子曰．學問之道無他也．知其不善．則
速改以從善而已．○程子曰．君子自脩之道．當如是也．游氏曰．君子之
道．以威重為質．而學以成之．學之道．必以忠信爲主．而以勝己者輔之．
然或吝於改過．則終無以入德．而賢者亦未必樂告以善道．故以過勿憚
改終焉．

37

[何]司馬牛問君子子曰君子不憂不懼孔曰牛兄桓魋將為亂
牛自宋來學常憂懼故孔了解之曰不憂不懼斯謂之君子己乎子
曰內省不疚夫何憂何懼包曰疚病也自省無罪惡無可憂懼

[朱]司馬牛問君子。子曰。君子不憂不懼。向魋作亂.
牛常憂懼.故夫子告之以此.曰。不憂不懼。斯謂之君子己
乎。子曰。內省不疚。夫何憂何懼。牛之再問.猶前章
之意.故復告之以此.疚.病也.言由其平日所爲.無愧於心.故能內省
不疚.而自無憂懼.未可遽以爲易而忽之也.○晁氏曰.不憂不懼.由乎
德全而無疵.故無入而不自得.非實有憂懼.而強排遣之也.

38

[何]子曰君子不器包曰器者各周其用至於君子無所不施

[朱]子曰。君子不器。器者.各適其用.而不能相通.成德之士.
體無不具.故用無不周.非特爲一材一藝而已.

39

[何]子曰富與貴是人之所欲也不以其道得之不處也
孔曰不以其道得富貴則仁者不處貧與賤是人之所惡也不以
其道得之不去也時有否泰故君子履道而反貧賤此則不以其道得
之雖是人之所惡不可違而去之君子去仁惡乎成名孔曰惡乎成名
者不得成名為君子君子無終食之間違仁造次必於是顛沛
必於是馬曰造次急遽顛沛偃仆雖急遽偃仆不違仁

[朱]子曰。富與貴。是人之所欲也。不以其道得之。
不處也。貧與賤。是人之所惡也。不以其道得之。
不去也。不以其道得之.謂不當得而得之.然於富貴則不處.於貧
賤則不去.君子之審富貴.而安貧賤也如此.君子去仁。惡乎成
名。言君子所以為君子.以其仁也.若食富貴而厭貧賤.則是自離其
仁.而無君子之實矣.何所成其名乎.君子無終食之間違仁。

造次必於是。顛沛必於是。終食者.一飯之頃.造次.急遽苟
且之時.顛沛.傾覆流離之際.蓋君子之不去乎仁如此.不但富貴貧賤
取舍之閒而已也.〇言君子為仁.自富貴貧賤取舍之閒.以至於終食造
次顛沛之頃.無時無處而不用其力也.然取舍之分明.然後存養之功密.
存養之功密.則其取舍之分益明矣.

40

[何] 子曰君子而不仁者有矣夫未有小人而仁者也孔
曰雖曰君子猶未能備

[朱] 子曰。君子而不仁者有矣夫。未有小人而仁者
也。謝氏曰.君子志於仁矣.然毫忽之閒.心不在焉.則未免為不仁也.

41

[何] 子曰朝聞道夕死可矣言將至死不聞世之有道

[朱] 子曰。朝聞道。夕死可矣。道者.事物當然之理.苟得
聞之.則生順死安.無復遺恨矣.朝夕.所以甚言其時之近.〇程子曰.
言人不可以不知道.苟得聞道.雖死可也.又曰.皆實理也.人知而信者
為難.死生亦大矣.非誠有所得.豈以夕死為可乎.

42

[何] 顏淵喟然歎曰喟歎聲仰之彌高鑽之彌堅言不可窮盡瞻
之在前忽焉在後言恍惚不可為形象夫子循循然善誘人循循
次序貌誘進也言夫子正以此道進勸人有所序博我以文約我以禮欲
罷不能既竭吾才如有所立卓爾雖欲從之末由也已孔曰
言夫子既以文章開博我又以禮節節約我使我欲罷而不能已竭我才矣其
有所立則又卓然不可及言己雖蒙夫子之善誘猶不能及夫子之所立

[朱] 顏淵喟然歎曰。仰之彌高。鑽之彌堅。瞻之在
前。忽焉在後。喟.歎聲.仰彌高.不可及.鑽彌堅.不可入.在前
在後.恍惚不可為象.此顏淵深知夫子之道.無窮盡.無方體.而歎之

也.夫子循循然善誘人。博我以文。約我以禮。循循.
有次序貌.誘.引進也.博文約禮.教之序也.言夫子道雖高妙.而教人
有序也.侯氏曰.博我以文.致知格物也.約我以禮.克己復禮也.程子
曰.此顏子稱聖人最切當處.聖人教人.惟此二事而已.欲罷不能。
既竭吾才。如有所立卓爾。雖欲從之。末由也已。卓.
立貌.末.無也.此顏子自言其學之所至也.蓋悅之深而力之盡.所見益
親.而又無所用其力也.吳氏曰.所謂卓爾.亦在乎日用行事之間.非所
謂窈冥昏默者.程子曰.到此地位.功夫尤難.直是峻絕.又大段著力不
得.楊氏曰.自可欲之謂善.充而至於大.力行之積也.大而化之.則非
力行所及矣.此顏子所以未達一間也.○程子曰.此顏子所以為深知孔
子.而善學之者也.胡氏曰.無上事而喟然歎.此顏子學既有得.故述其
先難之故.後得之由.而歸功於聖人也.高堅前後.語道體也.仰鑽瞻忽.
未領其要也.惟夫子循循善誘.先博我以文.使我知古今.達事變.然後
約我以禮.使我尊所聞.行所知.如行者之赴家.食者之求飽.是以欲罷
而不能.盡心盡力.不少休廢.然後見夫子所立之卓然.雖欲從之.末由
也已.是蓋不怠所從.必求至乎卓立之地也.抑斯歎也.其在請事斯語
之後.三月不違之時乎.

43

[何]子曰民可使由之不可使知之由用也可使用而不可使知
者百姓能口用而不能知

[朱]子曰。民可使由之。不可使知之。民可使之由於是
理之當然.而不能使之知其所以然也.○程子曰.聖人設教.非不欲人
家喻而戶曉也.然不能使之知.但能使之由之爾.若曰.聖人不使民知.
則是後世朝四暮三之術也.豈聖人之心乎.

44

[何]子曰參乎吾道一以貫之曾子曰唯孔曰直曉不問故答曰
唯子出門人問曰何謂也曾子曰夫子之道忠恕而已矣

[朱]子曰。參乎。吾道一以貫之。曾子曰。唯。參乎

者．呼曾子之名而告之．貫．通也．唯者．應之速而無疑者也．聖人之心．
渾然一理．而泛應曲當．用各不同．曾子於其用處．蓋已隨事精察而力
行之．但未知其體之一爾．夫子知其真積力久．將有所得．是以呼而告
之．曾子果能默契其指．即應之速而無疑也．子出。門人問曰。
何謂也。曾子曰。夫子之道。忠恕而已矣。盡己之謂
忠．推己之謂恕．而已矣者．竭盡而無餘之辭也．夫子之一理渾然．而泛
應曲當．譬則天地之至誠無息．而萬物各得其所也．自此之外．固無餘
法．而亦無待於推矣．曾子有見於此而難言之．故借學者盡己推己之目
以著明之．欲人之易曉也．蓋至誠無息者．道之體也．萬殊之所以一本
也．萬物各得其所者．道之用也．一本之所以萬殊也．以此觀之．一以貫之
之實可見矣．或曰．中心為忠．如心為恕．於義亦通．○程子曰．以己及物．
仁也．推己及物．恕也．違道不遠是也．忠恕一以貫之．忠者天道．恕者
人道．忠者無妄．恕者所以行乎忠也．忠者體．恕者用．大本達道也．此於
違道不遠異者．動以天爾．又曰．維天之命．於穆不已．忠也．乾道變化．
各正性命．恕也．又曰．聖人教人．各因其才．吾道一以貫之．唯曾子為
能達此．孔子所以告之也．曾子告門人曰．夫子之道．忠恕而已矣．亦猶
夫子之告曾子也．中庸所謂忠恕違道不遠．斯乃下學上達之義．

Glossary

Anchang　安昌

baixing　百姓
Bao Xian　苞咸
bei　背
beichen　北辰
beiji　北極
ben　本
bi　蔽
bing　病
bo　博
bu dang de er de zhi　不當得而得之
bu yi qi dao de zhi　不以其道得之
buhuo　不惑
buren　不仁

Can　參

Cao Cao　曹操
Cao Pi　曹丕
Cao Shuang　曹爽
Cao Xi　曹羲
Chan　禪
Chao Yuezhi　晁說之
Chen Qun　陳群
cheng (be perfectly true)　誠
cheng (promote, bring success
　　to)　成
Cheng, Emperor　成
Cheng Hao　程顥
Cheng Yi　程頤
cheng yi　誠意
chuan　傳
Chuci　楚辭
cong　從

cong xin suo yu bu yu ju　從心所欲
不踰矩

dan　憚
dao (lead)　道
dao (Way)　道
Daode lun　道德論
daxue　大學
de (get)　得
de (virtue)　德
di　褅
dianpei　顛沛

er shun　耳順

fa (enlighten; raise)　發
fa (rules)　法
fan (come back with; return)　反
Fan Chi　樊遲
fan shang　犯上
Fan Zhongyan　范仲淹
Fan Zuyu　范祖禹
fang　方
fei　悱
fen　憤
fu (lie down, bend)　仆
fu (repeat; return)　復
fu pan　弗畔
fuhua　浮華

gai　蓋
gang　剛
ge　格
ge wu　格物
gen　根
gong (respectful)　恭

gong (turn toward)　共
Gong, King　恭
Gongyang zhuan　公羊傳
goumian　苟免
gu　固
guan　貫
guang　廣
gui　歸
Guliang zhuan　穀梁傳
GuLun　古論
Guo Xiang　郭象
Guwen Lunyu　古文論語

Han　漢
He Jin　何進
He Yan　何晏
he you　何有
heyi　和易
hong　弘
Hong Xingzu　洪興祖
hou　後
hou su　後素
Hou Zhongliang　候仲良
houzhong　厚重
hu　乎
Hu Yin　胡寅
Hu Yuan　胡瑗
Huainan zi　淮南子
Huan Tui　桓魋
Huang Gan　黃榦
Huang Kan　皇侃
hui　繪
hui ye qi shu hu lü kong　回也其庶
乎履空
huishi　繪事
huishi hou su　繪事後素

ji (exhaust) 極

ji (foundation) 基

ji (self) 己

ji (worries) 疾

ji ji 汲汲

Ji Kangzi 季康子

jia (inflict; add to) 加

jian 儉

jiangu 堅固

jiju 急遽

Jin 晉

jin ji 盡己

jing (attentive) 敬

jing (classics) 經

Jing, Emperor 景

Jinxiang 金鄉

Jisun Fei 季孫肥

jiu (promote) 就

jiu (wrong) 疚

ju 矩

ju qi suo 居其所

junzi 君子

Kaogong ji 考工記

kaozhcng 考證

ke 克

ke ji 克己

keji fuli 克己復裡

kong 空

Kong Anguo 孔安國

kongkui 空匱

Kongzi 孔子

Lao 老

Laozi 老子

li (principle) 理

li (ritual) 禮

li (stand) 立

Li Sao 離騷

Li Yu 李郁

Liao 遼

libu shangshu 吏部尚書

Liji 禮記

limiao 立貌

Lin Fang 林放

ling 陵

Liu Xiang 劉向

Liu Xiaobiao 劉孝標

Lu 魯

lü 屢

Lü [Dalin] 呂大臨

Lü Zuqian 呂祖謙

LuLun 魯論

LunMeng gangling 論孟綱領

LunMeng jingyi 論孟精義

Lunyu jijie 論語集解

Lunyu jizhu 論語集注

Lunyu xunmeng kouyi 論語訓霥
口義

Lunyu yaoyi 論語要義

Lunyu yishu 論語義疏

Lunyu zhushu 論語注疏

Ma Rong 馬融

Mao 毛

mei 每

Mengzi 孟子

mian 免

mian er wu chi 免而無恥

min (earnestly) 敏

min (people) 民

Ming 明

mo 末

mu (details) 目

mu (long for) 慕

mu (simple) 木

na 訥

nan 難

neng yue shen 能約身

nu 怒

Ouyang Xiu 歐陽修

pan (all sparkling) 盼

pan (transgress) 畔

Pan Shiju, Zishan 潘時舉, 子善

Pei Hui 裴徽

peng 朋

pi 譬

qi (instruct) 啟

qi (psychophysical stuff) 氣

qi (raise up) 起

qi (regulate) 齊

qi (sorrowful) 戚

qi wei ren zhi ben yu 其為人之本與

qian (all dimpled) 倩

qian (hexagram) 乾

QiLun 齊論

qin 親

Qing 清

rang 讓

ren (man) 人

ren (true goodness) 仁

renzhe 仁者

renzheng 仁政

Renzong 仁宗

ru 如

Ru 儒

ru li he 如裡何

Sanguo zhi 三國志

shang (add to) 商

Shang (disciple Zixia) 商

shang (respectfully submitted; superiors; pass over) 上

Shangshu 尚書

shao 少

shen 身

shen hu 參乎

shen neng 身能

sheng 勝

sheng zhi 生知

Shenzong 神宗

shi (devote) 事

shi (gentleman) 士

shi (in due time) 時

shi (see) 示

shi (see) 視

shi shi 事事

shi xi 時習

Shiji 史記

Shijing 詩經

Shiren 碩人

shishuo 師說

Shishuo xinyu 世說新語

shu (empathy) 恕

shu (technique) 術

Shun, Emperor 順

Shun, Sage Ruler 舜

Si (disciple Zigong) 賜

si (shops) 肆

Siku quanshu 四庫全書

Sima 司馬

Sima Guang 司馬光

Sima Niu 司馬牛

Sishu 四書

Sizi 四子

Song 宋

songxi 誦習

su (white) 素

su (with urgency) 速

Su Dongpo 蘇東坡

sui 隨

Sun Fu 孫復

Sun Sheng 孫盛

Sun Yong 孫邕

Taixuan jing 太玄經

Tang 唐

tian zhi shu 天之樞

tianxia gui ren 天下歸仁

tiaojian 條件

tong 通

tongmen 同門

Wang Anshi 王安石

Wang Bi 王弼

Wang Su 王肅

Wang Yangming 王陽明

wei (constitute; practice) 為

wei (deep sigh) 喟

wei (inspire awe) 威

wei (yes) 唯

Wei, Dynasty 魏

Wei, state of 衛

wei nan 畏難

wei ren 為仁

Weishi chunqiu 魏氏春秋

weiyan 威嚴

wen (ornamentation) 文

Wen, Emperor 文

Wen Wang 問王

wo 我

wu (attend to) 務

wu (do not) 勿

wu (do not) 毋

wu (nonbeing) 無

wu (not, no) 無

Wu, Emperor 武

wu wo 毋我

Wu Yu 吳棫

wujing boshi 五經博士

Wuxing 五行

xi 習

Xi Xia 西夏

Xiahou Xuan 夏候玄

xian 鮮

xiang 向

Xiang Tui 向魋

xiao 效

xiaoren 小人

Xie Liangzuo 謝良佐

xin (mind-and-heart) 心

xin (true to one's word) 信

xing 性

Xing Bing 邢昺

xing ren 行仁

xu zhong 虛中

xuan 絢

xuanxue 玄學

xue 學

Xun Yi　荀顗
xunxun　循循
Xunzi　荀子

yan　偃
Yan Hui　顏回
Yan Yuan　顏淵
yanfu　偃仆
Yang Shi　楊時
Yang Xiong　揚雄
Yanzi　顏子
yao (keep to the essential)　要
Yao, Sage Ruler　堯
Yao Yue　堯曰
yi (resolute, firm)　毅
yi (serene; meticulous)　易
yi shi　以實
yifan zhi qing　一飯之頃
Yin Tun　尹焞
yindao　引導
yinjin　引進
yong (the Yong ode)　雍
yong (use)　用
you (being)　有
you (follow)　由
you (guiding on)　誘
you jiao wu lei　有教無類
You Ruo　有若
You Zuo　游酢
Youzi　有子
yu (are they not; allow;
　recognize)　與
yu (illustration, metaphor)　喻
yu (me)　予
Yu, Sage Ruler　禹
Yuan　元

yue (keep to the essential)　約
yue (pleasure)　說
Yue ming　說明
yue shen　約身
yue zhi yi li　約之以禮

zaoci　造次
Zengzi　曾子
Zhang Hou Lun　張候論
Zhang Yu　張禹
Zhang Zai　張載
zhangju　章句
Zhen Dexiu　真得秀
zheng (correct)　正
zheng (ruling; government; tools of
　government)　政
Zheng Chong　鄭沖
zheng ming　正名
Zheng Xuan　鄭玄
Zhengshi　正始
zhi (arrive, reach)　至
zhi (fulfill)　致
zhi (it)　之
zhi (set the mind-and-heart;
　will)　志
zhi (substance)　質
Zhi Dao　知道
zhi tianming　知天命
zhi yu shan　至於善
zhi zhi　致知
zhong (center)　中
zhong (doing the best one can; being
　true to one's nature)　忠
zhong (grave)　重
Zhong Hui　鐘會
zhongshi　鍾食

Zhongyong　中庸

Zhou (man's name)　周

Zhou, Dynasty　周

Zhou Dunyi　周敦頤

Zhouli　周禮

Zhousheng Lie　周生烈

Zhouyi　周易

Zhouyi zhu　周易注

zhu　主

Zhu Xi　朱熹

zhuan　傳

zhuan li　專力

Zhuang　莊

Zhuang Zun　莊遵

Zhuangzi　莊子

zhuo　卓

Zhuzi yulei　朱子語類

zi (given name)　字

zi (master)　子

zide　自得

Zigong　子貢

Zisi　子思

Zixia　子夏

Ziyu　子輿

Zizhang wen　子張問

Zizhi tongjian　資治通鑒

zuo luan　作亂

Works Cited

Balazs, Etienne. "Nihilistic Revolt or Mystical Escapism." In *Chinese Civilization and Bureaucracy: Variations on a Theme*, translated by H. M. Wright, edited by Arthur F. Wright, 226–54. New Haven, Conn.: Yale University Press, 1964.

Balazs, Etienne. "Political Philosophy and Social Crisis at the End of the Han Dynasty." In *Chinese Civilization and Bureaucracy: Variations on a Theme*, translated by H. M. Wright, edited by Arthur F. Wright, 187–225. New Haven, Conn.: Yale University Press, 1964.

Brooks, E. Bruce, and A. Taeko Brooks. *The Original Analects: Sayings of Confucius and His Successors*. New York: Columbia University Press, 1998.

Chan, Wing-tsit. *Chu Hsi: New Studies*. Honolulu: University of Hawai'i Press, 1989.

Cheng, Anne. "Lun yü." In *Early Chinese Texts: A Bibliographical Guide*, edited by Michael Loewe, 313–23. Berkeley: Society for the Study of Early China and Institute of East Asian Studies, University of California, 1993.

Cheng Yi 程頤. *Yichuan xiansheng wenji* 伊川先生文集. In *ErCheng quanshu* 二程全書. Sibu beiyao edition.

Cheng Yi 程頤 and Cheng Hao 程顥. *Henan Chengshi yishu* 河南程氏遺書. In *ErCheng quanshu* 二程全書. Sibu beiyao edition.

Dai Junren 戴君仁. "Huang Kan *Lunyu yishu* de neihan sixiang" 皇侃論語義疏的內涵思想. In *LunMeng yanjiu lunji* 論孟研究論集, edited by Qian Mu 錢穆, 141–60. Taibei: Liming wenhua shiye gongsi, 1981.

Daxue 大學. References are to standard chapter and verse numbers. See Daniel K. Gardner, *Chu Hsi and the Ta-hsueh*: *Neo-Confucian Reflection on the Confucian Canon*. Cambridge, Mass.: Harvard University, Council on East Asian Studies, 1986; and James Legge, *The Chinese Classics*. Vol. 1, *The Great Learning*. Rev. ed. Hong Kong: Hong Kong University Press, 1960.

de Bary, Wm. Theodore. *Neo-Confucian Orthodoxy and the Learning of the Mind-and-Heart*. New York: Columbia University Press, 1981.

Demiéville, Paul. "Philosophy and Religion from Han to Sui." In *The Cambridge History of China*. Vol. 1, *The Ch'in and Han Empires*, *221 B.C.–A.D. 220*, edited by Denis Twitchett and Michael Loewe, 808–72. Cambridge: Cambridge University Press, 1986.

Elman, Benjamin. *From Philosophy to Philology: Intellectual and Social Aspects of Change in Late Imperial China*. Cambridge, Mass.: Harvard University, Council on East Asian Studies, 1984.

Fingarette, Herbert. *Confucius: The Secular as Sacred*. New York: Harper & Row, 1972.

Gardner, Daniel K. *Chu Hsi and the Ta-hsueh*: *Neo-Confucian Reflection on the Confucian Canon*. Cambridge, Mass.: Harvard University, Council on East Asian Studies, 1986.

Gardner, Daniel K. "Ghosts and Spirits in the Sung Neo-Confucian World: Chu Hsi on *Kuei-shen.*" *Journal of the American Oriental Society* 115 (1995): 598–611.

Gardner, Daniel K. *Learning to Be a Sage*: *Selections from the* Conversations on Master Chu, Arranged Topically. Berkeley: University of California Press, 1990.

Henderson, John B. *Scripture, Canon, and Commentary: A Comparison of Confucian and Western Exegesis*. Princeton, N.J.: Princeton University Press, 1991.

He Yan 何晏. *Lunyu jijie* 論語集解. In Xing Bing, *Lunyu zhushu*. Sibu beiyao edition.

He Yan 何晏. "Lunyu xu" 論語序. In Xing Bing, *Lunyu zhushu*. Sibu beiyao edition.

Holcombe, Charles. *In the Shadow of the Han: Literati Thought and Society at the Beginning of the Southern Dynasties.* Honolulu: University of Hawai'i Press, 1994.

Hou Han shu 後漢書. Beijing: Zhonghua shuju, 1965.

Huang Gan 黃榦. *Huang Mianzhai xiansheng wenji* 黃勉齋先生文集. Congshu jicheng edition.

Huang Kan 皇侃. *Lunyu jijie yishu* 論語集解義疏. Congshu jicheng edition.

Kieschnick, John. "*Analects* 12.1 and the Commentarial Tradition." *Journal of the American Oriental Society* 112 (1992): 567–76.

Lau, D. C. *Mencius.* Harmondsworth: Penguin, 1970.

Legge, James. *The Chinese Classics.* 5 vols. Rev. ed. Hong Kong: Hong Kong University Press, 1960.

Legge, James. *Li chi: Book of Rites.* 2 vols. Edited by Ch'u Chai and Winberg Chai. New Hyde Park, N.Y.: University Books, 1967.

Liji 禮記. Shisanjing zhushu (Yiwen reprint) edition.

Lo, Yuet Keung. "The Formulation of Early Medieval Confucian Metaphysics: Huang K'an's (488–545) Accommodation of Neo-Taoism and Buddhism." In *Imagining Boundaries: Changing Confucian Doctrines, Texts, and Hermeneutics,* edited by Kai-wing Chow, On-cho Ng, and John B. Henderson, 57–83. Albany: State University of New York Press, 1999.

Loewe, Michael, ed. *Early Chinese Texts: A Bibliographical Guide.* Berkeley: Society for the Study of Early China and Institute of East Asian Studies, University of California, 1993.

Lunyu yinde 論語引得. Harvard-Yenching Institute Sinological Index Series, supplement no. 16. Reprint, Taibei: Chinese Materials and Research Aids Service Center, 1966.

Lynn, Richard John. *The Classic of Changes: A New Translation of the* I Ching *as Interpreted by Wang Bi.* New York: Columbia University Press, 1994.

Lynn, Richard John. *The Classic of the Way and Virtue: A New Translation of the* Tao-te ching *of Laozi as Interpreted by Wang Bi.* New York: Columbia University Press, 1999.

Makeham, John. "The Earliest Extant Commentary on *Lunyu: Lunyu zheng shi zhu.*" *T'oung Pao* 83 (1997): 260–99.

Makeham, John. "The Formation of *Lunyu* as a Book." *Monumenta Serica* 44 (1996): 1–24.

Mather, Richard, trans. *Shih-shuo hsin-yü: A New Account of Tales of the World.* Minneapolis: University of Minnesota Press, 1976.

Mengzi 孟子. Harvard-Yenching Institute Sinological Index Series, supplement no. 17. Reprint, Taibei: Chinese Materials and Research Aids Service Center, 1966.

Morohashi Tetsuji 諸橋轍次. *Keigaku kenkyū josetsu* 經學研究序說. Tokyo: Meguro shoten, 1975.

Nylan, Michael. *The Five "Confucian" Classics*. New Haven, Conn.: Yale University Press, 2001.

Sailey, Jay. *The Master Who Embraces Simplicity: A Study of the Philosopher Ko Hung, A.D. 283–343*. San Francisco: Chinese Materials Center, 1978.

Sanguo zhi 三國誌. Beijing: Zhonghua shuju, 1959.

Schwartz, Benjamin I. *The World of Thought in Ancient China*. Cambridge, Mass.: Harvard University Press, 1985.

Shangshu 尚書. Shisanjing zhushu (Yiwen reprint) edition.

Shijing 詩經. References are to standard Mao ode numbers.

Shinshaku kanbun taikei 新釋漢文大系. Tokyo: Meiji shoin, 1960–.

Sima Qian 司馬遷. *Shiji* 史記. Beijing: Zhonghua shuju, 1959.

Taiping yulan 太平御覽. Compiled by Li Fang 李昉 et al. Reprint, Taibei: Shangwu yinshuguan, 1968.

Tsai, Yen-zen. "*Ching* and *Chuan*: Towards Defining the Confucian Scriptures in Han China (206 BCE–220 CE)." Ph.D. diss., Harvard University, 1992.

Tu Wei-ming. *Centrality and Commonality: An Essay on Chung-yung*. Honolulu: University of Hawai'i Press, 1976.

Van Zoeren, Steve. *Poetry and Personality: Reading, Exegesis, and Hermeneutics in Traditional China*. Stanford, Calif.: Stanford University Press, 1991.

Wagner, Rudolf G. *The Craft of a Chinese Commentator: Wang Bi on the* Laozi. Albany: State University of New York Press, 2000.

Wagner, Rudolph G. "Lebensstil und Drogen im Chinesischen Mittelalter." *T'oung Pao* 59 (1973): 79–178.

Wang Baoxuan 王葆玹. *Wang Bi pingzhuan* 王弼評傳. Guangxi: Guangxi jiaoyu chuban, 1997.

Wang Baoxuan 王葆玹. *Xuanxue tonglun* 玄學通論. Taibei: Wunan tushu chuban gongsi, 1996.

Wang Mouhong 王懋竑. *Zhuzi nianpu* 朱子年譜. Taibei: Shijie shuju, 1973.

Watson, Burton. *Chuang Tzu: Basic Writings*. New York: Columbia University Press, 1964.

Xing Bing 邢昺. *Lunyu zhushu* 論語注疏. Sibu beiyao edition.

Yü, Ying-shih. "Individualism and the Neo-Taoist Movement in Wei Chin China." In *Individualism and Holism: Studies in Confucian and Taoist Values*, edited by Donald J. Munro, 121–55. Ann Arbor: Center for Chinese Studies, University of Michigan, 1985.

Yuan shi 元史. Beijing: Zhonghua shuju, 1976.

Zenshaku kanbun taikei 全釋漢文大系. Tokyo: Shûeisha, 1973–1980.

Zhao Shunsun 趙順孫. *Lunyu zuanshu* 論語纂疏. In *Sishu zuanshu* 四書纂疏. Taibei: Xinxing shuju, 1972.

Zhongyong 中庸. References are to standard chapter and verse numbers.

Zhouli 周禮. Shisanjing zhushu (Yiwen reprint) edition.

Zhouyi 周易 (*Zhouyi yinde*). Harvard-Yenching Institute Sinological Index Series, supplement no. 10. Reprint, Taibei: Chinese Materials and Research Aids Service Center, 1966.

Zhu Xi 朱熹. *Hui'an xiansheng Zhu Wengong wenji* 晦庵先生朱文公文集. Sibu congkan edition.

Zhu Xi 朱熹. *Lunyu jizhu* 論語集注. In *Sishu jizhu* 四書集注. Sibu beiyao edition.

Zhu Xi 朱熹. "Zhongyong zhangju xu" 中庸章句序. In *Sishu jizhu* 四書集注. Sibu beiyao edition.

Zhu Xi 朱熹. *Zhuzi yulei* 朱子語類. Edited by Li Jingde 黎靖德. Beijing: Zhonghua shuju, 1986.

Zhuangzi 莊子 (*Zhuangzi yinde*). Harvard-Yenching Institute Sinological Index Series, supplement no. 20. Cambridge, Mass.: Harvard University Press, 1956.

Zhuo Zhongxin 卓忠信. *Lunyu heshi jijie zhuzi jizhu bijiao yanjiu* 論語何氏集解朱子集注比較研究. Taibei: Jiaxin shuini gongsi, 1969.

Index